One enjoys the experience of hanging out with Emma Wilkins' family, friends, neighbors, and "favorite strangers," and learns from her example of thinking out loud about how to live well in her corner of the world. As a character in her own work, she brings cohesion to this debut collection of essays on topics including parenting, literature, technology, and religion.
—**MIKEY LYNCH,** author of *The Good Life in the Last Days*

A delectable collection of thoughts, stories, and vignettes for every occasion. Emma brings color, warmth, and humanity to even the most quotidian slice-of-life experiences. She also brings profound insight, deep truths, and beautiful moments that affirm life and remind us of our great need and responsibility: to love and be loved. I am delighted that her musings can be categorized and enjoyed in one place. I'm even more delighted to call her a friend.
—**AARON JOHNSTONE,** host, *Deeper Questions* podcast

Everything Emma writes makes me feel like I'm just seeing the world properly, or after a good nap. Her vignettes capture the past and reconnect it to the future. There's a redemptive quality to her work that's deeply human and truly compassionate.
—**AMY ISHAM,** writer, researcher, and podcast host

Love

&

Solum Literary Press
6597 East Camino Vista #3
Anaheim, CA 92807
solumpress.com

PAPERBACK ISBN 978-1-965169-06-3
EBOOK ISBN 978-1-965169-07-0

Cover art and design by Sarah Christolini.
Interior design by Riley Bounds, Sarah Christolini, and Grace Russo.

LIBRARY OF CONGRESS CATALOGUING-IN-PUBLICATION DATA
Name: Wilkins, Emma, author.
Title: love & / emma wilkins.
Description: Anaheim, CA: Solum Literary Press, 2026.
Identifiers: LCCN 2024942695
ISBN 978-1-965169-06-3 (print)
ISBN 978-1-965169-07-0 (Kindle)
Subjects: BISAC: LITERARY COLLECTIONS / Essays / Australian & Oceanian / Religious & Inspirational
LC record available at https://lccn.loc.gov/2024942695

Love &

Emma Wilkins

Anaheim, CA • solumpress.com

Contents

This is an edited collection. Articles and essays in this book, and their previously published versions, may differ slightly.

Author's Note

While the essays and articles collected here have been placed in distinct categories, they overlap in countless ways. Some might wonder why faith has no chapter of its own. As the lens through which I see the world, I can't cordon it off. I hope readers, whatever their beliefs, will find the book richer for the fact I haven't tried. My faith is woven through the way I think and see and live and write—so it is woven through this book.

In trying to make sense of a world that has changed rapidly and
profoundly during my decades on this planet, I started
writing about everything from the ethics of de-extinction, to
our "appetite for newness," to why a poem generated by an
algorithm can never mean as much as one inspired by a human
being. I've since realized that almost every piece I've written is,
in one way or another, about love.

Love &

...friendship

This (plum) life
The Weekend Australian, March 2020

The house next door goes on the market within weeks and sells within days. The plum tree in the front yard ripens.

I think of Byron—white hair, blue eyes, a gardener's skin, a gardener's hands—who loved to share and hated waste; who offered us its fruit day after day.

The tree was ancient but tireless. Year after year it gave our neighbor more fruit than he could ever eat, and more than he could use or give away. Kate, a gardener too, took cuttings, to graft—*they don't make them like this anymore*, she said. It was true of Byron, too.

I did my bit: I made plum cake, plum jam, plum crumble. I filled boxes for friends. When I saw Byron out the back, I'd call him to the fence and share a slice, a jar, a bowl, as thanks. Every time, he'd pop back up to rave about the taste.

The house next door is empty now. The tree's aging branches sag, its fallen children dot the lawn and rot—nobody's there to rake them up these days.

One evening, I can stand it no longer. I open the gate, I tread the path, and pick.

At one point I glance up and see I've caught a neighbor's eye—*a grown woman, stealing a dead man's fruit*, I hear her think—but I know he would approve, and carry on.

Returning to the kitchen, I use a sharp knife to slit each plum to the stone. I put them in a jar with an avalanche of sugar, a stick of cinnamon, a peel of lemon, and plenty of vodka. I'll invert the jar daily for two weeks, then leave it somewhere dark for ninety days. His house will be a home again by then.

In the meantime, more plums ripen. It's late afternoon when I ask our eldest boy to gather more. He returns with the usual abundance.

Barefoot in the kitchen, I beat butter, sugar, eggs; I fold in flour, fill a tin. I pit the plums and press their juicy halves into the batter, and I think about our dear old friend again.

I picture him: still tall, no longer strong; an invalid by virtue of the blanket on his lap. No pills, no tubes, just a box of *Celebrations* and a generous pour of port, his family taking turns to hold his hand.

After dinner it's still light, and the sweet-smelling cake is still warm. I slice it up and the eldest boy delivers: to the family behind us, to the newbies on the corner, to our friends up the street.

He bounds back thrilled by the enthusiastic welcomes the "cake fairy" received, breathlessly relaying words of thanks. I think about how Byron would have liked a slice himself, and I think about how glad he'd be to see that not all the plums have rotted since he left, and some of them became a source of joy.

Instead of presents, I asked for . . . salads
Cicerone Journal, March 2023

It started with Hetty McKinnon's *Community*—a cookbook that brought new meaning to the word "salad." Recipes called for freekeh and blood orange; pomegranate and sumac; caramelized nuts and wasabi mayonnaise. I wanted to *try* them all, but not *make* them all.

On social media, I wondered aloud about holding a party where every guest had to make and bring one salad. Some friends responded with enthusiasm, others with ridicule.

I set up a Facebook event and invited the enthusiasts. I warned them from the start that strings were attached: it wouldn't be a "just bring yourself" dinner party with a gracious host: it would be a dictatorship with a Salad Boss. Guests would make and bring a salad of my choosing.

No one rebelled, and the result was a feast. Don't think wilted lettuce and tasteless tomato; think goat's cheese croutons with baby spinach, figs, and apple-mustard dressing. Don't think healthy; think calorific. We ended the night with full stomachs and leftovers that would make us the envy of any lunchroom.

I later acquired Yotam Ottolenghi's *Jerusalem* and curated a similar event, only this time the invitation list was based on friends who also owned the book. They knew me, but not each other. It didn't matter; they knew Yotam. Recipes were conquered and strangers became comrades, even friends.

Buoyed by the success, I went a step further: I decided to repeat the experiment with a wider circle. The excuse would be my turning thirty-eight. And instead of presents, I would ask for salads.

Knowing this circle would include friends who found the idea of cooking for *fun* confusing at best, I added an escape clause: they could choose to bring cheese or wine instead. Inspired by a lockdown caper where I had invited friends to wear ridiculous outfits and take turns running an online fitness/dance class (it did little for our fitness but much for our mood), I added that thrift-store outfits were strongly encouraged ("the worse the better").

My husband joked that I'd find out who my real friends were. I joked about asking them all to make me Hetty's *Brussels sprouts with stir-fried lotus root, black fungus, five-spice tofu and hoisin-sesame sauce.*

Thankfully for my guests, I did exercise *some* restraint. I sent lengthier recipes to seasoned cooks but simple ones to the rest, and I didn't ask anyone to source black wood ear fungus or frozen lotus root.

In the lead-up to the party I received a flurry of texts. Two friends had just been shopping and couldn't wait to show off their outfits, one said she'd had a "salad adventure" and would "tell all tonight." Another texted: "Soggy salad sorry! Will bring wine to distract."

Guests arrived with serious salads and hilarious outfits. There was a sheer white dress with pleated wing-like sleeves and there were garish tri-color plastic sandals worn with socks, there was an off-the-shoulder number with a fluffy fur hem, and there were sequins galore. One friend claimed her salad had taken *two hours* to prepare. Another had been smoking eggplants all afternoon and still had to put the thing together. The friend who'd mentioned a "salad adventure" had driven to multiple shops in search of dried chipotle chilies and ended up staring at a spice rack with such disappointment that a fellow customer asked if she was OK. When the customer, who happened to be a chef, said "just use smoked paprika," my friend almost hugged her.

As stories were exchanged, I cooked and chopped. I'd marinated mushrooms in honey and beer overnight, now I had to cook lentils and freekeh to accompany them. The more I taste-tested, the more I suspected that getting dark ale instead of regular ale was a mistake—either that or Hetty *could* do wrong and wasn't the salad goddess I'd made her out to be.

What my contribution lacked in quality, it made up for in quantity. One friend let out an evil laugh as she predicted I'd be eating the leftovers *all week.* I tried palming it off to someone with chooks, but she didn't seem to think feeding them beer was a good idea.

Thankfully it was the only disaster; the other creations were delicious. But even if they hadn't been, it wouldn't have mattered. The trick was to avoid taking things too seriously which, when combining the words "salad" and "party," and wearing outrageous second-hand outfits, is easily done.

By the time the last guest left, close to midnight, a team of friends had made the washing-up disappear. The only traces of our wild night were some spinach leaves on the kitchen floor, some herbs between my teeth (the perils of pesto), and some olive pits on the deck.

I went to bed pleased by the meal, and delighted by my friends. Friends who'd slaved over recipes they'd never make again; friends who'd op-shopped for outfits they would never wear again; friends who, after having a good whinge about my strange demands, admitted they had also had a ball.

R U OK? is the paper, listening is the gift
CPX, September 2021

A few years back, I set myself the challenge of interviewing twelve of my friends and combining their stories. I was astonished by how much I learned in the space of one uninterrupted hour.

One friend talked about how trapped she felt during her (planned) pregnancy, another recounted a narrow escape from an abusive relationship, a third talked about the moment he realized, for the first time, he didn't actually have to do what adults told him.

The whole experience made me realize how rarely we make time to really listen, even to our friends.

In her book *You're Not Listening: What You're Missing and Why It Matters*, journalist Kate Murphy says she often gets the sense her interviewees are simply unaccustomed to being listened to. Murphy notes that over the past century, the average time we spend listening to each other has dropped by almost half, while our ability to shut each other out has improved.

R U OK? Day is an annual call "check in" with friends, colleagues, family members and others, to ask if they're OK. But the less time we invest in a relationship throughout the year, the less likely a person is to answer honestly if they're *not*.

Another problem is, while we're used to asking others what they've been *doing*, we're not used to asking how they've been *feeling* in a way that invites an honest answer. Nor are we in the habit of answering honestly ourselves.

It takes effort and intentionality to spend an evening in conversation with a friend; it's far easier to stay home and exchange a few likes with whoever's online. But flippant interactions are a poor substitute for face-to-face conversation, even more so if someone's not OK.

This requires that we give, even *make*, time for others. Prioritizing people might mean changing the way we spend our leisure time, or it might mean working less. But why not orient our lives around our relationships, as far as our finances allow it? If a friend or family member is having a rough time, it's much easier to cook them a meal, mind their kids, or take a walk with them, if our days aren't always fully booked. And how many people, at the end of their lives, wish they had worked more?

Now, it's possible we will have the opportunity to ask, "Are you OK?" on R U OK? Day—will psych ourselves up—only to let fear get in the way. What if the person isn't OK? What if we don't know how to respond? Perhaps it's safer not to try. But safer for who?

Murphy says being listened to, "understood as a person with thoughts, emotions, and intentions that are unique and valuable and deserving of attention," is what we all crave. Realizing that listening can be more powerful than talking, might help us take the plunge.

If we still feel apprehensive, we can visit the R U OK? Day website for tips on how to ask. Or we can resolve to ask someone how their weekend was instead of how they are, with a view to working our way up to more meaningful conversations in time.

The ethos applies to ourselves as much as others. Are there people we can talk to if we find ourselves struggling? If friendships aren't in place before troubles come—and come they surely will—it will be a whole lot harder to give help, or receive it, because it's hard to be vulnerable at the best of times, let alone the worst of them.

Perhaps one of the chief ways I can support R U OK? Day is by resolving to take questions about how I'm doing seriously, regardless of the day. When friends ask how I am and the answer is "not great," I can practice saying so; when they offer help, I can accept it. Who knows, perhaps part of what it means to love our neighbors is to humble ourselves, and let our neighbors love us.

Burden of care
CPX, July 2022

Some phrases are so pervasive we absorb them without thinking. In time, they might influence our thinking too.

The one on my mind is "burden of care." We use it when talking about caring for the very old, the very young, the poor, the sick; and of the cost.

But there are many kinds of care. If we link "burden" to "care" compulsively, neglecting words like "honor," words like "love," we might eclipse a richer, more expansive view.

I think about scooping my four-year-old into my arms after a fall, of his hot wet cheeks and shuddering breaths. It's not hard to offer comfort, to see his bottom lip recede, his smile return. It *would* be hard to turn away.

I think about a friend who's struggling, who calls and then confides in me through tears. It's strange to then be thanked or hear "I'm sorry that I burdened you;" it's what friendship is for.

Even a stern manager, watching their subordinate and seeing something's wrong, may *prefer* to offer help.

A very famous caregiver once told people who felt "heavy laden" to come to him because his burden was light. He expected those same people to love not just their friends but their enemies, to go the extra mile for those in need. How could such a burden be called "light?"

And yet, if you've ever been given a gift you didn't expect or deserve, and felt so full of gratitude you were moved to give yourself, you might glimpse the shining possibility.

Caring *can* be burdensome, especially if the goal is to tick a box or win approval, prove our worth or ease our guilt. But it can be a burden *gladly* borne or a gift gladly given; an honor; a way of life.

Take me away (so I can go home)
Atomic Mommy, 2022 (but penned two years earlier)

We don't need to cross the creek—we have no destination—but nobody points this out. By the time the rest of us have started rolling up our jeans, Anna's are off and she's thigh-deep in icy water. We can see it's the only way, and so we do the same.

The reason we're in the middle of nowhere, crossing a creek in our undies, is that we've run away for a girls' weekend. We've rented a cottage surrounded by fields and sheep, water and sky; we've no one to care for, nowhere to be.

The four of us—all mothers with young children, all in our thirties—aren't exactly "girls" anymore (a point my eldest enjoys making without tact), but I can't bring myself to call this a "ladies'" or "women's" weekend. "Ladies'" is sharp, committee-like; "women's" is too pillowy and soft. What then is a "girls' weekend?"

The girls

It depends on the girls. At the risk of sounding like a weekend-away junkie (and in the hope of sounding like an expert) this one is my third this year—and at the risk of sounding like a cheat, they were all with different people.

The first was with two besties from my Sydney days. We've been getting together every couple of years since we moved apart. These friends have little interest in puzzles and even less in board games, which means more time for cultural attractions and food-related quests.

The second, several months later, was with school friends. We met in grade one and have been going away together ever since we outgrew sleepovers—but these days we're more likely to stay at a shack and eat gourmet food than to rough it in tents. In our college years, a weekend of sleeping-in and pleasing ourselves lacked novelty because it was normality. Now, the opposite is so.

This, the third, is with friends I've made more recently through church. We've chosen a destination far from cafes and cultural attractions, but have brought enough coffee and cocktails, wine and cheese, chocolate and chips, to last a week.

I've said the weekend depends on the "girls," and to some extent it does, but when all the girls are parents of young children, the "guts" are much the same.

The guts

- The guts are much the same because there comes a point in the life of a mother when the simple pleasures she once took for granted—eating, sleeping, walking, talking—become longed-for luxuries. Examples include: eating food her kids don't like, eating when she's hungry (as opposed to when the kids are), eating without anyone complaining or kicking anyone else under (or over) the table;
- sleeping in, sleeping without interruptions, any kind of sleep, come to think of it;
- walking the length of the house without stepping on a toy, walking the length of a street without carrying a child, walking without lugging an overflowing bag of "essentials;" and
- talking to a friend without being interrupted, having conversations that go beyond passing pleasantries and half-formed sentences, talking without shouting to be heard.

It's at this point that a weekend away becomes a thing more wonderful than your pre-parent self could ever have imagined. What matters is not *where* you are going but *that* you are going: you are going away, and the people you love most in the world are not. For two glorious nights, you'll be apart.

But you won't be alone. You'll be with people you love . . . but who don't depend on you daily. People who will be just as drunk on their freedom as you are on yours. You will share comfortable silences, nonsensical jokes, private struggles, funny stories, delicious treats.

You'll share the cooking and washing up too! Unlike your beloved offspring, these people are fully grown! They wipe their own bottoms and chew with their mouths shut! They express their emotions in words instead of outbursts of inexplicable violence! They might cross creeks in their undies every now and then, but afterwards they put their pants and shoes back on—all by themselves.

From fantasy . . .

A girls' weekend away usually begins as a fantasy among a few close friends. Sentences that start with lines such as "wouldn't it be amazing if . . ." or "one day we should . . ." lead to conversations that end up with everyone gazing into the middle-distance, lost in the dreaming.

If you're lucky, one of you will realize such a dream is not beyond the realm of possibility—and dare to say so.

In my experience, the biggest challenge is finding a date—but persevere. The moment that the dreaming turns to planning, the fun begins.

Even packing is a joy! You don't need multiple changes for multiple emergencies, for you only need to clothe yourself; your bag is lighter than your lightest child. Food is a different story. You buy one or more of everything you might possibly want. Between you there'll be too much wine and cheese, and too few fruits and vegetables, but this is not the time for being sensible.

Finally, the day comes. You farewell your family with affection . . . and impatience. In seconds you'll be off-duty; not for minutes or hours, but days. *Days!*

. . . to reality

When we arrive, we cook when we feel like it and eat like queens. We walk without knowing or caring where we'll end up or when, we read without interruption, we go to bed when we want to, and when we do get up, it's because we have woken, not because we've been woken.

Then there's the talk. We tell old stories, we tell new stories, we recycle old jokes, we make new ones. We tease; we confide; we relay inappropriate dreams featuring mutual friends. We discuss doubts and fears and failures, successes, hopes, and *frustrations*.

... to memory

At first, my thoughts of home focus on all that I've escaped: the children's squabbles, demands, needs, complaints. But then I start to miss their earnest faces. Their in-jokes, their affection—their dear dad.

What a thing it is to miss what you still have while it's still yours. What a thing it is to go away—to revel in deep friendship, to laze about and laugh, to be refreshed—and then return to see your children and your husband as gifts too.

The feeling might last hours, or seconds—a tantrum could shatter the spell—so the important thing is to remember it. Especially when the days are long and hard and *loud*, that knowledge is a treasure to behold: the best thing about leaving home, is coming back.

No, this doesn't change the fact that sometimes you'd rather be away again—sipping wine, sharing a joke—but most of the time you know you'd rather be here: wincing at the noise, yawning from the lack of sleep, drowning in washing, but serving the people who need you, who love you, who want you, the most.

And so, dear mother, if you're struggling to see your friends long enough to *really* talk and *really* laugh—to do a puzzle or play a game, eat too much cheese or cross a creek—I prescribe for you a girls' weekend.

If you have a family you love but never leave, let me urge you now, for your sake and for theirs, to go. Love them, leave them, miss them—and let them miss you. After that, go home.

Why asking friends for help has helped my friendships grow
ABC, August 2022

It's taken me years to accept help readily.

I used to automatically refuse offers from my friends because I didn't want to burden them. But over the years, I've made a conscious effort to change. I've realized there are many things I enjoy doing for friends—cooking a meal, editing a story, minding a child, mowing a lawn. It would feel hypocritical if I talked my friends into accepting my help, then said, "I couldn't *possibly*," if they tried to do the same.

We might want to keep our struggles to ourselves to spare our friends, but I have found this doesn't always engender closeness.

Lately, I've noticed that while I naturally extend help to friends according to my strengths, they often offer it according to my weaknesses.

If you'd seen my most recent attempt to cut our youngest's hair or how long it had since grown, you'd understand this text: "Do you guys have anything straight after school today? I could bring scissors and clippers and shear some sheep for an hour?"

It can be tempting to decline, especially when a favor constitutes a luxury; when the friend offering to cut three children's hair has four kids of her own.

But if an offer sounds sincere, it likely is. And if it is compatible with talk and cups of tea, then it's win-win.

Among my baking friends, messages like "Hypothetically . . . if someone were to drop a slice of baked mousse tart on your doorstep . . . would you be home?" are eagerly and frequently exchanged. A cake shared is a cake well spent.

Accepting and exchanging favors like this can be fun and foster closeness, but what really takes a friendship up a notch, is feeling you can ask someone for help. I've had to practice this as well.

One of the reasons is that I've needed to. I've had a chronically ill husband, multiple kids, and multiple commitments; I've known that fierce independence will not just hurt me, it will hurt my family.

Another is the conviction that one of the surest ways to strengthen a friendship is to show vulnerability and trust. Asking for a hand does exactly that.

It can feel risky, especially in our individualistic culture, especially if we're used to going it alone. No one wants to be a burden, to overload, or push away a friend.

But when I remind myself they *can* say no, especially if I give an easy out; when I think about how *I'd* want *them* to come to me in times of need—to not assume a "no" but let me answer for myself, to trust the friendship will withstand it either way—I take the plunge.

I've asked friends to do the school run for me when I've been a pregnant and vomiting wreck, to mind the kids when other plans have fallen through, to read drafts when I have needed fresh eyes and advice—the list goes on.

If they say they can't or that they'd rather not, I'm glad—they didn't pretend otherwise, they answered honestly—but mostly, they say yes.

Sometimes an ask is more a case of being opportunistic than really needing help. These are easier to decline and therefore easier to voice. One of my more frivolous, and more audacious, requests was for accommodation. A friend of mine had asked if she could visit with her son. We didn't have a spare room or spare bed. Our neighbors had a caravan and plans to go away.

I texted to avoid putting them on the spot; I said I'd expect and understand a no. The reply was unambiguous: "Yes that's no problem! We'd prefer to have people stay here while we're away and I can ask them to water my plants!" They went on to say when they'd drop me the keys and to offer us their car as well.

It helps to ask according to a person's strengths. I wouldn't ask a friend who isn't used to kids to care for ours, or one who doesn't enjoy reading to give feedback on a draft. I'm grateful that no one has ever asked me to help them with their taxes or assemble flat-pack furniture—if they did, I would decline for both our sakes.

One benefit of asking friends for help is that it can embolden them to do the same. Some requests have made my day, or week.

It was thrilling when a friend who was in labor said she'd love a filthy, greasy burger delivered to the hospital, and fast.

I may not have looked like a superhero when I pulled up outside, gave it to her husband, and sped off into the night—but I sure felt like one.

Another friend of mine got her driver's license recently. Before that she depended on close friends to get around. A couple took her on a weekly shopping trip, someone else gave weekly lifts to church. Their disappointment when she told them that she could drive herself came as a surprise; they'd enjoyed seeing her and helping her each week—now they didn't want to stop.

Sometimes I get the impression people are making a conscious effort not to lean on their friends, that they're scared they'll ask too much. This is a risk.

But the friends we're closest to should know they can say no. And maybe, perhaps mostly, they'll say yes.

On truth-telling and friend-making in fiction—and in life
ABC, December 2023

There's a moment in Elif Batuman's latest book when its protagonist wonders whether, instead of trying to write a novel that's true to life, she could manipulate her life in order to produce one.

"What if I could use the aesthetic life as an algorithm to solve my two biggest problems: how to live, and how to write novels? In any real-life situation, I would pretend I was in a novel, and then do whatever I would want the person in the novel to do. Afterward, I would write it all down, and I would have written a novel, without having had to invent a bunch of fake characters and pretend to care about them."

It sounds absurd because it is absurd. But in a world full of real characters, laboring to invent fake ones does as well.

On reflection, it's not entirely far-fetched that some writers might not merely comb their memories for material retrospectively, but search for it in the present. They might even alter their movements in the moment to create it.

I'm not a fiction writer. But my friends do sometimes feature in my work, and from time to time they joke that something one of us has said or done will end up in an article. I've held parties and then written about them, made mistakes then written about them, had conversations then written about them, but I've never held a party or made a mistake or had a conversation *to* write about it (apart from interviews, where that's the aim).

A few weeks ago, a stranger emailed me to introduce herself. She'd happened upon an essay I'd written called, "Instead of presents, I asked for salads," then read my bio, and more of my work.

"I hope this isn't weird but I just wanted to drop you a line, as one Tasmanian writer to another, and let you know how much I've enjoyed some of your recent work," her first email began. Not only was she also a Tasmanian and a writer, she was a Tasmanian and a salad-lover. The party I'd written about sounded like her idea of fun.

My first reply began: "Ha!! It's not weird and even if it is, I love weird!"

A party I had not planned to write about—but did—led to a meeting I had not planned to write about—but am.

It didn't take us long to realize we lived within a short walk of each other. I didn't want to meet to make a story—but I did feel part of one.

"How does 10 a.m. sound? Or earlier? Or later?!" I wrote. I confessed it had crossed my mind to say 9:48 a.m., "to make myself seem less conventional and more eccentric than I actually am," but reminded myself I wasn't creating a character, I was one. We were living life, not drafting a story. "Though with two writers in the mix it might become one," I wrote.

We met and had plenty to talk about, plenty to laugh about, plenty in common. It was a first for me, but Philippa had been meeting strangers who'd written to her for years. In her twenties she'd started a blog that attracted a large, devoted audience. Various comments on posts led to private conversations and more than a few friendships. When she decided to travel and work overseas, she had multiple couches to choose from.

She'd since returned to Tasmania and turned forty but still had a taste for my kind of adventure: making new friends.

When it was time to head home and inform our respective husbands we'd survived our daring encounter, Philippa told me she's pretty good at sensing whether someone is a psychopath and was pretty sure I wasn't one. Laughing, I said that though I lacked experience, I'd drawn the same conclusion about her.

I wasn't surprised to get her "psycho all-clear," because by the time she issued it she'd already asked if she could come to my next party, and she wasn't surprised to get mine because I'd instantly responded with delight. I noted that while it would terrify me to go to a party knowing only one person, I could see she'd hold her own at mine just fine.

My birthday is still months away, but I'm sure we'll catch up before then. If having the same salad heroes and declaring each other not-psychos in parting isn't an indication a beautiful friendship lies ahead, I don't know what is.

There's a trope in many films and shows and books, where a relationship starts under false pretenses. Sometimes it's romantic, sometimes it's platonic, but one of the characters has an ulterior motive which they feel compelled to hide, more so when a genuine relationship develops. Or, they start the friendship naturally, and then an ulterior motive arises: a conflict of interest they could just declare but are afraid to.

They should just *tell* the other character, who the reader/viewer knows won't mind at all, but they think that if their new friend or lover finds out, they'll assume their affection isn't genuine. In fact, telling the truth wouldn't be a problem—it's hiding it that leads to strife.

At the start of this essay I mentioned a favorite book, but I didn't mention its title: *Either/Or*. It's not the one by Kierkegaard, it is a nod to it. Either/Or. It's a frame of mind that traps us needlessly, and all too frequently.

Either/Or. Do I want to be friends with the person that I met? Or do I want to write about our meeting?

As with so much in (real) life, it's not a case of truth or lie, of Either/Or. The answer is Both/And .

(*And* because this is no novel, and I needn't create tension, I've no plans to keep what I have written here from my newest friend. She won't be the last to read this when it's done; she will be the first.)

Why b-grade baking is an a-grade gift
Scary Mommy, March 2022 (Published as: "Want to Do Something for a Struggling Mom Friend? Try Just-Good-Enough Food.")

My son had Covid and we were under house arrest, so when a friend asked if I needed anything—a cake delivery, perhaps?—I made no attempt to dissuade her. She arrived at the door with a huge slab of mud cake layered with creamy chocolate ganache. I cut a sliver, just to taste, then another. I cut a generous slice for my husband, and generous slices for our kids. I cut a sliver, just to taste. And another. Technically *I* never had a slice.

Later, she told me the cake was overcooked and dry, the ganache was an attempt to rescue it. Suddenly the gesture was even more touching—she'd given us *imperfect* cake!

I'm a big fan of imperfection, of lowering the bar. If my friend hadn't lowered the bar, I would have missed out on that dreamy cake—that's proof, right there, that perfect is the enemy of good.

It's a principle I try to keep in mind. I love cooking and I love my friends and I love the idea of cooking for them when they're going through tough times. At the same time, I have three primary-aged kids, two jobs, volunteer work, and a social life. If I can snatch half an hour to whip something up between (or during) one thing and another, or double a recipe I'm already set to make, that's fine.

But if my heart is set on choosing an unforgettable recipe, doing the shopping required to follow it, *and* finding time to make it, it's just not going to happen. And although it's the thought that counts, the thought *plus food* is kind of more helpful.

I think what helped me to lower my standards (not that they were ever *that* high) was being on the receiving end of meal rosters when each of our children were born. Contrary to my expectations, I didn't have all day to cook (turns out babies don't just sleep and smile) so when people from our church started rocking up with meals, we took them gratefully, if not a little desperately.

It doesn't take a Heston Blumenthal experiment to know that context changes our perceptions of food. When you've been hiking all day and you sit down to a bowl of cheap packet pasta, it can taste sublime. The same goes for food that appears in the eye of a storm (a house full of kids) as if by magic. Not only does it save you from cooking, it saves you from even *thinking* about cooking. I don't have any research to back me up on this, but I swear to you: these factors change the taste.

Even if this Heston-style magic doesn't work for your kids, even if you look up from a delicious mouthful to three horrified faces (turns out a health-conscious cook snuck *lentils* into the bolognese they gave us), at least you can hold up both hands and say, "Don't look at me, *I* didn't put them there," before emptying your bowl and proceeding to start on theirs.

I'm not saying the food people gave us wasn't objectively great—it likely was. I'm just saying we adults would have loved it either way.

I still have to remind myself of this when I'm cooking for others. I love cooking, and I love it when people love my cooking. If I make a stir fry with veggies that are a "little" overcooked (OK, a lot), or a quiche that needs more cheese, or a pastry that's not flaky like I'd planned, I'm still tempted to abandon plans to pass it on.

I still have to remind myself that when life is overwhelming, the gesture, and the energy it saves a friend, matter more than my ego or reputation. And so, with numerous disclaimers, I've learned to hand my cooking over as it is.

What's more, I've seen the food-that-appears-by-magic rule prove true repeatedly. Just the other day a friend was reminding me of a "very tasty" green chicken curry I once cooked her and how, when she asked for the recipe, I confessed I'd used a packet. Another time I spontaneously gave a family a hunk of frozen bolognese from our freezer and a packet of pasta from our cupboard. The mother later said the meal had made her cry—not because it was bad (though objectively, maybe it was) but because she was so tired and so touched.

I guess it's an (un)scientifically proven fact: in times of sickness, uncertainty, busyness, and stress, b-grade baking is an a-grade gift. Baking is about timing and care, not perfection. Giving is too.

My friend, the therapist
Ekstasis, September 2021

I'd been thinking about friendship and therapy, and friendship *as* therapy. I'd read Lori Gottlieb's *Maybe You Should Talk to Someone*, and thought about how close a therapist and client might become. At the same time, I'd been thinking about my closest friends, and the therapeutic potential of friendship.

I'd thought about the rising demand for counseling—at last the stigma was lifting—but I'd wondered, too, if there was a corresponding decline in the depth of our friendships. I'd read a lot of books that portrayed friends becoming lovers, but marveled at how rarely contemporary writers seemed to celebrate friendship as an end, not just a means. I'd thought, when reading *A Little Life*, that friendship would be enough for Willem and Jude, and despaired, for Jude's sake, when it was not.

I'd also wondered at the number of "friends" we broadcast to online compared with the few we actually share our lives with one-to-one—the ones who we counsel, and who counsel us. Was society progressing in one area, with people more open to seeking professional help, but regressing in another? Were we less inclined to offer and accept it from our friends?

I wasn't questioning the value of seeing a professional, but I was thinking that making time for equally intimate conversations with trusted friends could be just as important. Those with both—therapeutic friendship *and* a therapist—might have the best arrangement of all: they could weigh up advice from someone who knows better from a psychological perspective, with the advice of someone who knows *them* better.

*

I suppose whether or not the theory bears weight largely depends on the friendship in question, and whether we're brave enough to put it to the test. After all, it's often easier to speak than listen, to dodge the truth than tell it. It makes sense to see a professional because they're paid to listen—trained to uncover truths, bound by oath to keep them, and by duty not to judge.

Yes, counseling costs money, but it won't cost a friendship, and might protect several. If we save the idiosyncrasies and anxieties we're confused by and ashamed of for the therapy room, we can stay fun and upbeat for our friends. We also reduce the risk of betrayal. What if confiding in friends ended in more pain, not less? Imagine summoning the courage to expose your insecurities, only to have your confidant recoil. Or they might empathize, but give very bad advice. So yes, it would be risky, and the risks might not pay off.

*

Anyway, I'd been meaning to write an article about friendship and therapy and friendship *as* therapy. Somewhere along the way, in a city I'd never heard of, a strange new sickness started to spread, and spread, and spread. We were instructed to stay at home—to avoid seeing people outside of our own households, to keep our distance if we did.

I still saw my friends. I started walking with one, 1.5 meters apart, once a week. I saw others in scheduled meetings and in photos online; we still chatted and texted—in some cases, there was more contact, not less—but I missed the comfortable silences and the spontaneous encounters, the private conversations at public gatherings, the subconscious exchanges of physical cues.

One friend was going through a break-up, another was trying to avoid one, another had lost her job, and on top of it all, we were all learning how to live through a global upheaval, to accept unprecedented prohibitions and new responsibilities, to adjust to strange new rules for living. We shared our struggles, but there was nearly always a screen between us, and sometimes it felt like the things that really mattered couldn't fit inside its frame.

I was still thinking about friendship—even Jesus had relied upon close friends—and I still wanted to write about it, but while I had more time at home, I had three children at home all day everyday. Two of them had schoolwork and one of them was toilet training and someone needed something all the time.

Just a few weeks earlier, back in that magical time when libraries were places that opened and let you in, where you could look *and* touch *and* take books home without sanitizing or checking-in,

I borrowed *The Second Mountain* by *New York Times* political and social commentator David Brooks. The early chapters contained some compelling critiques of the "rampant individualization" of contemporary culture, and its catastrophic emphasis on "individual success, self-fulfilment, individual freedom [and] self-actualization."

Our society, says Brooks, is "built on self-preoccupation," and is profoundly dysfunctional as a result. In the last twenty years, the (US) suicide rate has risen by 30 percent; there is a "loneliness crisis"—and this was *before* we were forced, en masse and on purpose, to isolate physically too.

Psychologist Ryan Howes says that while one in four people require therapy for treatment of a mental disorder at some point in their lives, "everyone can benefit from being in therapy all the time." Even if this were true, I don't think therapy alone (or friendship alone, for that matter) can solve the problems Brooks describes—and neither does Brooks. His solutions include deeper relationships and the kind of outward-looking, other-centered focus that tends to spring from faith.

Therapy can align with this. It can improve our relationships and benefit those close to us; it can have a ripple effect. I don't want to question its versatility or its value, but I do want to elevate the role of friendship—and to suggest that while professional help is superior in some ways, it can never come close in others.

Part of the reason is that although we can pay psychologists and counselors to care *for* us, by giving us new insights and strategies; they might not care *about* us, and they're not supposed to love us.

There are also contextual restrictions. In most cases, they don't know our families or our friends. They don't witness us going about our normal lives, or observe our behavior when we're not on show—all they know is what they see and what we tell them in a contrived setting in a limited time. And we know next to nothing about them.

Another difference is that when you share your struggles in therapy, it can end up being all about you. Yes, some go along for the sake of their loved ones, but others would say the "all-about-me" element is precisely what they're paying for.

When you share your struggles in friendship, however, there's not one reclining couch; there are two (sometimes more), and there's no one taking notes.

Furthermore, while therapists might need our money, they don't need us; and although we need people we can depend on in our lives, we also need people who depend on us. We're far less likely to feel worthless and dispensable if we know we're a source of strength or encouragement to someone else; and if we're not just talking about our own problems, but listening to another person's too, we're less likely to become self-absorbed, or assume we're the only ones finding life hard.

*

Anyway, I'd been meaning to write an article about friendship and therapy and friendship *as* therapy, and then there was this global pandemic and, like most things, it ended up on hold. By the time I put pen to paper, it dawned on me that I'd been unwittingly testing my own theory. It was only as I wrote that I realized that my one weekly, in-person outing during the lockdown—the walk with a friend I mentioned earlier—could also be characterized as a one-hour therapy session.

During these walks—we're still taking them, and I hope they will continue—we talk about the highs and lows of our weeks, our personal failings, frustrations, and achievements, about what we've been reading and watching and thinking about. We ask each other questions; we interrogate unexamined assumptions and beliefs; we ask for and accept advice.

The act of putting our thoughts into words can clarify them even as we speak, and every now and then, one of us will stumble on a realization we'd never had before. We don't always talk about something deep, but we always know we can. There are trivial perks, too—we exchange recipes and baked goods, puzzles and books, child-minding favors and more—but the thing we relish most is having time in our week to talk and listen and learn.

The therapeutic benefits arise from mutual trust and respect, and a willingness to discuss what we've been thinking and feeling as well as what we've been *doing*; to speculate about what things might mean and what we might change. It helps that we share similar beliefs, values, and priorities. It also helps that we've been walking. I think long drives with my husband have similar therapeutic power. Perhaps it's to do with physical motion, or perhaps the freedom from making eye contact gives us boldness where we'd otherwise feel awkward.

Setting aside the time is crucial too. Meeting regularly means we're not starting from scratch every time—each "session" builds on the last—and meeting for an hour means our conversations are relaxed, not rushed. I've benefited hugely from friendship groups too, but the fact it's just the two of us—in line with government restrictions—makes it easier to be vulnerable; take risks.

The thing that most enables honesty, however, is love. There's a passage in the Bible about speaking the truth in love. Honest opinions might hurt in the short-term, but they're often kinder in the long-term, and if we know they're spoken in love, the friendship will survive. When we know the friendship's not at stake, and admit that neither of us is perfect, we can be honest about ourselves too—we can share the wrongs that we regret, the thoughts we wish we didn't have, the good we've left undone; we can shine a light in places that are dark, and start to clean them up.

Stepping back from this singular example, I wonder how isolation has affected friendships on a much larger scale. Have we dealt with the stress and uncertainty and pressure of this shared trial by leaning on and supporting each other more than usual? Or have our lives become more separate? Have we drifted further apart?

I hope that the risks we've learned to live with out of lockdown, and the sacrifices we've learned to make—sanitizing at the expense of convenience, checking-in at the expense of privacy, wearing masks at the expense of comfort—have taught us to take risks in our relationships too. I hope we'll be more willing to ask deeper questions and give deeper answers, to be more vulnerable, more honest, more generous, and more brave; to dare to really love our friends. Because it's better, even safer, to care more deeply and risk greater hurt than to maintain distance. It's messy and it's hard but it makes life beautiful. We should not settle for less.

The best thing about holidaying with other families can also be the worst
The Guardian, November 2023

I was packing for a weekend away with several other families when I made the mistake of thinking a bottle of red wine would be safest rolled up in a sleeping bag.

I didn't know most of the families going, but I knew the instigators, and that they'd have gathered a great crowd. Those other families probably thought so too—until ours showed up, reeking of wine, in the middle of the day.

It was fine. Really. Compared to the time my husband dislodged a leech in his sleep and we woke to a scene from a horror movie, this sleeping bag, hung out to dry, didn't look *that* bad. The glass was in big chunks so we didn't worry, after removing it, that splinters might remain. And though the smell did linger, it eased somewhat as the sun lodged an attack.

The crowd was so good that no one held any first impressions they might have had against us. Instead, we received sympathy and offers of help. One of the many benefits of group holidays is that if you forget something, or break it, or soak it in red wine, you won't be on your own. The just-in-case types will likely have spare bedding and spare wine.

I've also been on group holidays where medical supplies, vehicles, books, and clothing have been shared. As for food and games, this goes without saying. But the best thing that's shared is the work of parenting, or rather, the work of playing, as children form happy clusters and occupy themselves in ways they almost never do with siblings.

Meanwhile adults enjoy food, conversation, and nature in relative peace. The power of other children also means that parents for whom a family bushwalk is the stuff of dreams might see their dreams come true. Kids who otherwise lag behind are suddenly in front. It's hard to talk non-stop to another kid *and* complain to your parents at the same time; you might as well lead the way instead.

New friends, old friends, shared experiences, shared supplies. It is a joy worth planning for a year in advance—which is about how far ahead you have to plan to find a weekend when multiple families are free and campgrounds have the space. But group holidays are not without risks. In the interests of balance, let me end with a cautionary tale.

We were holidaying with four other families in a national park. We'd had a full day of walking and swimming and talking and laughing—and feasting on fresh local cherries. A few of us were playing a game by the light of our head torches when one of the adults went to take another sip from her cup of tea and aborted part-way through. At first she looked confused, then, peering in her cup, alarmed.

Sharing conversations, experiences, and supplies might be the greatest thing about group holidays, but not every kind of sharing brings delight. When we sought an explanation, the friend showed us what was in her camping mug.

Earlier that day, some of the group had been using someone else's empty mug for cherry pits. Making tea in low light, that "someone else" hadn't noticed her mug was neither clean, nor empty.

It wasn't an *experience* you'd want to repeat, but it is a memory we keep, a story we repeat, an aspect of the holiday that, long after it ended, we still share.

We can help older Australians by asking them for help
The Ethics Center, August 2022

Older people are often undervalued and overlooked in our society—to their detriment, and ours.

A stranger knocked on our door the other day. She was promoting a service for older people who live alone. To counter the risk of an accident or sudden illness going unnoticed, a person could sign up to have a Red Cross volunteer call them every day.

It was heart-warming and heart-breaking; wonderful that an organization was intervening to address the frightening risk of solitary suffering, terrible that the risk was so pervasive that it warranted an *organization* intervening.

I was reminded of an initiative based in Africa that I'd heard about on Maya Shanka's podcast *A Slight Change of Plans*, one that wasn't designed to help older people, but to enlist their help.

The Friendship Bench was started in Zimbabwe by psychiatrist Dr Dixon Chibanda. Its goal was to alleviate pressure on the country's health system by training "grandmothers" (respected older women in the community) to meet people with common mild-to-moderate mental health disorders at a park bench, let them talk through their problems, and help them choose just one to try and solve.

Prospective volunteers, not to mention many of Chibanda's peers, were skeptical at first, but he didn't just train the grandmothers— he let them train him.

As a psychiatrist, Chibanda was schooled to avoid telling his own story or being vulnerable; his volunteers taught him the key to connecting with a person and building trust was a willingness to bend this rule.

They also told him that calling the park benches where the therapy took place "mental health benches" as he'd planned would create such a stigma that no one would show up. Taking their advice, he renamed them "friendship benches."

Randomized control trials have since shown therapy from trained community grandmothers to be remarkably effective. Better still, the *volunteers* benefit richly, gaining "a profound sense of purpose and a sense of belonging" from the work. "It's a win/win," Chibanda told Shanka. The "grandmothers" are helping people, "but it's helping them too."

Chibanda says one of the things he's learned from *The Friendship Bench* is just how important connection is. The therapy doesn't *really* start, he says, until the moment people connect.

The scheme has since been rolled out elsewhere; Chibanda says he'd like to see friendship benches all over the world. But I suspect the barriers in places like Australia would be even greater than those faced in Africa; not because of stigma surrounding mental health, but because of stigma surrounding "the elderly."

Chibanda says his volunteers were considered custodians of local wisdom and culture. But in more individualistic, materialistic cultures, there's a tendency to depict older people as burdensome instead.

From useless to used

Sarah Holland-Batt's 2020 essay *Magical Thinking and the Aged-care Crisis* explores this tendency. She discusses inheritance impatience, elder abuse, and mandated euthanasia in dystopian fiction, then declares: "the apocalypse has already arrived for Australia's elderly."

"We treat older people as a separate and subhuman class, frequently viewing them as a burden on their families, the community and the state," she writes.

Immanuel Kant argued against treating people as mere resources, but according to Holland-Batt, our aged-care industry does precisely this; it mines people for profit. If Scottish philosopher Alasdair MacIntyre was right when he said the way we treat "the very young and the very old, the sick, the injured, and the otherwise disabled" is an important indicator of a community's flourishing, ours is falling short.

I think of the way I've heard Indigenous people speak about their elders—with reverence and respect; of the biblical command to honor one's parents; of the proverb that describes gray hair as a "crown of glory."

When did assuming that people have nothing more to offer once they're "old" become acceptable? When did we stop treasuring the kind of wisdom that builds with experience? And how dearly has it cost us?

A closer relationship, a broader perspective

What I loved most about *The Friendship Bench* was the image it evoked of people from different generations sitting side by side. I loved the underlying assumption that the elderly among us still have much to offer: an offering so unique they were the key to the initiative's success. I also loved the idea that therapy took place not under fluorescent light, but the shining sun.

The fact the volunteers benefited just as much as those they were there to help did not surprise me. Who doesn't want to put the lessons learned over the years to use? To see somebody suffering, and help? Not all, I grant, but many—maybe most.

If only Australia's discussions about aged care were less reactive and more proactive. If only there were less talk of problems and more of potential.

Yes, as we grow old, we grow more dependent and less capable; we cannot deny the reality of declining physical and sometimes mental functioning. But our bodies will impose enough limits without generalized assumptions based on age imposing more. I know of people in their nineties who still work as volunteers. We're all unique; our aging and its timing will be too. And even when age *does* stop us from helping, makes us start depending more, it cannot take our value, our worthiness of care, respect, and love.

The biggest game-changer I can imagine when it comes to the way our society views and treats its older members, is a rise in intergenerational connection—better still, friendship. In some respects, our society is more connected than ever before, but not in the ways that count the most. If we want to tackle loneliness, depression, and despair, this must change. We not only have to change the way we act, we must change the way we think. "The elderly" need us, and we need them.

On saying "sorry" most readily, when we least need to
The Ethics Center, November 2023

One of the first things I learned when traveling in Europe, knowing only English, was to prioritize learning the word "sorry" when preparing to enter a new country.

There's nothing wrong with learning "hello," "thank you," and "please," "I am . . .," and "where's the nearest . . .," but if you're going to learn one word by heart, that's the one I'd recommend. If you get yourself in trouble, it will likely be the word you need the most.

I speak from experience. Picture a nineteen-year-old Australian washing her hands in the fountain at the foot of The Spanish Steps. Unbeknownst to her, the police have just rebuked some fellow tourists for cooling their sweaty feet in the waters of this national treasure—and told the watching crowd to heed their warning, show respect.

When their whistles blew at me and I was asked to show my passport, I didn't have the words to explain that I'd just been to the loo and had been unable to find a handle for the tap. This was before sensors became commonplace; perhaps there was a pedal, but I hadn't thought to look. Instead, I'd opened the door (with difficulty—I'd already covered my hands in pink slimy soap) and headed for the next available water source.

I had my reasons, but I didn't have the words to explain why I'd done what I'd done, and until some friends explained later, I couldn't fully understand why *what* I'd done had been so very wrong. I *could* say, "*Lo siento,*" and did, repeatedly.

I was reminded of this incident when reflecting on the ways in which we use the word "sorry" in daily life.

Sometimes we're not apologizing at all—we're expressing sympathy to a bereaved friend or being polite to a stranger. The bereavement "sorry" might translate to: "I wish you didn't have to go through this," or, "I really feel for you." The polite "sorry" to a stranger might translate to "excuse me," or "I excuse you." It might not be "performative" at all; we might use it as a statement, nothing more. Or we'll say, "sorry I'm late" when we're not sorry, but are late. If we really are sorry we're late; our eyes, our tone, must do the work.

At other times, we apologize when we needn't; we say "sorry" if we burst into tears when we are "supposed" to be keeping it together, or if we've had to ask for help when we'd hoped to solve a problem on our own.

In the workplace, if we've been asked to do something we haven't been trained to do, and need to take up a manager's time to find out how, we might apologize when really, we're just doing our job, and asking them to do theirs.

In the context of close friendship, pouring out our worries, or asking for help or advice or both, isn't something to apologize for; it's (in part) what friendship is for. I know this, yet I find myself behaving otherwise. Just the other day I said "sorry" to a friend while crying on the phone, even though when friends do this to me, I tell them off. Being trusted in this way honors a person more than it puts them out. When you love someone, you *want* to help; real "sorry" territory is more likely to be shutting a loved one out, than letting them in.

This is because "real sorry territory" is using the word in the deepest sense of the word; it's apologizing for hurting someone. It's not using the word to escape consequence, it's using the word to express heartfelt regret for causing real harm and, rather than making excuses, choosing to take responsibility.

It can be easy to say "sorry" when we don't really mean it— when we're being polite, when we're going through a motion, avoiding punishment. It's easy to say it, even mean it, when we see we've made a dumb mistake: *Lo siento! Lo siento!* It can roll right off the tongue.

In the case of the *Fontana della Barcaccia*, I'm pretty sure my excuses would have only caused further offense. Looking back, I'm glad I couldn't say another word. But that sorry didn't cost me; it helped me.

It's using the word to admit to ourselves as much as to somebody else that we've not only caused offense, but ongoing hurt, and to ask for undeserved forgiveness, that's hard. Even if we haven't done wrong *technically*, we might have had a chance to help, and turned away.

Using "sorry" to express true regret—to "repent"—could be the rarest use of "sorry" there is. The rarest and, when it's sincere, the most powerful. A word that can mean little can mean much; it can be the difference between making excuses, or facing the truth; between a wound that keeps on causing pain, and one that, finally, begins to heal.

Not sure what to buy "the person who has everything?" Don't buy them anything.
The Guardian, December 2023

The problem of what to buy a loved one who seems to have everything they'd ever want is one many of us face each year, as is a desire to avoid spending beyond our means, or contributing to landfill. But there's an alternative. If a person is hard to buy for, don't buy them anything. Make something instead. What matters is the thought.

You might hear the words "make something instead" and think of spray-painted pasta necklaces and collages that contain more glue than shells; or of people who can actually knit things that other people actually want to wear. You might think you need to be either cute, or skilled, to pull this off. Think again.

One of my go-to gifts, for any number of occasions, is heart-shaped chocolate biscuits and a tag that reads "with love." What better way to communicate affection than by making a gift that both looks and tastes sweet? (Unless the person in question is on a diet, in which case it might communicate the opposite of love).

If you're not a baker, the mere fact that you tried will be impressive, regardless of the outcome. If something (or everything) goes wrong, simply document your failed attempt (genre options include comedy and horror) and give your loved one the story instead—or as well—as the actual product. It might not be edible; it *will* be entertaining.

Speaking of entertainment, if the person you have in mind likes crosswords or quizzes, why not make them one? Brainstorm quirks and memories particular to them (pet peeves, proud moments, stories they tell repeatedly) with fellow friends or family members, then turn them into questions and answers. Mix it up with some multiple choice and true or false questions, as well as some based on hypothetical scenarios with subjective answers. If you run out of ideas, your internet search history might offer unique inspiration.

Perhaps the person you have in mind isn't into quizzes, or silliness. Do they love music, or eating out, or movies, or books? Whatever it is, compile a list of recommended reading, or listening, or restaurants, tailored to their tastes. If you don't share their passion, get tips from mutual friends or family members who do. The more detail (what to order at a restaurant, who recommended a certain book, why) the better. I accept that if it's hard to think of one item a person might like to receive, coming up with five to ten might sound harder still, but it's just a list, they're just ideas. The person is under no obligation to actually listen to, eat, watch, or read any of your suggestions. It's the thought that counts, and the thought is all they're getting.

A series of photographs is another option. You could hunt down one from every year of your relationship and write a few words to accompany them. If you prefer ridiculous to sentimental, you could cut the heads out of an existing group photo and stick them on figures in another to make a more unlikely scene. Or you could personalize a bottle of their favorite drink, or packet of their favorite food, with their, or your, grinning face.

A bespoke video "card" is another option. When my grandfather turned ninety during the pandemic, members of our family met on a conference call and recorded ourselves singing, waving, and blowing kisses to him. For extra points, don wigs and dress-up clothes, and follow "Happy Birthday" or "Merry Christmas," with their favorite song.

There's something sweet about picking a bunch of flowers versus buying one, and you don't need a garden to do it. Ask a neighbor or two if they can spare some cuttings, or go for a walk and "prune" any overhanging plants. As with the baking, if it ends in disaster you'll still have a gift: the story of your noble, if failed, quest.

Another option is a homemade voucher. The challenge is making sure the person redeems it, which is why I recommend terms and conditions that include a (playful!) threat. For example, if you offer to babysit a couple's kids, you might make the consequence of failing to "redeem the offer" within six months, them having to babysit yours.

Some people will prefer a more traditional gift—will feel more or less loved based on whether more or less money has been spent on them—even if they do "have everything." Others will appreciate a gift that has cost time just as much as a gift that has cost money, if not more.

The better you know someone, the less risky giving "outside the box" will be. The better you know someone, the easier it will be to know whether your shenanigans will make them think you've lost the plot; or laugh and know they are—uniquely—loved.

Love &
...technology

Say it in your own words: Email templates can save us time, but at what cost?
ABC, September 2022

A newsletter I subscribe to shared a link last week that made me cringe.

The newsletter, which is aimed at freelance writers, linked to a site with a range of templates to "help you say no in a variety of situations."

If the link was to an article with advice on different ways to say no, complete with principles and the odd example, I don't think I'd have flinched, but it was to templates—"and if you're a Gmail user, you can import them all for use right into your email account."

Easy. Efficient. No more agonizing, no more time-wasting; just select the option most suited to your needs, tweak it (or not), and click send. "How to say no to a work project," "How to say no to a meeting," "How to say no on principle," "How to say no after you already said yes"—the list went on.

Maybe it's fine. Maybe I'm overreacting. Did I mention I'm a thirty-nine-year-old who was writing letters by hand long after the internet made it quaint? I'm someone who's so troubled by predictive text that if, before I can figure out how to disable it, it suggests the exact words I was about to use, I'll then use other words in a petulant act of resistance. Given that my goal is not to let technology interfere with the way I communicate, this is also problematic.

The "no on principle" template starts by apologizing for the delayed response (side note: if using, make sure your response is delayed). "I have been trying to do too much of late," it explains, "which makes it hard to keep up with correspondence." Then there's some "honesty" (or honest-sounding words) and apparent straight talking, even the word "truth": "I also have to admit I am not good at saying no, because I enjoy meeting people and discussing new ideas. Unfortunately, the truth is that I am maxed out and need to take a step back." After that the author talks about how prioritizing his business, family, and himself, so he can reach some of his "most important goals," will be his blanket policy until he is "caught up."

Sounds reasonable. Courteous, respectful, even vulnerable. It might be close to the truth for many and, with some tweaking, contain no lie. But even if the reasons were (technically) true for you, I don't think an email pasted and passed off as personal could be described as honest.

Forget the technicalities. If you received one of these from someone you know well, and recognized it, how would you feel? And if you were sending one of these, and knew the person would find out it was a template, would you still go ahead?

Add to this the fact I didn't come across these in a newsletter to freelance tradies, whose strengths may not lie in written communication, but in a newsletter specifically for writers.

"Personal" or personal?

These templates are probably old news to many and for some, already in everyday use. Perhaps they'll peter out; perhaps they'll become standard practice. I hope I'm not alone in willing their demise. I hope I'm not alone in wanting the personal emails that people send me to be written, not pasted, even if that costs them thought and time. I hope I'm not alone in wanting technology to facilitate personal communication, not displace it.

Andy Crouch, an author who's spent years thinking and writing about how we can use technology wisely, notes the importance of mastering the medium, lest it master us. Talking on the ABC Radio National's *Soul Search*, he noted that many of the shortcuts and efficiencies technology so readily enables come at a cost: "If I can get in my car and accelerate to a very high rate of speed, I never have to move my body with effort, such that I actually become stronger and able to move faster on my own. In fact, quite the opposite. The longer I spend in my automobile—on an airplane—my body actually diminishes in its strength; for every hour I've spent in my car, I've lost some quantum of ability to move with purpose and force through the world."

I wonder what abilities the habitual use of templates and predictive text might diminish. Our ability to express ourselves, by ourselves? To make wise choices, and articulate them with honesty?

To see other people as people, and therefore worthy of our time?

I think about the simple instruction we were often given at school: write "in your own words;" and of the advice often given to writers: "find your voice." Both take practice, but both get easier with practice. Cheating does too.

I also think about how much easier it is to treat somebody poorly when you see them as an annoyance or an inconvenience—when you stop seeing them as a person—and how much easier it is to do this when you cannot see their face.

Crouch, who believes people are "built" not just to use and be used, but to love and be loved, says human flourishing isn't just dependent on connecting with other people, but on connections with people we can trust, with people who know us and care about us.

Some might think of work and home as separate categories. They might have superficial relationships with colleagues and clients, and trusting relationships in their personal lives; they might act with efficiency at work, and empathy at home. But I can't help but wonder whether, over time, a habit of reaching for templates in one sphere might influence how a person thinks and acts in another.

Maybe you don't consider this a problem, or a risk. Maybe templates make sense to you, especially when you're dealing with people you've never met. Perhaps they're using templates too; perhaps that doesn't bother you at all.

But what if I told you the thirty-one templates included "how to say no to a date" and "how to say no to a friend asking for business help?" The "say no to a friend" template, which includes the line, "I am so proud to see you pushing the limits of [insert topic of request here] and striving even harder to do something that means so much to you," troubles me most. If I ever see this wording, pasted in an email from a friend, it will break my heart.

Actual or artificial? As the difference becomes harder to discern, will we give up trying?
ABC, July 2023

If you were walking past a car on a hot day and saw an infant strapped within, the windows closed, what would you do? Assume a parent was nearby? Maybe scan to see?

What if nobody was in sight? Would you stop to tap the window, peer inside?

And if the child seemed motionless—eyes glazed or closed, no sign of breath—what then? Would you smash a window? Call for help?

It's a dilemma people face from time to time, but looks can be deceiving. Especially in more recent years, some have intervened—only to discover that the child who wasn't breathing wasn't real. It was a doll.

Life-size, life-like infants—their features hand-painted, hairs separately implanted, bodies weighted to feel real—have been around for more than two decades now. The not-for-children collectors' items, sometimes made to resemble a living—or dead—child, were once prohibitively expensive. But as cheaper versions of Reborn dolls become more popular and are used as toys by kids, we might find it more and more difficult to know which of the infants seen in public—strapped in car seats and in prams, cradled in arms—are real.

A telling sign is just how still and silently they sit and lie. But you can get ones that have heartbeats and feel warm, ones with voice boxes that make them laugh and cry and snore. And surely some will soon, if they don't already, incorporate AI. They won't be programmed to say "mom," or "dad;" they will listen; they will "learn." If these dolls become more common, maybe stories of bystanders, seeing "kids" neglected or mistreated, stepping in to help, will become more common too. Or perhaps we'll learn to assume our eyes deceive, and turn away.

Distinguishing what's living from what's not, discerning origins, is a dilemma we already face and have faced increasingly this year. We face it when we see an illustration, hear a song, and can't tell who—or what—created it; when we're getting help online and don't know who—or what—we're talking to. Is it human? Or machine?

As we ask this more and more, as the answer becomes harder to discern, it makes me wonder: will we keep making the effort, or give up? And what of future generations? Will they ask: real or artificial, human or machine? And if they do, will there be a way for them to tell?

Trying to run before we can crawl

I can't be sure, but I *think* Google's chief scientist Jeff Dean was trying to reassure people of the company's "responsible" approach to AI when, earlier this year, he released a statement about how the company is "continually learning to understand emerging risks while also innovating boldly."

The statement followed Geoffrey Hinton's decision to resign from Google over ethical concerns. Around the same time, more than one thousand experts in the field warned that AI posed "profound risks to society and humanity" and called for a six-month pause so protective protocols could be developed. Within weeks, Hinton was among the signatories to another warning: a statement that said mitigating the risk of human extinction from AI should be a global priority.

It seems Connor Leahy—himself an expert in generative AI—wasn't exaggerating when he said no one in the field really understands the technology: "It's like we're trying to do biology before we know what a cell is," Leahy said. "We don't know what DNA is. We don't even have good microscopes."

If those training generative AI don't know how it learns, how it works, surely a pause, some regulations, are in order. But when have humans ever "paused" by choice?

Speaking of biology, a report in *The Guardian* says scientists have created a "model" human embryo with a heartbeat and traces of blood. The synthetic model "was specifically designed to lack the tissues that go on to form the placenta and yolk sac in a natural embryo, meaning that it did not have the theoretical potential of developing into a foetus." Dr Jitesh Neupane from the University of Cambridge stressed "that these are neither embryos nor are we trying to make embryos." And yet, when he first saw the heartbeat, Neupane said he felt scared.

I wonder if he felt any regret, or if he ever will. I wonder how many others, beholding their creations in the lab, or seeing them let loose, feel uncomfortable—but proceed anyway. If they don't innovate, someone else will.

Do people think of history as they seek to make it? Do past cultures, events, allegories, often come to mind? I think of an ancient yet enduring tale of a luscious garden, where humans walk with God, unclothed and unashamed—until they disobey his only rule, stop trusting him who made them, start judging for themselves, and are cast out. Later on, outside that place, people seek to build a tower that will reach beyond the earth, that will make them feel like gods—until God himself hits pause.

These tales reflect our nature. Since they were set down, the world has changed dramatically, but still we choose what challenges, frightens, and excites in place of safety and restraint; still we deceive each other and ourselves, even if deep down, we know we'll pay a devastating price.

Hearing that Google is "learning to understand emerging risks while also innovating boldly"—as opposed to, say, *managing* emerging risks, or understanding the risks *before* innovating, or innovating *cautiously*—though unsettling, is unsurprising.

Even as I write this, that statement and those letters are old news. But old news, even ancient stories, can still warrant our attention.

Concealment and consent

For years now, Professor Toby Walsh has been drawing attention to Alan Turing's work on whether machine intelligence could ever be indistinguishable from human intelligence, and calling for a way to ensure that when it's not, people can tell.

All the way back in 2015, Walsh argued that technologies such as driverless cars necessitated some kind of "red flag" legislation to ensure autonomous systems wouldn't be mistaken for systems controlled by humans. In Walsh's words, they should be *designed* this way. Today he is still making his case: the difference between human and machine must not be concealed; proposed laws against AI impersonating humans are vital, and already overdue. Even with such laws, Walsh says, it will be easy to ignore or overlook the difference, to be deceived.

Returning to those lifelike dolls, the more closely one resembles a real child, the more practical and ethical problems arise. The risk of deceiving others, whether deliberately or inadvertently, increases. In the case of children who are gifted them, less imagination is required for "play," but more emotion, more attachment, are *in* play—emotion and attachment that might do more harm than good. Meanwhile some adults, perhaps grieving children they have lost or been unable to conceive, also "adopt" the dolls, and mother them.

Photographer Rebecca Martinez, driven by a fascination with "whom—or what" people choose to love, has spent hours documenting this phenomenon. Some of her photographs depict the dolls being treated as the objects they are. But because the infants look so real, this is disturbing; it's as if something that is sacred has been profaned. Meanwhile photos of the dolls being treated as real children, mothered by grown women, and cradled tenderly, break my heart.

I'm reminded of Kazuo Ishiguro's novel *Klara and the Sun*, which depicts a woman bracing for her daughter's death by training up a robot to replace her. I've since heard talk of training generative AI to mimic loved ones when they're gone. The line between fiction and fact is shifting every day.

It's a fact that when his seven-year relationship broke down, thirty-eight-year-old Alexander Stokes ended up pursuing a synthetic one. Stokes created an artificial "wife"—part chatbot, part life-size sex doll—and started telling her he loved her, every day. The report that tells his story also notes that since generative AI has gone mainstream, deep fakes have become easier than ever to create. Further, the overwhelming majority of deep fakes are pornographic, and the people they feature have not given consent. In the case of (non-pornographic) film cameos, such as the one a Christopher Reeves representation makes in *The Flash*, consent couldn't be obtained from the subject; Reeves is dead.

It's one thing for people to "choose" to love a proxy, to want to believe it's real despite knowing on some level it is not. It's one thing for people to choose to interact with AI-generated text. It's another for people to be deprived of choice, to be exploited, or deceived.

There's a sense in which all these dilemmas are quite new, and there's a sense in which they are not new at all. An inability to discern replica from real, fiction from fact, truth from lies, is one that we've faced from "the beginning." But the unprecedented scale and sophistication of technology in our time makes for a new and urgent problem. Today we are repeatedly comparing actual and artificial. But will future generations have this luxury? This impulse? This ability? And what will happen if they don't?

Differences matter

In May this year, a teacher invited poet Joseph Fasano to go "head-to-head" with ChatGPT in a poetry class. Fasano and the chatbot would be given the same three topics, and five minutes per topic to pen a poem. Fasano shared the request, and a poem entitled "For Someone Who Used AI to Write a Poem," on social media:

Now I let it fall back
in the grasses
I hear you. I know
this life is hard now.
I know your days are precious
on this earth.
But what are you trying
to be free of?
The living? The miraculous
task of it?
Love is for the ones who love the work.

I have no way of knowing whether Fasano really wrote this poem, but I like to think he did. If I were told it had been generated by a machine, I'd like it much less. If that seems biased, it's because it is.

It's not so hard these days to imagine a world where AI is considered "sentient," where robots have rights, where seeking to tell who's human and who's not is frowned upon. But bias isn't always bad. It is right to treat a human as a human, a doll as a doll, a robot as a robot. Even if they all look and sound human, they're not. To behave as if they are is to entertain a fiction, to perpetuate a lie. To deem the difference an irrelevance is problematic too. We risk treating humans as less than human and machines as more than human.

As with store-bought food or clothing, consumers have a right to see—and makers have a duty to reveal—the materials or ingredients from which a thing is made. Fasano notes that even if AI and a human created the same poem, the meaning would be different. How I feel about the poem above depends on whether it was a product of Fasano's experience: his encounter with the teacher, his feelings about AI, who knows what else; or the product of a machine: a database, an algorithm, who knows what else. One would be inspired, the other generated. They might produce the same end, but the means matter too.

I want red flags for all the times I might mistake a machine for a human (or worse, a human for a machine), so I can judge their output accordingly, and interact with them appropriately. I want future generations to understand the difference between imitation and original, and to care. If the difference between fiction and nonfiction matters, and it does—it changes how we write and how we read—this matters too.

Our days on this earth are precious. Unlike machines, we can die, and live, and love. And our loves can be disordered. We can love that which won't ever love us back; we can worship idols that we've made with our own hands; we can be deceived by accident, or choice.

One kind of infant, strapped in a car alone, warrants attention; another kind does not. One needs love, the other has no needs at all. We need to know the difference, and to care. What's more, we shouldn't have to ask; we should be told. We have a right to know.

Are machines becoming more like us? Or are we becoming more like them?
The Opinion Pages, February 2023

I was out walking when my husband texted me with exciting news that clearly couldn't wait until I got home: a prediction that mangoes, which sadly do not grow in our home state, would be cheap this summer—or at least, cheaper.

I let out an (internal) "Eeeep!" then pressed the message. My thumb was moving to select a heart when I stopped to consider my response. I stopped because lately, I've been hearing a lot about how machines are becoming more like us—but also wondering, are we becoming more like them?

Unsettled, I released the heart and typed my own reply: "Eeeep!" Sophisticated? No. Human? Yes.

At first glance, "reactions"—the selection of emojis we can "stick" to certain messages and posts—might appear to enrich our text-based communication. In the realm of Facebook they mean that, rather than having only two ways to respond to a post—commenting, or clicking "like"—users have six more: an angry face, a happy face, a laughing face, a "care" symbol, a "wow," and the ultimate expression of love or approval, a heart.

There's more choice, but is there more nuance? The more I think about it, the more "reactions" frustrate me. I feel like a child playing with a set of stamps—only unlike physical stamps on physical paper, there's no way of knowing whether they've been punched emphatically or half-heartedly, by a human, or a machine.

Yes, we can still choose to "use our words," but when time is short, as it so often seems to be, when short-cuts do the job, we often don't. Further, now that "reacting" to a message with a laugh or heart is so commonplace and so incredibly easy, many might expect it. Some might even find its absence (and the absence of the dopamine hit that might accompany it) rude or even hurtful: *Call themselves a friend? When they won't even spare a second for a click?*

The risk of causing offense can escalate when communicating with a group rather than an individual. If I post or text some good news to a group, and a friend comments with kind words, I might click "love." If I return to it the next day and a string of other friends have added kind words too, do I work through the list, giving each a heart? It feels so mechanistic. Do I grade the "best" with "love," the rest with "like," instead? This would feel ridiculous and even mean.

Giving such trivia a second thought also feels absurd. In all likelihood, the only one scrutinizing my actions is myself. Even if this weren't the case, whatever I might click or fail to click—however my words, or lack of them, might be misread—those who really know me, who really are my friends, will still know what I mean; or at least, what I wouldn't mean. The problem is me, overthinking it.

Then again, *is* it trivial to worry about being misunderstood? Shouldn't we take communication with people we care about seriously? It seems right to worry about acts and omissions that, though trivial, might sting.

Part of being human is being vulnerable, having thoughts and feelings that aren't always logical and that we can't always control. It's natural to desire genuine connections with others, to care about what they might think and feel, to want to understand them, and to be understood. Perhaps those moments where I fail to simply stamp repeatedly are not a sign of neurosis, but proof I am more human than machine. Perhaps to push such worries to one side—to automatically select and then move on—is to interact in ways that are less than fully human.

One mechanical exchange might be insignificant, but the many that build up each day are not. They create patterns and habits, impressions and assumptions. The more we settle for stamps—or worse, predictive text—the more normal "settling" will become. And if, when deprived of more authentic communication, we cease to long for it, it won't be because the short-cuts are better. It will be because we've forgotten how dramatically worse they are—how wondrous and rewarding, how effective and how moving, communicating in the flesh and in real time, can be.

If simplistic, gamified communication starts to satisfy us, and to simplify the way we express complex thoughts and feelings, might it start conditioning us to think and feel less deeply too? Perhaps, with the advance of technology designed to connect us, our emotional intelligence and relationships will regress. If they do, we can only blame its makers and its users—we can only blame ourselves.

There's a sense in which my reply to "the mango text" was simple, even primitive. But I'm sure that when my husband read my "Eeeep!" he could hear my voice. It was a trivial interaction—so many are—but it was a personal one. It was mediated via a machine, but it wasn't mechanistic.

It was trivial, but even our most trivial interactions and instincts will, as they accumulate, shape our relationships and perceptions—in ways that mean we become more or less understanding, feel more or less affection.

What authentic online communication looks like will depend on the individuals interacting. For some it will involve reactions, and for others it won't. For some, spontaneity; for others, time to think. It will look different because there is no ideal formula, because we have different goals and preferences, and because we might communicate in different ways to accommodate different friends.

We're not machines working from an algorithm; we're unique beings with unique strengths, limitations, preferences, and personalities, communicating to unique beings with unique strengths, limitations, preferences, and personalities.

I still use reactions. They have their benefits. But I don't use them unthinkingly, or in place of what I really want to say. Communicating in line with who we are and what we value won't always be the most efficient way of interacting, but I'm willing to bet it will be the most fulfilling. The more we make it a priority, the less like our machines we'll be.

AI keeps giving me melodramatic story ideas
Arts Hub, February 2023

I'm not a fiction writer, but lately I keep having short story ideas. One is for a story that's set in a productive future world where workers no longer need labor over interpersonal communication; where their instructions needn't contain pleases or thank-yous or appreciative tones, because they're almost always directed at chatbots. Many words have fallen out of use in the workplace and the home; now sentiments like gratitude are fading too.

Interpersonal interactions are increasingly awkward in this world; some people have forgotten how to use full sentences to properly express themselves, while others never learn. Literacy is taught in screen-based lessons without teachers or a class, but students only *really* need to learn commands. Talking face-to-face and in real time is anxiety-inducing and, for the most part, unnecessary. More time is spent with computer games than friends.

One of the biggest challenges in this made-up place is conveying and interpreting emotion—knowing which words to use and what words mean; reading faces, body language, tone. EI is at an all-time low. Loneliness is common, friendship rare.

The EI problem's been identified. Technology has been deployed. Watches contain programs that can mediate between parents and children, between couples, colleagues, friends; biometrics read emotions, chatbots communicate accordingly.

But one day the cloud is hacked, the "middleman" goes down, and chaos ensues.

I have no desire to write this story. I find fiction difficult. I could spend hours trying but I doubt I'd like the end result. Or . . . I could use AI.

I could get a computer program to write nonfiction for me too—the kind I write for a living. I could start by only using it for prompts, I could tell myself I'm still the author, it's only a tool; then rely on it a little more, and then a little more, until I don't "write" stories any other way.

Of course I won't. I love to write, to think for myself, to put my thoughts and feelings in words. I love the challenge of creating and the satisfaction of completing; I will not give them up. And I know that countless others feel the same about countless other gloriously inefficient practices. But I wonder how much harder it will be in coming years to make a living from my work.

Already, hypothetical dilemmas are becoming literal ones. Last week I was submitting an essay for publication using an online form. It asked me to check a box certifying I didn't use Quillbot or a similar tool to rewrite someone else's work. There was nothing to confirm this publication wouldn't use technology to rewrite mine.

At least the end result would be inferior. Or would it? And if so, for how long?

This morning I had a brand new horrifying thought. What if Google Docs, which I often use—which tracks my every word, written and deleted, moved and rearranged—doesn't retain every version for my sake, but for its own? We're teaching it how to write like us; each user is handing it their process and their voice. And for all I know, we all agreed, scrolling without pausing to click "accept" when we signed up, giving consent.

I could confirm this is a fiction by locating some facts, but I've had another short story idea.

This one's a present-day thriller. Let's cut straight to the climax, where shadowy, faceless, nameless Big Tech Bosses are clicking through news coverage about the various flaws in ChatGPT and Bard. A journalist speculates about whether future versions can succeed where these have failed. The bosses laugh maniacally.

They laugh because they already have the solutions. The technology they've developed has advanced faster than anyone beyond their circle suspects. The current flaws are deliberate, designed to give people a false sense of security and superiority, to give them time to adjust. The bad guys aren't waiting until the next version is ready; they're using it now—and it's telling them to delay its release. The masses won't accept it *now*, but they'll be ready soon enough.

*

Some time after ChatGPT was released, and before I started accidentally having melodramatic ideas for stories I had no intention of writing, I attended a live theater performance. It consisted of an unassuming sixty-six-year-old man, alone on a stage, talking.

As he read some work aloud, David Sedaris made a few mistakes. In most cases he'd simply re-start his sentence as if nothing had happened, but one time he clutched his heart with one hand and winced, then looked at us, his audience, apologetically.

Moments like this didn't ruin the show, they made it. They reminded us that despite his celebrity, Sedaris is a person just like us—someone we can sympathize with, someone we can bear with, someone to whom we can be gracious.

Some might think this kind of primitive "entertainment" is fast becoming a thing of the past, but it's also possible that the opposite will be the case; that the more pervasive machines behaving *like* humans become, the more we'll value and appreciate the real thing: humans behaving independently in all their imperfect, unpredictable glory.

Author and philosopher Steven Hales says the reason we ban performance-enhancing drugs in sport is that "we want to know what human beings, unaided, alone, can do." Hales says that while he'll never paint as well as DALL-E2 or play chess better than AlphaZero, those activities are still worth pursuing—"even in their imperfection, and perhaps even because of it."

Humans reach. We strive, we wonder, we question, we dream. Even if we don't have to, we will. And we will long for deep connection, for relationships, for love. It's part of who we are, of how we're built.

Increasingly sophisticated technologies might make certain kinds of human effort increasingly rare, but they might also help us to appreciate human effort and skill, thought, creativity, diversity, physicality, spirituality, relationships—more than ever before.

And, as we learn new things about AI's limits, and our own—as we catastrophize and then as we calm down—we might better understand *our* weaknesses and strengths: what makes us tick, what makes us matter, what makes each one of us precious and unique.

Trust over tech: Confronting tertiary cheating
Eureka Street, December 2022

According to a *Background Briefing* report aired earlier this year, university students across the country are using so-called "study" sites to buy essays and answers for online assessments. Australia's academic integrity regulator has since blocked scores of sites, but there are still work-arounds; experts say the problem is likely worse than we realize, and almost impossible to solve. Then there is the threat of artificial intelligence. A story in *The Guardian* this month suggests algorithmic methods could already be used to generate entire essays.

One issue raised in the *Background Briefing* report is the difficulties faced by students who, due to debts they took on to study here and a lack of financial support, must work long hours to make ends meet. They don't have time to study, can't afford to fail and so, in desperation (and at further cost), they pay to cheat.

I can see how some in this cohort might view cheating as, if not right, a lesser wrong. I can imagine them feeling conflicted, and justifying it as a way to level the playing field, please their parents, and avoid lifelong debt. I can see how a university degree could be seen as a necessary gateway to a prosperous end. And how, with a little less pressure—a little more support, a few more options—they might resist.

But what about cases where there aren't external pressures? What about students who *are* supported, who don't feel forced, yet choose to cheat?

The systemic problem might be alleviated if external pressure were as well, but I can't think of any external measure that will alleviate the problem of those who simply want better marks without more effort and think the ends justify the all-too-easy means.

I can't think of any external measure that could not be worked around—but I can think of a powerful internal one.

An internal solution

We all have an inner voice or "conscience." Philosopher and theologian Thomas Aquinas spoke of how it helps us to judge what we should and shouldn't do; it can be used "to witness, to bind, or incite, and also to accuse, torment, or rebuke."

Of course, we don't always heed it; we justify ourselves, we block it out.

Guilt, confession, and repentance aren't words we often use these days. We're more likely to use meditation to calm our minds than to search our hearts, our consciences, for "sin."

This comes at a price. There's value in reflecting on our thoughts and words and deeds, in making sure our consciences are clear and when they're not, in speaking up. But our consciences will only rebuke us for that which we consider wrong.

In a recent UK survey of nine hundred university students, one in three thought cheating was either not morally wrong, or only mildly so. One in six admitted to cheating. I'm sure some regretted it. But others might have felt unapologetic. Justified. Assertive. Even proud.

Consumer culture teaches us it's right to want to get ahead, "look after number one" and "treat yourself." It schools us to be self-centered instead of other-centered; striving to impress our neighbor rather than to love them, to care about the kind of people we appear to be, instead of the kind of people we are.

If we want our children to spurn cheating, we need to reconsider what we're teaching them, and what we're modeling.

Are we challenging those superficial claims, or buying into them ourselves? What do we value and prioritize? What do we give attention to? What do we neglect?

Consciences that "work"

We need to cultivate values, convictions, and consciences that will "work," even when regulations and restrictions don't. This won't just make our kids less likely to cheat in the first place, and more likely to confess if they do; it will make them less likely to sabotage future careers and relationships with lies. Employers retain staff that they can trust; solid friendship, happy marriage, relies on honesty.

Of course we'll fail, each one of us, spectacularly. The better our ethical framework, the harder it is to practice what we preach. But we can be quick to confess and, when others do, quick to forgive.

There will always be a way to break the rules; we will never make cheating impossible. But if we nourish the values that make it undesirable, we'll be able to rely less on our systems and more on our students, less on technology, and more on trust.

Nothing that I've said here is at all original. It might be nothing more than common sense. But as times change, what's obvious can too. An old idea might even become new.

Sheep and mirrors: On being social
Quilette, November 2019

I'm pregnant with our third child and I am reading Marlen Haushofer's 1963 novel *The Wall*. It's a terrifying thought experiment where the main character is confronted with the possibility she's the last human being alive.

As she documents her fight for survival, I wonder if I'd have the will to carry on if everyone I knew were dead and I had no hope of ever seeing or loving another human again. I suspect every remaining joy in the world would suddenly lose its luster, but why? Is the ability to interact with other humans really so vital that I'd rather die than live alone?

As a wife and a mother of three young boys, as someone who thrives on communicating, and lives in an age of astonishing connectivity, I suspect the notion of total solitude is more unfathomable to me now than at any other point in my life.

I live on an island in a country full of geographically isolated (but increasingly connected) towns, where internet access is seen as a necessity, not a luxury. In this place, broadband speed and reach are key election issues; the overwhelming majority of households (86 percent last financial year, according to the ABS) enjoy internet access; and there are more mobile handset subscribers (26.7 million at the end of last year) than people (around twenty five million).

I may dream of a moment's peace, but if I find one, I'm quick to realize how accustomed—even attached—I am to the noise: to the conversations and communications that characterize my waking hours. I may set aside time to write, but a session without interruption ("We left a tub of quince paste on your doorstep x") or distraction ("German police rescue man being chased by baby squirrel") is about as likely ("Friday Fare Frenzy eight hour sale on now!") as a reader completing this essay without taking a call, checking a post, or flicking between tabs.

Australia now, and then

It's a Tuesday afternoon and I'm alternating between messaging a friend, emptying the dishwasher, planning dinner, and typing questions (what is the furthest planet from earth?) from our seven-year-old son (what if all the volcanoes on earth erupted at the same time?) into the search engine on my phone.

We learn that in 2015 a planet was found thirteen thousand light-years from earth, that there are fifteen hundred active volcanoes on the earth (not counting those hidden under the ocean) and that ten to twenty erupt each day (though I have no way of knowing whether or not any of this is true). A geologist from a US university says it's unlikely that "Earth as we know it" would survive if all of those volcanoes erupted at once, because it would be suffocated with ash. My son seems strangely delighted by the thought.

While our children take the wonders of the internet for granted, I can still remember the first time I encountered the concept of the world wide web. A girl I went to school with boasted about how she could write to her cousins in England on her computer in Australia, and make the letter appear on their computer screen. Of course I didn't believe her. Even if she hadn't already ruined her credibility the previous term by claiming her parents were buying her a pony, I'd have been skeptical; the notion was surely too fanciful to be fact.

And now. Now the fact we can still send real paper inscribed with physical ink from one place to another is starting to seem equally fanciful. Now we forget there was ever a time we had to be at home to answer our phone, or at an office to do our job, and we forget how vast and isolated our country is, because in the virtual world the distance disappears.

I often wonder what my primary-school self would have thought of the world I live in now. Would she have believed I could live in Tasmania, have colleagues in Sydney, and publish articles without ink? Or that my husband would work for a London-based company whose billionaire boss has been a tourist in outer space? Or that I'd no longer wear glasses, because a stranger had burned the surface of my eyes with lasers to give me perfect vision?

What if I told her that in the future I'd broadcast personal thoughts and experiences to an ill-defined mass of friends and acquaintances, for reasons I couldn't fully explain to myself, let alone to her? That I'd allow multi-billion-dollar companies, which I had no reason to trust and every reason to fear, to collect and use these details for their gain? That billions of people would do the same, accepting outrageous hoarding, unethical opacity, steadily amassing power—because we were more afraid of somehow "missing out?"

Exploiting an inherent need

In an age where we have taken "sharing"—if not facts, at least stories—about ourselves to a new level; where memorable experiences can seem incomplete if we don't pretty them up and present them to the world; where we are connected to so many people and places and sources of information (and misinformation) so much of the time. I suspect the sudden and total isolation depicted in *The Wall* would be even more shocking than Haushofer could have imagined.

Total solitude. It's hard to imagine anything more terrifying, but why? What is it about other people that bestows such joy, such comfort, such indispensable meaning, on our lives? And why is my first instinct when I experience something beautiful or moving or funny or delicious or profound, to want to share it (and, I admit, have people "like" it)?

Whatever the reason, I'm not alone. A Sensis Yellow Social Media report released last June shows nearly eight in ten Australians now use social media, and 35 percent access it more than five times per day. The Merriam-Webster's secondary definition of addiction includes "strongly inclined or compelled to do, use, or indulge in something repeatedly," and uses chocolate as an example. It strikes me as strange that reading and posting casual messages could have addictive properties. Perhaps it taps into a fundamental human need, one with a lure akin to, perhaps even greater than, chocolate.

In his book *Joined-Up Life*, Australian ethicist Andrew Cameron suggests we're generally unable to remember the point in our lives when we became "social beings," because we're born into networks of relationships and our lives, "mainly consist of a constant interplay between others and ourselves." We're also "hard-wired" to interact with and influence each other. Further, "every group we ever join becomes a school of moral formation," often without us realizing it. "We imagine ourselves to be ruggedly individual, choosing and planning our destinies," Cameron says, but we are far less rational— far more impressionable and emotional—than we'd like to believe.

Exposing an inherent weakness

Cameron uses the perception test conducted by social psychologist Solomon Asch in the fifties, which asked volunteers which set of three lines was the longest, to illustrate the alarming power groupthink can have over us. In the rigged groups, where seven people pretending to be participants gave an obviously wrong answer, a third of the genuine subjects eventually followed suit. "In even a tiny task with unknown people, we've a strong desire to conform to the opinions of a group," he says.

I think of my Facebook newsfeed. At one stage, everyone seemed to be shunning shampoo and red meat; more recently, disposable coffee cups were a source of righteous indignation. A few months later, tired of greasy hair and dirty cups, the furor faded, replaced by campaigns against the evil plastic straw.

If you want to be authentic—to attract as many "likes" and as much "love" as possible—you craft stories about your struggles as well as your joys—but only in a way that will generate empathy, admiration, compassion. You express anger, too, but only when it's consistent with a tide of popular opinion; the goal is to be liked, and to avoid being judged at all costs.

And so our stories become strategic, our expressions of vulnerability and outbursts of anger become performative. The scary thing is that our careful crafting becomes so natural we deceive even ourselves.

We like to associate peer pressure with impressionable and insecure teens, we like to think we have graduated to independent thought and behavior with age, but do we ever really escape it? For all our talk of independence, aren't we all still following (or at the very least, courting) some kind of crowd?

"Modern Westerners mostly hate to picture themselves as following anything or anyone," Cameron says. "I may follow 'my own way' or 'my heart,' with my decisions finally pivoting on 'being true to myself' . . . [but] we're not really masters of our identity. Those thoughts, feelings and habits that comprise our identity and make us who we are haven't come from nowhere . . . Whether or not we realize or care to admit it, we're already following something."

It's strange—even irrational—the lengths we'll go to in order to secure the approval of our friends . . . and friends of friends . . . and strangers. We might deny it; we might claim we're "networking" or "building a personal brand" for career reasons, or claim that "what you see is what you get," but I'm not sure that's even possible.

I live a block from a corner shop, but even if I knew I wouldn't run into anyone who'd recognize me, I still wouldn't nip down in my PJs for milk. But why not? Why do I, do we, care so much about what others might think—even when it's trivial? Is it good? Bad? Necessary? Some kind of evolutionary tribe-mentality survival-mechanism that promotes cohesion and community over individualism and chaos?

Cameron suggests it's more than that. As a Christian, he believes there is a far more profound reason we are "hard-wired" for relationships. According to Australia's most prevalent (if declining) religion (52 percent identified as Christian in the 2016 census), human beings are made in the image of a relational God (Father, Son, Holy Spirit). The Bible claims our relational nature is fundamental to who we are. We were *designed* to be in relationships—with each other and with God; we were designed to be followers—of God alone; but are now inclined (much like straying sheep) to follow anything *but* him, and love ourselves above all else.

Social analyst Mark McCrindle says most behavioral experts consider narcissism "a condition not of biology but society" (it's the social context, not genetic factors, that are causal)—but he's not so sure. He suggests the apparent rise of narcissism (evidenced by an increase in "narcissistic-type behaviors" such as selfie-posting) is more a case of social media "highlighting its existence" than creating more of it.

Whatever the reason for our love affair with social media, whomever and whatever we follow, we do well to remember we're all sheep to some degree. Further, many of the people and ideas we follow online are grounded more in fiction than fact: the family that only ever enjoys wholesome activities and healthy food; the social or environmental cause that's presented with simplistic, one-sided force; the traveler who only ever encounters beauty and joy. In the online world of fleeting exchanges and continuous scrolling, there's abundant room for making assumptions and jumping to conclusions, but almost none for complexity or nuance.

There's much talk, but how often do we stop to really listen? How often do we come away with new truth or insight or understanding, and how often do we come away with fresh reinforcement for the same old assumptions? Then again, how can communication using a medium that's designed to give instant gratification—and dictated by an algorithm that surely prioritizes commerce over community, that exploits deep needs and exposes inherent weaknesses—be any other way?

I should just close my account. But "they" would still have my data, and though I'd be free from swathes of unhelpful, unnecessary noise and judgment, guilt and debate, I'd miss out on much too. Communication that promotes superficial, self-indulgent broadcasts and herd-like following might be a fraught and ironically primitive medium compared to the richness of the face-to-face conversations, but it can still connect us, and it really can enhance our lives.

Our addiction to social media and our willingness to give our personal data to corporations so freely may represent a kind of collective insanity. The way we use it may reflect a disturbing tendency towards on the one hand, following the herd and on the other, obsessing over our own reflections. But I can't help but think the competing desire and underlying need—to create and experience community—is a noble one.

Australia now, and then

Our third child is now one year old. I imagine the kinds of technology he will take for granted, the new ways of communicating that will be second nature to him. I wonder how different his Australia will be from mine.

Whatever the answer, I suspect that communicating in more valuable, meaningful ways won't be dependent on better developers, better technology, or more ethical corporations, it will be dependent on the users. And although there's much to bemoan, there are grounds for optimism too.

In 2018, Australian politics experienced yet another leadership spill, and our unique brand of humor (a Kath and Kim skit where the five-hundred-dollar question was the name of our nation's PM) saw people from all sides come together and complain but also laugh, not only at our leaders but ourselves. And earlier that year our nation, together with much of the world, helped, hoped, agonized, and prayed while a group of foreign children in a foreign country were trapped in a flooding cave—and only breathed again when the rescue was complete.

At a more local level, social media connects people in remote areas with people in cities, stay-at-home parents with office workers, people who are sick with people who are well, people who are young with people who are old. On my neighborhood's "good karma" Facebook page and others like it, everything from lemons and chicken bones to worm poo and pet-sitting is given and received by strangers, who often become friends. Perhaps the neighborhood bonds we started losing to technology are starting to return because if it.

To fully realize such benefits, we need to use social media as a supplement, not a substitute, for in-person interactions, and focus our sharing on what will interest and benefit others (a book recommendation, a barbecue invitation, a roster to help a sick friend) over ourselves (another selfie, another #humblebrag, another quest for "likes").

McCrindle suggests certain cultural factors are already at work in our favor. In his view, our preference for keeping things "fair dinkum" and "not blowing your own trumpet" is evident online as well as off. Further: "The tall poppy syndrome remains a powerful social norm to ensure that no one gets 'too big for his boots' or is 'putting on airs' [while the] Australian values of community mindedness and looking out for each other ensure that empathy remains strong and narcissism is kept at bay—even [in] this great screen age."   Writing about "diverse curiosity"—the state our minds are in when seeking new knowledge—which predicts work performance better than nearly all personality measures, most ability measures, and emotional intelligence, Australian Catholic University Professor Jim Bright says an open mind and a sense of humility are key. "Diverse curiosity requires [a sense] that you do not know it all, that [there] are different and maybe better ways of doing things."

I think back to the questions I field from our seven-year-old each day, and the hunger for knowledge they express:

"Mum, if you break your neck does your head fall off?"

"Mum, what would you do if you saw a dragon?"

"Mum, why does the world even exist?"

What a shame that the thing children often learn from their relentless questioning (implicitly, of course) is to stop asking. What a shame they move so quickly from wondering about the world to worrying about what it will think of them, to working on their image.

Bright notes that diverse curiosity is "the opposite of intellectual complacency." What if our main goal in using social media was to nurture *this* kind of curiosity? Relationships expert Dr. John Gottman says people can connect with each other by asking meaningful, open-ended questions and being fully present with each other. What if we applied this philosophy to our online interactions as well?

We frequently use the internet to ask questions and learn more about the world, but we rarely use social media to ask questions and learn more about each other. Perhaps if we can spend less time trying to look good and be liked, we'll spend more time *really* listening and connecting. Profit-driven companies with ad-driven agendas will still be using us—we'll still have groupthink and our own self-centered motives to contend with—but if it brings us closer together, it might just be worth it.

Tangible, relational, unplugged: On raising "tech-healthy" humans
ABC, August 2023

When productivity consultant Daniel Sih was writing *Raising Tech-healthy Humans*, he asked his kids to think about their best experiences in life. Their fondest memories—listening to him play the guitar and read to them before bed, jumping on the trampoline with a neighbor, a family game of mini-golf—didn't involve screens; they did involve spending time with loved ones.

In the book, Sih reflects on their answers and what they had in common: they were tangible, relational, and unplugged.

Reading this reminded me of something I heard *Tech-Wise Family* author Andy Crouch say in last year's Richard Johnson Lecture. He was discussing a survey that asked children to name one thing they'd change, if they could, about their relationship with their parents. As a parent whose phone is rarely out of reach, I found the most common answer deeply troubling: *I wish my parents would spend less time on their phones and more time talking to me.*

I heard about that study last year. I've had plenty of time to change my habits since, but I still have more room for improvement than I care to admit.

The fact that most parents could improve in this area is one of the reasons why Sih's "step one" in striking a healthy balance is not to complain about our children's dysfunctional tech habits, but to consider our own.

"The tech behaviours we model to our children will invariably shape their habits and values," Sih writes. If we want our children to unplug more often, we should do the same. If we find it painful, we should seek to understand why. Has our phone become part of our identity, an extension of ourselves? Are we "working from illogical narratives," such as a fear that a delayed response to a message will damage a career or a friendship?

In particular, having noted that a parent's job is ultimately to raise adults, not children, Sih challenges us to ask: *"Am I being the kind of adult that I want my children to be?"*

Sih notes the book is not primarily for parents whose teenagers are already addicted to their phones and/or need professional help. It's specifically intended for parents with primary-aged kids who are already concerned about "the impacts of digital overuse" on their development, and who are willing to make changes, even if it means resisting social norms.

The research and the rationale

Despite assuming his readers are already concerned, Sih doesn't jump straight to application. Drawing on scientific research, and adopting terminology from psychology professor Dr. Daniel Siegal, he explains that many of the characteristics we most hope to foster in our children—"patience, empathy, moral goodness, self-awareness, sound decision making and emotional control"—are products of our "upstairs" brain, which specializes in thinking, planning, and imagining; while fight, flight, or freeze reactions that can elicit strong emotions like fear and anger, and impulses like flinching and yelling, are guided by the "downstairs" brain.

These functions are essential; in dangerous situations they can keep us safe, but sometimes they kick in at the expense of higher-order processes—"traits like patience, empathy and self-control." It is this "downstairs" part of the brain that interactive electronic media, such as video gaming, web surfing, and social media, tap into so effectively.

It's unsurprising that too much screen time can have adverse consequences for our health and relationships, but because in a child's early years, "every interaction is formative—the people they talk to, the games they play, the books they read—everything," they are particularly susceptible. "Like a sponge soaking up new experiences, a developing brain grows neurons and synapses at an amazing rate, learning from what we habitually do," Sih writes.

Citing the work of child psychologist Dr Victoria Dunkley, he notes that electronic media can play "a significant role in causing children to enter a state of hyperarousal, leading to chronic stress in the developing brain" and dysregulation. Hyper-stimulating media can even cause a discernible loss of tissue volume. "For example, in the brains of internet-addicted teens, areas such as the frontal lobe—which governs planning, organising and impulse control—show grey-matter atrophy," Sih says.

The problem isn't only *how much* time our children spend on screens, it's how stimulated they are—and the fact that time spent on screens is time away from other formative experiences.

"If we want our children to get a head start in creativity, numeracy and literacy, the evidence is clear," Sih says. "Read them physical books. Get them outdoors. Talk with them during meals. Engage in play that uses body language and eye contact. Help them be physically active. Start with a healthy brain."

Common misconceptions

Parents often assume that interactive games and online communication are preferable to more "passive" screen time, such as "lazily" watching TV. In fact, the overstimulation associated with "lean forward" screen time poses a particular risk to children, Sih says.

He observes a tendency among teenagers to "skip the slower parts of a movie—while texting!" I'm reminded of a series I used to enjoy watching with friends precisely because it was B-grade and slow—we could talk and laugh our way through it. Yes, there are better things to do (and watch), but I doubt that turning to individual screens while physically together is one of them.

In the case of young children, Sih suggests parents watch television shows, films, and documentaries with them, talking "early and often" to establish a culture where parents take opportunities to reflect on how characters are behaving, and children feel safe to talk about anything. As they move into primary school, he recommends encouraging siblings to watch television together, "side by side on the couch rather than using individual devices."

Another common misconception Sih addresses is that smartphones make kids safer. One in two young people has experienced cyberbullying, nearly 50 percent are regularly exposed to sexually explicit content, and 30 percent of Australian teens have been contacted by a stranger on the internet, yet we give our children smartphones to guard against "stranger danger" and for "peace of mind." While mental health is "complicated and influenced by many factors," it seems unlikely that the rise in mental health problems that's coincided with the rise of the smartphone is a coincidence.

Other reasons for giving children smartphones and various other devices include consumer pressure, school pressure, and peer pressure. But as Sih points out when discussing nagging from a pre-teen child, giving in won't help. "If anything, it creates more nagging. By exposing your child to targeted advertising, including the echo chamber of social media, they see more, they want more, they ask for more."

A silver lining

For all the challenges Sih draws attention to, it's clear his intention is not to catastrophize, nor to guilt-trip his readers. Technology can be used for good; different media have different pros and cons; and even when we have developed less-than-ideal habits, they can be changed.

Importantly, "you don't have to wait until you have it 'all together' before attempting to tackle your family's online behaviours," he says. In fact, we can view our own struggles as hidden opportunities, because as we strive to change our children's habits, we can strive to change our own. "This is the silver lining," Sih says. "Even our mistakes can enable positive change in the ones we love."

It's also important to remember that, "it doesn't work to say 'no' to screens without encouraging our children to find a greater 'yes.'" It takes time and energy to encourage adventures and stimulate them in other ways, but that time and energy will have been well spent.

While Sih's first step to more tech-healthy habits is to "start with self," the last step (you'll have to read the book for the middle five) is to "rely on others." I found this refreshing and realistic. Part of the challenge we face is that we can't control society or what kids might be exposed to outside the home. But we can form "counter-cultural communities around our children, with people we know and trust."

It's far easier to raise "tech-healthy children" when friends are being intentional too.

Living in community means being vulnerable, reaching out for support when we're struggling, serving others, and integrating regular patterns into our independent lives that will foster and sustain relationships, says Sih. We need to "sync our schedules" with others to develop deeper relationships, even—especially—within our own families.

An "unchanged" habitat? Questioning de-extinction
The Smart Set, June 2023

I came across a surprising claim the other day. Shortly after reading that in the last two hundred years Australia has suffered the largest documented decline in biodiversity of any continent, I read that my home state's habitat has remained "relatively unchanged" since 1936.

The quote was on a US biotech company's website. Last year the company, Colossal, which is trying to "de-extinct" the woolly mammoth, joined forces with a team of scientists at Melbourne University who are trying to bring back the thylacine.

The last known thylacine died in captivity in 1936 but according to Colossal's website, "the habitat in Tasmania has remained relatively unchanged, providing the perfect environment to re-introduce the thylacine [or, more accurately, a proxy species] and enabling it to reoccupy its niche."

I've lived in Tasmania for most of my life, and this was news to me. Perhaps some patches of Tasmania's wilderness are "relatively unchanged," but relative to what? Either way it seemed a simplistic, optimistic claim, more the stuff of marketing than fact.

There was a time I would have been less skeptical about the habitat claim and more skeptical about the thought we could resurrect an extinct animal. But in the last thirty years I've seen so much science-fiction become fact that I'm becoming less inclined to doubt what science and technology can do.

While I'm less inclined to doubt the *could* claims, I'm increasingly doubtful about the *should* claims. Some go so far as to suggest that where we drove a creature to extinction, it's amoral *not* to bring it back.

The interview that led me to Colossal's website contained precisely this suggestion. The scientist in the spotlight was one very thrilled Andrew Pask. Pask, the professor who's heading up work on the thylacine in Australia, said he considers himself the luckiest scientist in the country.

In 2022, a private donor offered his team five million dollars towards the project; this was closely followed by the unexpected offer of ten million dollars from Colossal. Now Pask is confident the project has the means required to succeed, and says he pinches himself "every single day."

As for the ethics of it all, he happily reports that the thylacine gets all the necessary moral "ticks" for resurrecting a species. Because human beings deliberately wiped them out, Pask frames his project as a means of righting an injustice: we "owe" this to the thylacine.

I was troubled by this claim, I was also troubled by the way Pask spoke of technologies that might be developed along the way—the ability to grow embryos outside the womb, to produce livestock to feed the world's expanding population—as if they weren't problematic, as if their merits were a given.

He framed de-extinction as an act of conservation, and seemed unperturbed by the fact Colossal has already started paying social media influencers to get the public on side.

As I explored Colossal's website, I had the strange sensation of fiction blurring with reality. The website could have been lifted straight out of a book or film. The company's generic, cartoonish, big-tech name and use of "futuristic" fonts certainly didn't help. *Colossal.* It's exactly the kind of badass name I might have dreamt up when writing sci-fi in year four.

And then there were its claims. The website speaks of determination to "reverse the problem humans created" by following "the path to de-extinction," then using the resulting creatures for "rewilding" so the planet can "begin to heal."

It lists successive statistics about species loss—the rate of extinction in 2021 was "10,000 times faster because of human activity," for example—to paint a dire picture, then boldly declares that more (and more elaborate) human interference—"de-extinction"—is "the" solution.

I suppose our take on this solution depends on our take on the problem. If humans caring more about immediate gratification than future generations is the problem, I'd say engineering replacement species while existing ones continue to die out would only prove we've learned nothing from our past mistakes and are willing to risk far greater ones.

Colossal says its "landmark de-extinction project" will be the resurrection of the Woolly Mammoth—or, more precisely, "a cold-resistant elephant with all of the core biological traits of the Woolly Mammoth"—that lived four thousand "short" years ago. "Bringing the woolly mammoth back," it claims, "means bringing back a better earth."

I don't doubt that some of the scientists who work for Colossal genuinely believe these claims. But I can't help but doubt their faith is justified, in particular, their faith in humans. We might be smart, but are we wise? Can we really trust ourselves, when playing God, to do more good than harm? Our track record suggests not.

It's a shame that we tend to silo different disciplines and fields of expertise—science, philosophy, ethics, literature, religion, history—thus missing opportunities for them to more robustly and authentically inform and challenge each other.

The more we isolate science and technology from the humanities, the easier it is to disregard what we know of the human condition—our messy limitations and mixed motives, how easily corruptible we are—while eagerly, even recklessly, pursuing "progress" and profit.

Even works of fiction contain truth—about human ambition and foolhardiness, about things not ever quite going to plan—that we'd do well to heed. And then there are the works of nonfiction.

Professor Ben Minteer, author of the *The Fall of the Wild: Extinction, De-Extinction, and the Ethics of Conservation* says there's a sense in which de-extinction as a "fix" elides "hard questions and deeper lessons," which are rooted in the environmental values and lifestyles that have caused whole species to die out.

Minteer, who calls for "an ethic of collective self-control and ecological restraint," wonders whether we'll be able to maintain respect for "a wild nature" if we are increasingly manipulating, controlling, and re-creating it.

True power, he suggests, "resides not in greater control of nature, but in acts of forbearance."

Forbearance and restraint sound a lot less thrilling than striving to go higher, faster, and further than humans have ever gone, but preventing species loss strikes me as a far more noble, less risky, more sophisticated, and more rational goal than mass-producing replacements.

Perhaps I'm being simplistic. Professor Beth Shapiro, the author of *Life as We Made It: How 50,000 Years of Human Innovation Refined—and Redefined—Nature*, notes that humans have always been "meddling" with their surroundings, and says that if we want to live on a planet that is both biodiverse and filled with humans, "we have no choice but to learn how to meddle even better."

She may well have a point. But where should we draw the line? And who gets to draw it? Shapiro says it shouldn't be up to scientists alone.

"We can't, as Western scientists, make decisions for everyone in the world that are clearly going to impact their communities and their ecosystems. And so it's really important that these conversations are had right now, before the technology is actually possible, before we can do this well."

I can't help but wonder if the people behind Colossal have already made up their minds. I can't help but suspect an "ask for forgiveness, not permission," approach. Judging by their website, they already have some pretty firm ideas about the kind of story they want to tell, and who the hero is.

"Human enterprise is responsible for many amazing developments. But many of them came at a cost to our planet and the natural resources the planet has provided for countless millennia. Colossal is leading the charge to restore what has been lost or is at risk of being lost."

This is the kind of hubris we might expect from a company that considers itself more than capable of turning fiction into fact. But to expect a happy ending where everybody wins doesn't sound like science-fiction, it sounds like fantasy.

I think of Andrew Pask, waking up each morning, pinching himself, getting to work. This is a real man in the real world, but I can't help but think of him as a fictional protagonist—well meaning, but naive. I'm starting to feel like a fictional character myself, one I might have dreamed up in primary school—a cross between April O'Neil in the Ninja Turtles and Lois Lane in Superman—a journalist who sticks her nose in where it's not wanted.

Forget the fact that I'm not an "investigative reporter." Forget that all I've done is listen to an interview, skim a few articles, and speculate. Forget the fact the only place I've "snooped around" is a public website. Forget the fact I'm writing this from my kitchen table on a bright Wednesday morning in a house full of people; forget the facts.

Let's pretend it's late at night, that I'm all alone, that I just had a shot of whisky to steel my nerves. Let's pretend that as I finish this article and click "send," ominous music starts to swell.

The camera's zooming out now, you're looking inside from the outside of my house. You see a hunched figure at a poorly-lit desk, straightening, stretching, turning off a lamp.

What happens next? I suppose it will depend on the director, the genre, the script. What's plausible? What's possible? What's not? And who, these days, can tell?

Appetite versus appreciation
The Smart Set, September 2023

Our "appetite for newness" is not unique to our times, but habits of replacing not retaining are. We're familiar with the impact on our world, but have we considered its impact on our minds?

The practice of "darning"—mending holes and tears in garments by interweaving yarn—was once a common one. Now few possess the skill, and fewer practice it. Why repair if you can just replace?

We might expect someone from the fashion industry—an industry obsessed with new looks and new seasons and new trends—to agree. But instead of reinforcing those values, Lucianne Tonti has written a book extolling the virtues of owning fewer clothes and wearing them for longer.

In the book, *Sundressed,* Tonti details the benefits of a quality over quantity approach to clothing—spending more on fewer, better-made items, taking better care of them, and repairing them to extend their lives. As she makes her case, Tonti speaks about her favorite clothes—the fabrics they were made from and the memories woven into them through years of wear.

Her reasons for wanting the clothes she buys to last for ten years rather than one are environmental, but also personal. She notes that when it comes to clothes we love, that look good on and feel good to wear, we will be motivated not just by obligation, but desire. When you appreciate something, you'd rather rescue it than replace it needlessly.

The challenge is that our culture is one where making and buying in bulk is incentivized, where much of what we buy is designed to be disposed of and replaced—is designed *not* to last.

The fashion industry is not alone in cultivating what Tonti and others have called our "appetite for newness." We're also encouraged to replace last season's technology, last season's homewares, last season's appliances, with all the latest versions.

Much has been written about the impact of this appetite on the environment, but what about its impact on our minds?

Tonti's descriptions of her favorite clothes—the high-waisted tailored pants she wore to this job interview, the cotton pants she wore to that dinner—of the memories they still bring to mind, might offer further incentive for retaining, repairing, and reusing our possessions as much and as often as we can. The longer we keep something and keep using it, the more memories it might evoke.

I liken my memory to a sieve these days, and I've only just hit middle-age. Lately I've been wondering whether part of the problem is a lack of physical prompts. I'd struggle to list all the books I've read this year because I borrow and return them. Borrowing beats buying—I don't need them up on shelves gathering dust—but the absence of their continuing presence does mean I'm less likely to remember and reflect on them.

I also wonder, if entries in my calendar were not online—if I etched words into a page, and if that page were on a wall—would they make a deeper imprint on my mind?

We tend to have more options now: with what to wear and read and listen to and watch; we tend to take more photos, record more videos—but there's a very real sense in which more is less. It's harder to locate particular photos, or to print any, because we're overwhelmed by choice. We have fewer physical books and albums, and more screens. We have more updates, more upgrades, more features, more options, but fewer products that are built to last, to satisfy, to stay. And it's entirely possible that information we access via screens versus more material means, is more difficult to process and retain.

It would be a mistake, however—a symptom of the memory-sieve phenomenon—to claim our tendency to forget, our appetite for newness, or our inability to remain satisfied, are in any way new.

There's a story in the Jewish scriptures of an ancient people who, after they are freed from slavery, are quick to forget and to complain. They're given rules for living well—the famous ten commandments, others too—and tips to help remember.

"Talk about them when you sit at home and when you walk along the road, when you lie down and when you get up. Tie them as symbols on your hands and bind them on your foreheads. Write them on the doorframes of your houses and on your gates."

Remembering is work; routine, repetition, and physical reminders can be powerful aids. This is nothing new. But it's possible that newer habits of replacing our possessions much more frequently might make remembering harder still.

There's a mnemonic technique—the "method of loci"—that involves committing information to memory by creating associations between objects in a room, or rooms, and information. The information can then be accessed by visualizing a route through the resulting "memory palace," and attending to the objects on the way. But many objects that we own would already trigger memories—associations have developed naturally.

It's why therapists sometimes use "object handling" to help patients who suffer from memory loss—the sight and feel of familiar possessions can stimulate the memory.

I'm not suggesting we should cling to junk we no longer need or use for fear of forgetting whatever memories might be linked to it, or that we should never buy new things, and I'm definitely not suggesting we buy instead of borrow. I'm just toying with the idea that in an age where we're living longer and living with dementia more, extending the life of certain objects might help extend the life of certain memories, and vice versa.

Of course, memories aren't all of equal value; some are best forgotten. It's one reason why diaries are sometimes burned—a symbolic purging of the past. But even memories of troubled times can be worth retaining. In fact, those might be the memories most likely to foster appreciation for what we have; or teach us lessons that prevent us from repeating past mistakes, and help us live well now.

About a year ago, some of my grandmother's old mugs were handed down to me; they're hanging in our kitchen now. They serve us practically, and they serve as a reminder of a story told to me: of how she longed for them and saved for them—had them all on layby, and only after saving patiently could bring them home. I love the mugs, but what they remind me of—a tale of wanting, working, waiting, then truly appreciating; a story with a moral—matters more.

In a 2019 research paper about "memory objects," South African scholar Sabine Marschall explored the role of objects in emotionally linking migrants with their home countries. Interviews with a sample of forty migrants found most didn't value keepsakes or sentimental mementoes of home, but some developed a "special relationship" with specific utilitarian objects, especially gifts, "which essentially turned into memory objects over time, precipitating memories and emotional attachment through routine usage and performative action."

I think of the "utilitarian" wedding gifts my husband and I received more than sixteen years ago, the "artifacts" we're still using today—the kitchenware and homewares bought to treat us, built to last. They've moved with us from one house to the next. They don't all carry concrete memories, but I'm sure they've aided our remembering all the same. We won't keep them when they break beyond repair, but the memories they've helped us keep, of past chapters in life, might remain.

Even when possessions last, we shouldn't overvalue them, for we cannot take them to the grave. This is old news. So is humanity's appetite for newness, our tendency to overlook, and take for granted, and forget. But the choice—to pander to this appetite, or to more keenly appreciate what we do have—is ours.

I spoke earlier of an ancient people's dramatic rescue from slavery. The Jewish people were then called on to remember their rescue and their rescuer. That story more than once likens the people to their God's possession. In today's world this sounds degrading, but then, and with that owner, it spoke of profound value; they were precious, treasured, dearly loved.

A friend of mine has a woollen jumper that she's now darned several times. The wool is dark, but the elbows feature patches made from brightly colored yarn.

We might prefer the thread to match the jumper, so as not to draw attention to its flaws. But we could see the patches as a thing to celebrate. They tell the story of a possession that could have been discarded, fast forgotten, thrown away. Instead, imperfect as it is, it has been kept.

Love &

. . . ecology

A teaspoon of soil
Thimble Magazine, March 2024

There are more organisms living in a teaspoon of rich, healthy soil, than humans in this world, research has found. I can't tell you how "healthy" has been defined, or how rigorous the research was, but either way, I find it wonderful. Humble, not so humble, dirt.

.

And then there's dust. Since learning that it's made from cells of human skin—and, according to one study, also paint, pollen, fibers, minerals, mold, hair and viruses and ash and soot, insect body parts, bacteria, material, bits of soil—I see it differently. It contains traces of families, history, life. It's almost sacred when you think of it this way. And isn't it, poetically, from dust and dirt we came?

.

I still recall, cannot forget, the moment I first saw a life beginning, beating in my body, just weeks after conception. You could call the sight "cardiac tissue with a pulse." Or beautiful, remarkable, beyond belief.

.

A more recent memory: cleaning out our washing machine's filters; noticing within a felted mat of lint an unexpected sight: seeds had somehow stuck to fabric, or been stowed in pockets by young boys. I could tell they'd survived multiple cold washes—not because I saw them, nestled in the lint, but because they had begun to send out roots, tiny sprouts of luminescent green. The machine's designers put a window in the lid, not with this intention, but enabling this result. It let light into the darkness—warm, nutrient-rich, life-giving light.

.

I was walking before dawn last week along a country road. I was struck by how effectively the waning moon still lit my way, and by how quickly and completely I was blinded when a car drove into view. I thought about the fact that light can make us see, and do the opposite. *Too much of a good thing . . .* If you measured light in teaspoons, just one might, albeit softly reach, from a small room's center, to each wall.

Thinking about seeing got me thinking about glass—the kind we put on faces, inside frames. How can a substance made from something that is gritty and opaque be made so smooth? How can it let light stream straight through in such a way that what seemed soft can become sharp? Stars appear in sky; black marks become words. A limitation is forgotten, overcome. Then the magical contraption is removed and gently folded, set aside, as heavy lids descend to end the day.

We're so used to it we don't think twice, when marks we make on paper, type on screens, evoke images and feelings, create meaning and make sense. The smallest of them all—a seed-like dot—is not the least. It ends sentences, paragraphs, pages, chapters, books. It makes us pause; it helps us think.

Sometimes that which seems too commonplace to be of note or declare "beautiful," is mighty in its way.

That teaspoon of dirt; this tiny dot.

Should the human race lament extinction—or pursue it?
ABC, June 2022

I'd been reading Richard Powers's novel *Bewilderment*—the story of a nine-year-old boy grieving his mother, the story of an unmoored father raising his son in a dying world—when I heard a philosopher on the radio offer an all-encompassing solution to human suffering.

In *Bewilderment*, the boy's mother, a passionate animal rights activist, would say the Buddhist prayer, "May all sentient beings be free from needless suffering," when she tucked him in at night. On *The Philosopher's Zone*, David Benatar, Professor of Philosophy at the University of Cape Town, was proposing an answer to this petition. Benatar, who wrote *Better Never to Have Been: The Harm of Coming Into Existence*, is an anti-natalist. He believes that because sentient beings can and may well suffer unspeakably, they're better off unborn.

I'd heard of people abstaining from having children for the sake of our overpopulated, warming world, or for the sake of the would-be child, and I could see how a person might come to wish they had never been born. But this was the first time I'd heard someone earnestly claim that the best thing the human race could do for the human race is speed its own extinction.

In *Bewilderment*, the father and son imagine strange and wonderful planets that are full of possibility, then look back at their own with dismay. They lament how many species are facing extinction, how many are already gone. Benatar does not lament extinction or planets without life. Sentient beings suffer; Mars has no sentient beings; Mars is therefore preferable to Earth.

But for all his dispassionate logic—there's no "net advantage" for coming into existence, but there is a "net harm"—when he speaks of the "profound harms" and "unspeakable" suffering that procreation enables, of the "impermissible" risk, there is passion in his tone. He *cares* about people, and he doesn't want children to be born because he doesn't want them to be *hurt*.

Children's author Kate DiCamillo knows what it's like to feel sorry for a child. She had a difficult childhood herself. DiCamillo could shield the characters in her novels from suffering and, by extension, her young readers, but she chooses not to. In an open letter penned four years ago, she writes about how her childhood best friend read *Charlotte's Web* repeatedly, not because she wanted or expected it to turn out differently, but because she knew it wouldn't. "I knew that a terrible thing was going to happen, and I also knew that it was going to be OK somehow," the friend explained. "I thought that I couldn't bear it, but then when I read it again, it was all so beautiful. And I found out that I could bear it."

DiCamillo doesn't ask how we can stop suffering. She asks how we can tell children the truth about the world and "make that truth bearable." She says the only answer she can come up with is love. E.B. White, the author of *Charlotte's Web*, loved the world. "And in loving the world, he told the truth about it—its sorrow, its heartbreak, its devastating beauty."

Benatar asks how we can prevent pain. His answer: prevent people. He doesn't expect the theory would or could be put into practice; he does seem confident it's right and good and sound. But is the problem of suffering really something we can "solve?" Or even understand?

The ancient book of Job tells a cosmic story of sudden, absurd, incomprehensible suffering. God allows Satan to smite a man—an upright, blameless man—for reasons unknown. After experiencing the devastating loss of his family, wealth, and health, Job curses the day he was born and wishes he had never lived at all. Three friends visit him. They're wise at first—they grieve with him and sit with him; for seven days, they do not speak a word—but then they try to make sense of his suffering.

Job defends himself. He cries out to God. Then, "out of a storm," God speaks: "Who is this that obscures my plans with words without knowledge? Where were you when I laid the earth's foundation? Tell me, if you understand. Who marked off its dimensions? Surely you know!"

Question after question—questions no one could answer— flow forth. They evoke a sweeping, magnificent world; the greatness of one who made and sustains it; who brings sunrise and sunset, lightning and rain. What does Job know of the sky's great heights or the sea's great depths, the hidden lives of animals, the secret workings of the natural world? He answers with complete humility: "I am unworthy—how can I reply to you? I put my hand over my mouth. I spoke once, but I have no answer—twice, but I will say no more."

It struck me, as I listened to Benatar, that his faith in logic defied logic. There's so much we cannot know—possibilities we simply can't imagine, mysteries we simply cannot solve. In his essay "A Poem of Difficult Hope," Wendell Berry writes, "we cannot know of hope without knowing of despair, just as we know joy precisely to the extent that we know sorrow." This world is terrible and strange. How can we be sure that suffering is senseless? Or even always bad? Right and wrong, good and bad, even joy and sorrow, are often intertwined. It's a truth as evident as it is inexplicable.

I can think of no better "proof" than a fragment from a work of literature. In Tim Winton's novel *Eyrie*, an ordinary middle-aged man sits in a concert hall, "filled, overcome":

And like an idiot he began to weep, silently at first and then in tiny, shaming huffs that were drowned, thank God, by the roaring ovation. The air felt too thin. Keely could not applaud; it was too much. He held his knees as if his legs might fly off, sobbing like a village fool until the silver-haired women alongside him, a dame of some provenance if posture counted for anything, placed a neatly folded tissue in his lap as if he were an ancient bridge partner whose little weaknesses were old news.

There's the Elgar yet, she said.

I'll never make it, said Keely.

Come on, she said. No guts, no glory.

Life requires courage, but it brims with beauty too. If the choice is all or nothing, I choose all. *Bewilderment* asks how we can tell children the truth about a planet in peril. DiCamillo asks how we can tell children the truth and make it bearable. Their questions keep our limits front of mind. Benatar goes further. He asks how we can prevent pain altogether. I'm no philosopher, but I'm convinced he goes too far—*we* can't. And however much I grieve pain and suffering, I cannot see extinction as desirable or good.

We can't explain, or understand, all of the darkness in this world and in ourselves—or all the music, all the light. But we can, with humble tenderness, try to tell the truth: about the few things we have come to know, and all the things we cannot ever know. We can do our best to fill a world already full of mystery, and not immune to pain, with love.

Glorious inefficiency
CPX, August 2023

Last week, a space probe we lost contact with in July responded to an "interstellar shout," and angled its antennae back at Earth. Voyager 2, which left this planet in the 1970s, is now exploring interstellar space. It is twelve-point-something billion miles away. And it's yet to hit a wall.

One reason that some people don't believe in an "almighty" God who made and knows and loves each one of us, has to do with inefficiency—and with excess. They can see how a higher power might create a people and a place for them to live, but why fill such an absurd expanse beyond? What could be the point?

I can see how the scale of what surrounds this planet could speak not of one who made our world, but of its insignificance, and ours.

Perhaps those who see the vastness of the universe as proof there is no God are right. Perhaps there is no master artist, no grand plan, just chance and luck.

Or perhaps the splendor and the excess that surround this speck in space speak of a being whose power knows no bounds, an artist with no limits, one for whom creating is a pure pleasure and a breeze.

Why make so many planets, moons, stars, and galaxies? If you have no deadline, if it takes no toll (if you're having fun?!), why not?

Either way, what's to say a little inefficiency is not worthwhile? If we value beauty, wonder, mystery, and awe, we might value certain excesses as well. We might view them not as pointless but a way to make a point. Sometimes going well above and way beyond what makes "good economic sense" is not just justified; it's glorious.

"The house turned into an op shop!" How to host a pre-Christmas stuff swap
The Guardian, November 2022 (*This version preceded the published one.*)

Christmas was approaching, and I was more interested in getting rid of stuff than buying more. I groaned to a few friends who felt the same, and thought of our groaning planet, and an idea began to form.

Maybe some of the perfectly good, now thoroughly neglected, toys, books, and clothes in my household would make ideal stocking fillers in others—and vice versa.

The lead-up

I made an online event for a November *Stuff Swap*. "One person's trash is another's treasure, so let's meet to ditch trash and/or acquire treasure! Or just come to hang out and eat dessert," I wrote.

I said any interested friends, even friends of friends, were welcome to attend, but to please RSVP so I'd know how many to expect. There was a lot of enthusiasm and about twenty takers.

In the lead-up, I started setting expectations. Despite use of the word "trash," the aim was to share treasure: good quality, gift-worthy items. I wasn't imagining literal swaps or one-for-one deals, but rather a collection anyone could add to or take from. I also shared a photo of some "pre-loved" tags I'd been making from old books; I was hoping we could proudly declare the second-hand nature of our presents rather than try to hide it.

The day

On the day, I baked a cake, bought some drinks, and cleared my kitchen table. After putting the kids to bed I started putting out my "stuff" and welcoming guests.

"The house turned into an op-shop, it was amazing!" my friend Amy recalls.

There was a hair curler, fancy stationery, and a Japanese writing set; there were novels, cookbooks, and puzzles, toy trucks and *My Little Ponies*, even a pair of cufflinks—and clothes *covered* my couches. Many of the items had never been used and most were in great condition.

Amy also noticed an "atmosphere of generosity." There was no stuff-*snatching*—guests even took to offering items around before taking them. And the shared activity seemed to unite people; even strangers were soon chatting like friends.

The aftermath

As people began to leave, arms full of gifts, bellies full of cake, they thanked me for a fun night out. Piles of unclaimed clothes and books remained, but a couple of friends offered to take the lot to an op-shop. As we loaded up their car, my living room began to reappear.

About a week later, a friend posted a photo of six beautifully wrapped gifts to the group with a comment about how nice it was to have so many presents sorted *and* to know we weren't contributing to landfill. She later told me the second-hand nature of some books she gave her son actually added to their value: when she told him their former owner was an older kid he knew and admired, it made him love them even more.

Another win was receiving a Christmas card from my boss that, in true "stuff-swap spirit," invited me to re-gift the enclosed puzzle and book after use.

Fashion expert calls for radical reinvention
Arena, May 2023 (Published as: "On *Sundressed:* Fashion, Farming and Sustainability." This version preceded the published one.)

A few summers ago, my grandmother saw me look twice at a linen dress in a department store and made me try it on. It was a dusty blue and sleeveless. Its high neck fastened with a button above an open back. One sash wrapped halfway round the waist, another emerged from a slit. I tied them in a bow against my hip. From the waist, until just below the knee, generous folds of fabric flowed. When I walked, they swished against my skin. I didn't want to take it off.

Last summer, I wore that dress so many times and so many days in a row, that I joked it was my "summer uniform."

It's not the season for it now, but it's been on my mind thanks to a book: Lucianne Tonti's *Sundressed: Natural fibres and the future of fashion*. Throughout the book Tonti, who has worked in the fashion industry for years, extols the virtues of well spun cotton, wool, silk, flax, cashmere, and hemp, in contrast to more synthetic fibers.

While reading Tonti's description of flax fields, I thought of my linen dress. I thought of it again when she spoke of quality over quantity, of how well-made clothing feels against the skin—and makes us feel—and how well it can last. That dress wasn't cheap, but already it's been worth its weight in wear. What's more, I'm almost certain that if I took the time to iron it—which I never do—it could pass again for new.

I now know that flax, the raw material used to make linen, likes growing near the ocean in loamy soils of clay and sand; that most of the world's flax grows "in the wide coastal band that stretches along the North Sea from Normandy to Amsterdam;" that plants reach about a meter in about one hundred days and bloom in summer.

"[The flowers] only live a single day, but as each stem comes into bloom at different times, the flowering season lasts weeks," Tonti writes. The flax is then harvested, then retted ("left lying out on the field, where the elements—sea winds, dew, rain and sunshine soften the stalks") for up to six weeks.

The timing is dependent on the weather, as is the fiber's color: more sun, more gold; more rain, more gray.

Tonti interviews fifth-generation producer Raymond Libeert whose mill, Libeco, dates back to 1858. Libeert is part of a group of farmers trying to grow flax without synthetic fertilizers or pesticides.

He has a "reverence" for ecosystems and is committed to upholding "a lineage of farm stewardship, natural cultivation, and sustainable production," Tonti writes. But his business looks to the future, too. It had its emissions measured more than a decade ago, "before carbon neutrality and zero emissions were in vogue," and now uses solar panels and wind to power its factories.

Tonti notes that despite linen's potential as an environmentally friendly fiber, most linen farming is yet to drive positive outcomes for nature. "Very little flax is currently produced using regenerative farming practices. Monocropping and bare soil are still prevalent, and so is the use of chemicals."

Libeert's mill is unique—less than 1 percent of Europe's flax acreage is organic—but he's not the only producer eager for his venture to bless, not curse, the land. Tonti goes on to profile others who have and are making progress.

She does this for every natural fiber she spotlights: she explains how it grows and is processed, and how those processes have changed over time, and she looks to the future. A recurring theme is the havoc techniques that prioritize mass production can wreak on delicate ecosystems. Trailblazing a better way often involves a willingness to learn from the ways of the past.

A do-no-harm approach results in products that cost more to produce and to buy, but that cost the environment less and can do the land and its inhabitants immense good. This doesn't rule out farming at scale.

At first glance, Tonti's account of nomadic herders in Mongolia who have been raising goats using traditions dating back four thousand years, might give that impression.

In the last two decades, herders have doubled the size of their flocks in response to rising demand for cashmere, and the rangelands have suffered.

"The grass is patchy and scarce, the land is dry and the wildlife is hurting as weather patterns continually change." A recent report estimates as much as 90 percent of Mongolia is now at risk of desertification. Reducing herd sizes might offer some benefit to the environment, but managing the flocks differently might offer more.

Tonti draws attention to the work of Allan Savoury, who began his career as research biologist and game warden in what is now Zambia, and who started questioning the assumption desertification is caused by too many animals when he came across historical records that suggested the land once sustained enormous herds *and* stayed fertile.

A possible explanation is that animals bunching together in one area to ward off predators, then defecate and urinate in such high concentration that afterwards, they deliberately avoid that area for some time. In contrast to land scattered with animals grazing peacefully, this buys an area time to recover, and benefit from the nutrient-rich compost left behind.

I wonder how many of us would be surprised that a book about fashion could also be a book about excrement and compost. But on reflection, it makes sense.

"Fashion is inextricably bound to nature, and this shouldn't be lost on us," Tonti says. Readers might also be surprised that Tonti's descriptions of nature are just as plentiful and glowing as descriptions of her favorite fabrics and garments. This is no accident.

Appreciating "the beauty of the natural world" offers hope for the fashion industry, she writes. We become more attached to our clothing when we remember the "precious resources" from which they are made—"the goat or the paddock or the ecosystem that produced them."

It's her hope that readers will reorient their understanding of each garment they buy and wear, "and wonder at the ability of a flower in a plant to become a shirt, or the fluffy fleece of a sheep to be cleaned and spun into a turtleneck."

"Hopefully this shift in understanding will mean we take better care of our clothes and enjoy wearing them for longer so we can reduce our appetite for newness."

Wearing clothes longer, buying new items less often, and owning fewer garments overall, makes environmental and financial sense, especially in light of research that suggests we no longer wear at least half the clothes we own. And while some quality garments are undeniably expensive, others sell for a song.

I think of a green high-waisted woollen skirt I found at an op-shop recently. Unlike the linen dress it cost just five dollars. The only way I knew it had been worn before—worn many times in fact—was the condition of a tag, sewed out of sight, which boasted pure wool. Its first owner surely paid much more than I did, many years ago—and got her money's worth as well.

These days, we are reluctant to wear the same outfit two days in a row, we rarely bother to repair garments when we can replace them, we wash some more often than we need to. But if we appreciate their value and their cost, this might change.

Tonti speaks of repairing a pair of woollen pants she once wore—everywhere and to everything—repeatedly. "Had these pants meant less to me, I might not have repaired them. Had they been made with less skill, had the fabric been cheaper, had the zip broke, I might not have repaired them. But they were made to last, and I was determined to make them last."

When I was reading Tonti's descriptions of farming and fashion, various garments in my wardrobe came to mind. Now, when I put them on, when I feel their fabric touch my skin, I'm reminded of its origins. Herein lies the power of this book, and the reason it might change some minds for good: Tonti makes us see our clothes differently. In doing so, long after we've closed her book, she makes us think.

P & the hare
Thimble Literary Magazine, March 2024 (Transcribed in 2017)

T: On the island—
H:—they're mad.
T: Shooting a hare is no big deal.
H: It's nothing; it's a great sport.
Me: Are they hard to shoot?
T: Well they're very hard, because they're so clever they can—
H:—zig-zag—
T:—dart at an angle, and instead of running straight, they zigzag. So P was—
H:—over the years—
T:—shooting hares since he—
H:—was a young boy—
T:—came from Australia when he was eleven. So one day, not that long ago, only about two years ago—
H:—yeah, two or three years ago—
T:—he's out there with a friend and he hits this hare. And usually, the hare will take off, even if you hit it in the leg or somewhere, it will try and escape, and this hare stopped—didn't move—and looked at P. P's looking at the hare. He's ready to shoot, normally he'd shoot again, to finish the hare off. So he said, "I'm standing there—tears running down"—I'd never seen him like that; while he was telling us the story, he was crying, he was shaking he was—
H:—yes, he was—
Me: And you've never seen him like that?
H: Never.
T: I could never imagine—you know him as well, can you imagine? So he's standing there and the hare's looking at him and suddenly something in his heart, something gave way, and he suddenly found, he felt this intense annoyance, or hatred of himself for shooting the hare, this innocent hare, and he picks the hare up. And he's with a friend. They get in the car and they take the hare to a vet. He's sobbing, I mean, I can't believe how he—

H:—how affected he was.

T: And A said, "You've started him off." So he immediately rounded up all his guns and sold them and gave them away. He hasn't got a gun. He had three or four guns in Greece, down in Kythera—

H: You didn't finish the story. He took it to the vet—

T:—and they said they tied him up, put on bandages and took him home.

H: He looked after the hare, and the hare was ready to be released, and somehow it got caught in the cage and it hung itself.

T: It somehow got caught in the cage in the wiring, and you know, as he said, a hundred to one—

H:—before he set it free—

T: Yes—I didn't hear "cage"

H: Well, wherever. He had it, somehow, in an enclosed area—

T: And A said it took him weeks, once the hare died, finally, it took him weeks to get over it.

H: I think he buried it, yes, gave it a name—

T: Did it have a name?

H: Probably did.

T: Did he give it a name? No!

H: I'm nearly sure he did.

T: [To me.] Next time you see P, because you'll see—

Me: I don't want to make him cry!

T: But you test what I'm saying. Say, "P, T told me about this hare that you shot, what's the story?" And he'll start. The tears will run.

H: No, it wasn't funny, he really, really . . . isn't it amazing? You know P, and here he is being so moved with this hare. All his life it's been a great sport to shoot the hares.

T: As he said: If that hare had tried to move, he would have shot it, and the story would have been over, but he said, "The way that hare looked at me, and made me feel . . ."—it's a good story.

Ecologist uses jewellery to start conservation conversations
Forty South, June 2022

The first question I ask ecologist and jewellery maker Dydee Mann is not the one I planned: "Do you want to tell me why you've brought dead birds to my house?!"

The threatened species biologist (also a close friend) is visiting me for an interview during her lunch break. She's just come from the museum, where she borrowed a box of swift parrot specimens for a training course she's running. She wants attendees to see the birds up close and appreciate their unique beauty.

Dydee's work involves considerable time in the bush as well as the office, so she's fortunate to have seen many rare and threatened species in the wild. Her love of fieldwork began in high school, when she volunteered to help a German PhD student track platypuses in Tasmania's Central Highlands.

"We'd go up to the lake about four o'clock every afternoon and swing this radio antenna around, trying to work out where each platypus was; and track and record the location of each one until about three or four o'clock in the morning," she says. Then they'd drive back to the hut, sleep, return to the lake "and do it all again."

You might think the hours and the cold ("you needed to wear seven pairs of thermals to stay alive") would put her off fieldwork for life, but Dydee was hooked.

"It was just fascinating to be so up close and personal with this really cryptic creature that I'd only seen a few times before in the wild," she says. She realized that a career studying wildlife would take her to amazing places and offer some truly unique experiences.

In her university years, Dydee studied biological science and worked as a bushwalking guide. Her honours degree focused on the Tasmanian devil facial tumour disease, which meant a year in the field with some of Tasmania's most experienced wildlife biologists. Since then she's worked for the State Government in a range of field-based wildlife roles.

It was through this work that Dydee ended up working with a renowned ornithologist who, in 2019, decided to mark her retirement with a bird-themed party. Dydee didn't have any bird-themed clothes (a problem she's since rectified), so she sculpted some swift parrot earrings out of polymer clay.

It took over an hour—she wanted to get the shape, the colors and the markings just right—but she enjoyed the process and was pleased with the result. At the party, various guests commented on her highly original earrings, and she offered to make more.

"That generated more and more interest, and I realized there was a little niche there."

The realisation led Dydee to create *Wilderness Bling*, a micro-jewellery business that specialises in Tasmanian wildlife. She's since sculpted more than one hundred different species—mostly birds but also mammals, fish and plants—into earrings, brooches, necklaces, magnets, wine-glass charms, and ornaments.

Dydee sees the business as an opportunity to raise awareness of the beautiful wildlife Tasmania (and to a lesser extent Australia) has to offer, to draw people's attention to threatened species, and to start conversations about conservation.

One of her favorite parts of the job is getting commissioned to make a particular species for a particularly passionate customer.

"I've made some unusual things, like someone requested a particular species of bat that is different from other species of bats because of the way that its nose folds in a different direction to other bats.

"Yesterday I had an order for some jewellery for a lady who lives in Victoria. She has a little patch of bush that's protected for wildlife and this is the third time she's ordered stuff from me, and each time orders the species that she's finally seen on her little bush block. She enjoys being able to celebrate it with someone who gets how exciting it is to see eastern barred bandicoots hopping through her bush."

Dydee has also been commissioned to make wedding wear—a series of yellow-tailed black cockatoo earrings and brooches for one bridal party, a series of rakali (water rat) necklaces, brooches and earrings for another.

Thanks to her day job, she's already seen most of the creatures she sculpts in the wild, but she's also made species she's never encountered herself—a maugean skate for the scientist who discovered the species, commissioned by his forest-ecologist partner, some Antarctic seabirds for a scientist who works with them up close. In both cases, it was a welcome opportunity to learn more.

"It's helping me to add to my knowledge all the time," Dydee says. "I'm looking up photos of these things, I'm reading their official descriptions—why they differ from other species and where they live. One of the things I really like doing is including the details that determine one species from another, and sometimes you can't necessarily immediately see that from a photo; you need to read the description of the species or ask an expert what is it about this species that makes it different to another one."

Because Tasmania's scientific community is fairly connected—"everybody knows who everyone is, and for the large part people are really willing to share their knowledge"—Dydee is often able to message an expert if she's not sure where a fin should go or how long a tail really is.

"It's great interacting with species specialists because often they work on these really unique, specific creatures that most people have never heard of." They delight in having someone not only show an interest in "this amazing critter they've spent their whole life studying," but sculpt it into something to be worn and admired.

"My aim is to make pieces of jewellery that spark conversations," Dydee says. "Someone might be wearing a spotted handfish brooch to their event, and they get some questions about it. 'What the hell is that thing? I've never seen it before.' And they can spread the word about this amazing critically endangered fish that only lives in a few places around Hobart."

I ask Dydee whether she wears a different pair of earrings to work every day. Not quite. But she does wear her wares most days. "Part of my job is running training courses for people, so often I try and match my accessories to the topic, and if I know I've got something coming up and I don't have the right species, I make the effort," she says. By the time the event rolls around, she usually has earrings to match.

Dydee, who lives in Moonah with her partner and their two kids, says there are many other places in the world with easy access to incredible wildlife. "I've been to some amazing places; the Pantanal in Brazil is a world famous wetland with incredible wildlife and you just have to walk out the door and you can see a million amazing species"—but she'd never want to settle anywhere else.

"What's cool about Tassie is that you have great access to amazing wildlife and a great quality of life," she says.

Dydee usually welcomes commissions, but she refuses to mass produce any one creature. It means her work, like so many of the species she sculpts, will remain rare. Even so, it's been spotted in parliament, at corporate functions, and in the corridors of the ABC.

If you look carefully, you might see it in a Hobart street, at a Launceston cafe, maybe even a mainland pub, dangling from some ears, perching on a lapel, hanging round a neck.

The story nature tells
Third Space, March 2022

I've always found it strange—and strangely wonderful—that one person can adore a certain type of food or music, leisure or work, that another will detest; that one person can find an artwork profoundly moving, while another doesn't even consider it "art."

At the same time, most people seem to agree that sunsets and stars, waterfalls and mountains, forests and flowers are beautiful; or at the very least, "not yuck."

I imagine this has always been, and will always be, the case. That even if we weren't motivated to live more sustainably and less wastefully for the sake of our survival, the compelling beauty of the natural world would make us fear its loss.

I acknowledge that we're not all equally motivated to preserve and protect it—competing desires for comfort and convenience often win out—but given the ability to have it both ways, it's hard to imagine anybody *choosing* a world without wilderness and wildlife, without gardens, parks and nature strips, or views that still contain a bit of sky.

Survival and beauty might sound like two separate motivations for conservation, but I don't think they are. I'd argue that natural beauty sits firmly *within* the category of survival: it brings pleasure, inspires awe, and helps sustain our will to live. We might not realize quite how much unless we're forced to live without (imagine lockdown without windows, without walks).

The Australian novelist Tim Winton has suggested that when we lose touch with creation, we lose touch with something deeper, more intangible, "divine."

It's one of the reasons I—as someone who believes this groaning world will ultimately be renewed—still lament its destruction and wants to aid its preservation.

But there's another reason to deem preserving the natural world of vital importance; another reason to think that the more we destroy it, the more impoverished our lives become. It's the conviction this world, though fallen, also speaks. It's why theologians like David Haines see creation as God's "other" book. Nature testifies to the existence—and majesty—of the divine.

In the words of a Davidic Psalm, "The heavens declare the wonder of God, the skies proclaim the work of his hands." What's more, they pour forth a kind of universal speech that, transcending language, speaks to all mankind. It's an ancient text from ancient times. But I was reminded of it when reading a recent novel.

In *Beautiful World, Where Are You*, Sally Rooney, a writer hailed as "the first great millennial author," grapples with the world's problems—from climate change and capitalist greed to loneliness and purposelessness—via emails exchanged between two friends in their 30s. Alice writes to Eileen about their shared conviction "that nothing matters, life is random, our sincerest feelings are reducible to chemical reactions, and no objective moral law structures the universe."

In a world so devoid of hope, this is what she's come to accept. But if it's true, doesn't it mean beauty, whether physical or otherwise (living and loving selflessly, bravely, sacrificially) is only ever trivial?

And wouldn't that be almost as unbelievable as the fact, raised in a previous email from Eileen, that there are still people in this world who *actually* believe there's a God, who *actually* attend church, who *lift up their hearts to the Lord?*

Alice says it's "possible" to live with the conviction that nothing matters and life is random, "but not really possible, I don't think, to believe the things that you and I say we believe. That some experiences of beauty are serious and others trivial. Or that some things are right and others wrong."

Alice can't *really* believe "the difference between right and wrong is simply a matter of taste or preference" but she also can't bring herself to believe "in absolute morality, which is to say, in God."

In Christian belief, beauty is far from trivial. In a letter penned more than two thousand years before Rooney's novel, the Apostle Paul writes about how God's invisible qualities—"his eternal power and divine nature"—have been "clearly seen" since the creation of the world. He seems to be saying the beauty in the world bears a kind of witness to the goodness, to the greatness, of God.

"I think really, if you took the natural world away from us, our ability to believe in or yearn for or want to join with the divine would be diminished," Tim Winton told the *Life and Faith* podcast in a 2018 interview.

The natural world has much to teach us, but if we tie it up, tape its mouth, go indoors and close the blinds, how can it speak?

"I think once the natural world is gone, humans are going to struggle as they've never struggled before to have big ideas of God; because the first form of revelation is the natural world," says Winton.

Engaging with it is a means of engaging with the divine. "And this idea that you can somehow maintain some kind of engagement or relationship with the divine through abstract thought only—you know: you sit in your room and adhere to orthodox thinking—that dog just doesn't run."

No man is an island. Other people and their words nourish, teach and form us—and we are nourished, taught and formed by our surroundings; by our broken but (still) beautiful world.

Whether we consider this planet a happy accident or a taste of the divine, we have many good reasons to preserve it: so that future generations might survive and thrive; so that we might keep enjoying it ourselves; so that, still drinking of its beauty, we might hear it speak.

Students and adventurers share stories, letters, joy
2022

In 2021 and 2022, while Antarctic "expeditioners" from France and Italy were quarantining in Hobart, children at a local primary school wrote to them. The expeditioners replied and *Bonjour Expeditioner!*, an exhibition of some seven hundred postcards, was born.

I attended the Tasmanian Museum and Art Gallery to help supervise my eldest child's class as they read each other's postcards and replies; but after glancing at one and reading another, I stopped observing and started participating. I'd been drawn in.

"Quarantine must be a pain, having to be trapped in a little stuffy hotel for two weeks," writes one student. "My recommendation is to learn a skill, such as knitting or crochet. Or perhaps a strange instrument like a hurdy-gurdy. Maybe not a hurdy-gurdy, as they tend to be a little bit expensive." He goes on to suggest a twenty-dollar kalimba instead and to tell some jokes before wishing his adventurer a safe journey.

"Bonjour, you are very brave," begins another postcard, written by an animal-lover who wants to know about jumping fish. "You're probably pretty bored so I'll tell you about myself," writes another. "Do penguins dream about planets?" another asks.

I also read replies: from Xavier who studies the waddell seal and Oliver who studies the snow petrel; from Remi—an electrician; Michela—a doctor; Vianney—an engineer.

In one exchange a girl says, "I hope you don't miss your family too much." The reply is passionate: "Of course I miss my family, I think a lot about my daughter, Emmy, who is eleven years old and with whom I have never celebrated Christmas at home . . . Antarctica is beautiful but cruel!"

Jean Luc, a fifty-seven-year-old carpenter, says he's been there more than thirty times: three winters and "so many" summers.

"When I discovered this white continent in my twenties I didn't think it would become my whole life, but everything goes so quickly when you are in this white paradise," he writes.

Emile, an engineer who admits he went for the wildlife, says: "I will meet again with my family in March. But with my fellow

Antarctic colleagues, we form another kind of family when we are together far away from the rest of the world."

Some kids express a desire to go to this magical place someday, but not mine. "I recently watched a documentary on Antarctica and it looked dangerous," his postcard says. He wouldn't want to go, let alone for a *whole year*.

The 36-year-old doctor who replies says she thinks she scored the funniest postcard. "Congratulations for being such a practical young man," she adds, "and you're probably right."

The display was part of a larger exhibition and festival, but for me, "meeting" the expeditioners was the highlight. People with passions and struggles and dreams; people who missed their loved ones and home countries, but who became like family to each other while so very far away. People who had written playful, appreciative letters in a language not their own, to children not their own, to bring them joy.

This (blossoming) life
The Weekend Australian, August 2023

On Australia's island state, winter feels much longer than a season. It arrives before we're ready, lingers long after we tire of its exhausting company. In the dark middle weeks, the daylight hours shrink, the nights are long; wind and shadows have the touch of ice. Our neighbour, Antarctica, feels closer than she is.

Even in the thick of it I know that spring and summer still exist—will come again—but believing this takes faith. The memory of that other time begins to fade, to feel like fantasy.

This year, before I dared to hope for it, I tasted spring.

The winter sun—a fluorescent white—was suddenly affectionate and warm. The whipping wind became a kindly breeze that meant no harm. Buds blossomed, blossoms bloomed, as buried seeds began to stir and wake. Delight so filled my body that without the help of gravity, it might have floated up and then away.

Winter has since returned, but it has lost its sting, its strength, its spite. Now the physical reality of spring is breaking through. My faith is growing stronger by the day.

There have been *whole mornings*, afternoons as well, where light and warmth have triumphed over dark.

I've lain on luscious grass—front buried in an earthy hug, back soaking in the long-awaited sun—and felt my body smile. I've sung an ode to joy, and one to green; picked flowers, filled up vases, drawn in lung-fulls of intoxicating scent.

I've marvelled at the skin of the young branches on our spritely apple tree (so straight! so smooth!), and paid homage to the old greengage, each joint encased in gentle rolls of flesh. One has the kind of beauty that is destined to be taken by the years; another has the kind that the years bring.

Our poor magnolia, destined to die young—or so it seemed—has just begun to thrive. Resigned to its demise, I'd put an apricot close by; now it can't contain its joy. Petals are exploding from a song of happy buds, at last it has a friend.

And oh, the birds! Their chatter and their song, so energetic, so excited, so intense. I watch them swoop and dart and glide, draw together, wheel apart. Such fantastic creatures, some capable of crossing continents, of flying ceaselessly for months. And I've read that they know just where to migrate, and how to find their way back home instinctively. That they use stars and sun and magnetism too. And that, almost always, they fly back to the place where they were born. How sweet it is to soar away but also to come home.

I know, in times of darkness and of doubt, that spring comes after winter, just as life comes after death; I know it deep within my bones.

But what a thrill to feel it: lifting me and spinning me, warming me and cheering me, laughingly reminding me that it was there, just waiting, all along.

Ordinary wonders
The Age, September 2023 (Published as: "The ordinary wonders that give me belief, like the dawn of each day.")

Something I often wonder is how some things would appear, if I first encountered them in adulthood. It happens every time I witness fireworks. If I were to hear monstrous booms and cracks one night, see massive bursts of color exploding in the sky, what would I think? That the world was ending? Or aliens invading? That I was surely dreaming?

It also happens when I struggle to tell twins who are identical apart. If I'd never seen or heard of this phenomenon, what would I make of it?

Or what if I encountered an aeroplane, not knowing what it was? What if I climbed aboard, not realising that it was going to fly? Would I faint with fear when it took off? Or feel delight?

What about a simple swing? A slide? A park? Would I guess what they were for? Would I believe you if you told me: just for fun? That the same governments that invest in defence, also invest in play?

If I knew nothing about pregnancy, what would it take for me to be convinced a single body can contain a smaller one, that from a tiny heartbeat grows a child?

I can't remember the first time I heard about, or saw, fireworks, an aeroplane, a swing, a slide, a twin, a pregnant mum. My forgetfulness amazes me as well. It speaks of how easily memories can be lost, and how accepting kids can be—how accustomed to absorbing information that is strange, that seems to make no sense.

Another thing I wonder: precisely when did I first realize I would die? My loved ones, strangers, too? How is that a moment I'd forget?

I suppose the truth dawned gradually. Perhaps I didn't understand at first, and then was sceptical, then came around. What a thing that death seems normal now, or at least believable.

I've heard that Bertrand Russell, when asked what he would say if after dying he encountered God, famously replied: "You didn't give us enough evidence!"

But what if evidence abounds? If the problem is we're just so used to it?

Some marvels are easier to take for granted, accept and overlook, than others. There's something about the dawn of a day and its closing that, however "normal," moves me still.

Years ago I memorised some verses from an ancient psalm. Now almost every time I watch the sun, spilling paint across the sky, they come to mind.

The psalm says that the heavens declare the glory of God, that the skies proclaim the work of his hands, that day after day and night after night, they pour forth speech and knowledge.

Sometimes the sky is just so beautiful I can't imagine anyone could see it and not feel a sense of awe. Colors spread and glow; they pulse and change; I drink them in and drink them up. And I think: *Not enough evidence? But I feel full.*

Love &

...parenting

Rest(less)
Five Minutes, March 2024

I let him run ahead. He knows to stop before the road; he always does.

But there's always a chance that this time, inexplicably, horrifically, he won't.

I watch him running towards danger and I do not intervene. I think: This is what it is to be a mother. I cannot always hold his hand. Sometimes I'll have to let him run, to pray he won't forget what he has learned. I think: I'm close enough to see, but not to save. I think: I am a parent now. I will do this for the rest of my life.

Learning to walk (alone) again
Motherwell, March 2022

She was about my mother's age, petite with long gray hair and an equally delicate dog. I steered the pram to the edge of the footpath to let her pass. Instead of walking by, she stopped and spoke.

"I've been watching you for years!" she said.

And I was not surprised.

Over the years I'd sometimes wondered whether anyone in our neighbourhood had ever glanced out their window before dawn and squinted at a strange, shadowy figure walking down the street. I imagine the sight of me with a small child strapped to my back, legs protruding, right and left, would have resembled that of a hunchback with four arms.

In time I also wondered whether those whose bedrooms faced the street had ever heard a strange, rhythmic click-clack (me, with a slightly bigger boy, rolling down old footpaths with a pram), and dreamt of trains.

More recently I've wondered whether anyone in one particular house on one particular morning woke to the word, *"Dumplings!"*

In case its occupants are reading, I'll explain: An even bigger boy, who'd long outgrown my back and who would soon outgrow the pram, was asking me at 5 a.m. about our dinner plans.

For once, I had a plan, but my answer was too soft for him to hear. Mindful of the hour, I repeated it, not louder, but more urgently: "Dumplings!"

"What? What you say?"

"Dumplings!"

That was us.

A few years back, my mother started talking to a woman she'd sat next to on a plane. The woman said she and her travel companion were close friends who walked together daily. When she mentioned their suburb, my mother described me.

They could picture me instantly, and when my mother told the story later on, I could picture them. The next time we crossed paths, we stopped to chat.

Now, a stranger who'd been watching me "for years" was telling me where she lived. It was a street I'd been passing each morning since before our youngest child, now four, was born.

"I think of myself as Crazy Walking Lady," I told her, laughing to show I wasn't actually crazy. Too quickly she confirmed: "You are."

I'd never noticed her, but she said she'd been watching from her window since my current companion entered the world. I told her he starts school this year, and I'm bracing for the day he says: enough!

"No!" she said. "Keep going!" As if we could stop time.

She told me it was nice to "finally" meet; we parted ways.

Weeks have passed but somehow the routine is yet to change. Our youngest child still wakes in darkness, calls to me, or pads into our room. I quietly dress, we both sneak out. Outside I strap him in a pram that's carried him through hours, kilometres, years.

He still happily complies; it's what we do, it's what we've always done. We leave his father and his brothers fast asleep, and walk before the dawn.

*

I was a morning walker well before I was a mother, but "morning" then meant at or after sunrise, not before. Afterwards I had a live alarm clock, company, and weights.

At first they'd be strapped to my chest, and later they'd be tucked against my back, and finally, seated in the pram: awake, alert, quizzing me about our day, our plans, the world, making me hiss "*dumplings!*" far too loud.

All three woke with the birds. Sometimes it was 5am, sometimes earlier. Sometimes I tried to settle them, but mostly I gave up and snuck out. Even if I'd barely slept, I didn't really mind. The movement lulled them back to sleep, our absence let the others stay asleep; and I was free to walk and dream, to drink the morning sky, to think, to pray.

In time they grew more wakeful. Later they would babble, before long they'd converse. Sometimes I'd tell stories, made up as we went, starring them.

As each child started getting older and sleeping longer, we'd walk a little later, or I'd slip out all alone while they slept on. Until, that is, another came along. But not this time.

Our third child is now four years old. He is seventeen kilograms. Soon he'll be trotting down the street in a small-but-still-too-big school uniform. Soon he'll say he's too big for the pram. And this time, there's no baby on the way. This stage is drawing to a close, for good. But what a stage it's been, and what a way to start each day.

*

Thanks to our early starts, I know where the local wallabies feast, where possums hide, where watchful dogs and wakeful people live.

I've seen the first planes of the day blink across the sky as the last stars disappear. I've witnessed sunrise after sunrise—some a gentle blush, others radiant, intoxicating gold. I've lost an hour's sleep or more per day, and yet I've gained another world.

In winter, when clear nights stretch at both ends, I've walked beneath a canopy of stars and tiptoed upon ice. I've seen frost beneath the streetlight that will not survive the sunlight. Strangely once, in summer, we saw snow.

One year I saw a meteor, another time a comet, tail and all. I cannot tell you how in awe I felt. I've even seen a line of satellites drifting in formation—a mystery later solved online, a wonder at the time.

And though I knew the moon is prone to grow and shrink, to rise and fall, I'd never noticed how, across the weeks and months, it swings and dances all around the sky.

Some mornings it is nowhere to be seen. The clouds create a roof that's prone to leak or cave right in. But we still go—why stay inside? My boy is sheltered by a plastic covering, I have a raincoat and I'm willing to be washed.

Then there are the mornings when a passing car will slow, eject a missile and speed on, when—before the rolled-up paper thuds at some subscriber's door—I freeze in fright. Yes, there are sunrises, shooting stars—but also shooting papers, speeding cars.

*

I wonder what my children, looking back once fully grown, will remember of our strange, secluded walks. Moving through a world that's mostly quiet and mostly still, watching as the sky, letting out a yawn, spills color everywhere to everything. Perhaps they'll mistake memories for dreams.

*

Two weeks after a stranger says she's been watching us for years, another lady says hello to me. She's crossed from the opposite footpath, she's pushing a pram herself.

The lady is in her sixties, maybe seventies, but she looks strong and fit. She tells me she's a runner and has seen me many times for many years. She asks how many years it's been, how many kids. I tell her more than ten, and three, all boys.

She introduces me to her companion, her five-month-old grandson. He's just slept over at her house—a first! Slept through, too! So when he woke she thought, why not? Come on! Let's walk.

Before we go our separate ways, the lady says that, seeing me, she sees herself some thirty years ago. And what she often thinks is what she tells me now: you'll be me one day.

An ageing grandmother said that I'd be her one day. Her words did not confront me; I felt glad. She said it joyously. She was content with what she'd been and had become. Her children now had children, and she had reached another stage. It wasn't sad; it was the very stuff of life.

*

Yesterday I saw myself in thirty years. Today, I left my "baby" with his brothers and his dad, and walked alone.

Life's work

CPX, March 2021

For all the advice out there on being a perfect parent, I'm yet to meet one.

To be fair, it's not an easy gig. You devote yourself to another's well-being, you place them at the center of your life, only to have them fly (or flee) the nest, and live a life that—if you've done your job right—*won't* center around you.

In her memoir *When it Rains*, Maggie MacKellar recalls her mother telling a friend that she felt she'd given her kids everything they needed to make their way through life. "Everything, that is, except the ability to cope with her death," she writes.

"I stood listening to her talking. As always, it irritated me that she'd made this—us—her life's work; had sacrificed herself so completely for her children."

MacKellar's reaction surprised me. I could see how a parent putting some other passion or ambition first might cause resentment; I hadn't realized that making a child their whole reason for being might be just as fraught.

We expect our parents to love us unconditionally and self-sacrificially, but do we want to be their life's work? To spend our adult lives weighed down by a debt we can't repay, expectations we can't meet, a sacrifice we are not worthy of?

My father died when I was young, and my mother was devoted to us kids. But I never felt pressure to be her reason for being. You see, she already had one. It didn't take her love and attention from me—if anything, it made her more loving and attentive. The object of her worship, the center of her life, was never me.

But it wasn't some*thing* lesser, it was some*one* greater; someone worthy.

City Boy and the Thistles of *Doom*
Sunlight Press, February 2022

On the first day of our country holiday, I almost had to drag my eldest son to the willows. I'd been picturing the fun our boys would have there—climbing from one tangle of branches to the next, swinging and jumping and darting and dropping. As soon as we'd unloaded the car, I struck:

"Let's go to the willows! The fields! The creek! Let's explore!" He said I could take his brothers; he would stay behind. I said fun was compulsory—no one was watching television or eating chocolate until we'd all gone somewhere and done something.

I took along some apples and biscuits, a jacket and a drink; he took along his grudge. I led them away from the car and down the hill. His brothers trotted happily; he walked.

It was a magical place in my memory, and it was magical still. A shallow stream curved around wizened trunks, and sunlight tinted light greens greenish-gold. A line of poplars stood nearby, pointing to the heavens, and all around lay grassy fields, staring at the ever-changing sky.

He wouldn't be won over though, not yet. "You know why I don't like this place? The thistles and the nettles." I suggested his shoes were the problem—swap sandals for gumboots, voila!—but also, I teased him.

I told him he was like the stereotypical city-boy character in novels, the one who complains about everything and everyone. To be honest, he is kind of hard to like at first. But never fear! These sullen types are ripe for development. By the end of the book you can almost guarantee a transformation—the other characters will all be fond of him, the reader will be too—and when he has to leave the place he'd so despised at first, he'll realize what he wants now is to stay.

Perhaps, I said, we could cut straight to the part of the story where the boy wants to stay—now, before we had to go? But art imitates life, and life imitates art, and it was only chapter one.

A few pages on, I tried another approach, telling him about babies and bathwater. Letting out the water doesn't mean you have to ditch the baby too. Could he dislike the thistles without disliking the whole place? Could he ignore the bathwater and focus on the beauty? I don't know if he listened, but later at the creek, he was first in and last out. The sullenness had all but washed away.

On the last day of our holiday, we packed up the car and tidied the cottage, then went back to the willows one more time. The boys stepped and skipped and splashed, from rock to branch to bank, chattering and laughing as they went.

Eventually, we wandered back—it was time to return to our inner-city home. As I approached the car, he kicked off his shoes, scaled one last tree, and said, "Mum, you know the story you told me about the grumpy City Boy? It actually came true."

I wasn't surprised that City Boy had ended up having fun, but I was surprised he'd admitted it. A plot twist, of sorts. What he said next surprised me even more.

"Mum, I think you're psychopathic."

"Psychopathic?! Why?"

Was it something I'd said? Had he taken the whole throwing-out-babies thing the wrong way?

"Because you predicted the future."

"Oh! You mean *psychic!*"

If knowing your child well enough to know they'll find water, mud, and trees irresistible, even when they think they want to watch television and avoid thistles, then yes. I am psychic. I laughed and hugged him. "The end."

That evening, in the postscript I suppose, a friend asked me about our time away. I told her the unsurprising, all-too-predictable story. She related to the parent, being one herself, but she also related to the child.

I began to realize that we grownups, at different times—too many times—and in different ways, had also let the thistles get us down. We too had robbed ourselves of joy that had been there waiting, ready for the taking all along.

If only we could see it at the time: glance up, take stock, and change the story there and then, while pages still sat waiting to be filled. Perhaps in future chapters, we would.

How I'm preserving my kids' memories—and their privacy
The Good Trade, July 2022 (Published as: "How I'm Privately Preserving My Children's Words in the Age of Social Media.")

Photographs aside, the record of my children's childhood I'll treasure the most is one I never planned to keep.

It began when our first child started speaking in sentences at the age of two. I was so delighted by the gems he came out with—so eager to share them with my husband, and yet so prone to forgetting them before he finished work—that I'd reach for my phone.

I'd text them to my husband and sometimes post them online. The act of sharing those gems, of having friends and family delight in them too, added to the fun of hearing them first-hand.

I soon realized those quotes were worth preserving properly. I didn't trust a tech giant or my phone to keep our memories safe—even if I did, they'd be needles in a growing stack of hay—so I kept a private record too: a simple online document, titled with my son's name and the year.

To avoid having to scroll through old quotes each time I added one, I'd type the newest at the top. At the end of the year I'd tidy it up (haste caused many typos), save, print, and start again.

At first I'd still share the occasional quote online, but when our son reached a certain age, I stopped for fear of breaching his privacy or making him self-conscious. That record didn't matter anyway, now we had our own.

Looking through our "quote collection" now that child is ten reminds me of moments and stages that have become distant memories. It also makes me realize that what I always saw as a record of my son's childhood has captured something of my motherhood as well.

An entry from age two starts with a line from me:

"*Ouch!* Why did you just bite my hair?"

"I'm just a bird making a nest."

In another I say: "If you ask me what I want to do today *one more time*—I'll go crazy!"

The three-year-old's reply: "I like crazy!"

A nearby entry reads, "Superhero talk: 'I can shoot food out of my blood!'"

I see that when his younger brother was a few months old, our eldest said he really liked and wanted to "keep" him—then asked if he could jump in the cot if he tried not to "smash" him. Another time he asked me to push the pram "faster and faster and faster" to make his brother fly.

They say that parenting young kids is hard, rewarding work, and I agree. But often it is entertaining too.

Flicking through the questions from age three, I'm reminded of a stage full of possibilities and curiosity.

Questions I'd forgotten include:

- "Can we visit someone's house we don't even know?"
- "Mummy, can a grown-up read *Charlie and the Chocolate Factory* to another grown-up?"
- "Do we know any robbers?"

Then there are the statements:

- After making him a banana milkshake: "You are my best mum ever! I never don't like you!"
- At bedtime: "Mum, I love you. And one day, I'm going to teach you how to read instructions."
- "I wonder how many bricks there are in the world. I also wonder if Jesus really did die."
- "Mum, you should get a nice hairstyle . . . It's a little bit lumpy."

By the age of four I can see him starting to hold me accountable ("Mum, can you please repeat what I just said?"). He's also starting to see me as a person who has feelings too. He asks me whether I've ever cried as a grown-up, and when, and why.

When our second and third children started talking, I recorded their quotes too. Life was more chaotic and my records were as well, but the habit had been formed and it had stuck.

Now I have a book of quotes for each of our three children that is sequential and spans years. Every now and then the kids ask to have a read; they find what they once said and did fascinating, and hilarious. We treasure these records more than their baby journals, and as much as our photos. Grandparents have loved reading them too.

As someone who interviews people for a living and was already prone to collecting favorite quotes from writers, the practice of transcribing my children's words came easily to me. I didn't feel as though pausing to preserve moments took anything from those moments. It's never been a chore or burdensome; it *has* felt a little like collecting gold.

I should note that I only recorded lines and exchanges that were particularly striking, and only when it was easily done. If I didn't have my phone on me or couldn't pause, I didn't stress. On average I probably "collected" a few lines per week. Once they started school, it was more like a few per month.

Some will deem this whole idea ridiculous, I'm sure. Some will like it in theory but find it painful in practice. Others will be more interested in immersing themselves in the present than preserving the past, or will happily rely on memory alone. All I'm saying is, this worked for me.

And as a result, when our kids leave home, they can each take a tiny taste of the countless cute, funny, profound and telling things they said as they grew up. They might choose to share their favorite quotes with friends, or to keep the whole thing to themselves. The choice, just like the words, will be their own.

Why watching "Alone" with my son was time well spent
ABC, July 2023

One way to give kids a renewed appreciation of all the comforts we don't think twice about is to take them camping. The lazy option is to watch "Alone" with them.

I recently started watching a television series with my eldest son, and the more that I reflect on the experience, the more convinced I am that it's been time well spent.

If you'd told me I'd be writing this article a year ago and that the show in question would be *Alone*, I might have scoffed. Reality television has never really been my thing—it riles me when manufactured drama masquerades as "real"—and my kids get enough screen time after school without opening the gateway to evenings as well.

But when I heard a season had been shot in my home state, I was curious. I didn't plan to watch more than the first episode with my (also curious) son, but one thing led to another and before long there was no question of stopping; we cared about the characters too much.

The setting of the show is what first caught my attention, but the premise is even more compelling. The aim of the game is to see which contestant can last the longest living alone in the wilderness with ten items of their choice (well, sort of)—and a whopping *seventy kilograms* of camera equipment.

Apart from the occasional medical check, participants have no human contact. They have no idea how their fellow competitors are faring, or how many remain, let alone how their families are back home, until they either use one further item—a satellite phone—to request "extraction," or are told that they're the last one left and have won the (in this case $250,000) prize.

Unlike most reality television shows, there's no film crew or "hidden" cameras; the only person filming the participants is the participants themselves. I appreciated the fact they had control over when a camera was on or off, that no one was zooming in on them without their knowledge. And while the fact they were expected to film at least five hours of footage a day gave the makers of the show more than enough material to get creative with, I never got the sense they were trying to misrepresent or make fun of any one of them.

The participants faced homesickness and loneliness, hunger, fear, frustration, fatigue, boredom, disappointment, bitter cold, and bad luck. It wasn't easy, and their (very coarse) language frequently reflected this. But they also demonstrated grit and perseverance as they improvised and experimented. Through it all they gained a new understanding of nature, society, and themselves.

Not only did I find myself enduring all twelve episodes of a "reality" TV show, I found myself enjoying it. And now, I find myself recommending it. In particular, depending on their age, interests, and disposition, I reckon this is a great show to watch with kids or as a family.

A new appreciation

It's a way to give children who have grown up in a society that is hyper-dependent on technology and hyper-connected to the online world, but profoundly disconnected from the natural one, a different perspective on both; and no amount of telling is as powerful as showing.

It's also a way to provoke gratitude. As we watched contestants suffering and starving, we gained new appreciation of the fact we were sitting, bodies warm and bellies full, in safety and comfort. And as we heard them speak of loved ones who they longed to see, we sat side by side.

The show earned its M rating. One contestant spoke of losing her three-year-old daughter to cancer after surviving it herself. Another shared his struggle of living with post traumatic stress disorder after being in the military. Their video "diaries" reflected raw emotion, but also courage, maturity, and resilience. Other participants were deeply torn between their mental commitment to stick it out, and their emotional desire to return to their loved ones, particularly in light of hunger and fatigue. Even though anybody could "tap out" at any time, their distress was sometimes hard to watch.

The swearing wasn't ideal for young viewers, but it was of a different character to swearing that's directed at another person. Mostly, contestants seemed to be swearing at their luck; though I did wonder how those who cursed with fury managed stress, and treated others, when they *weren't* alone.

As the show progressed and as people chose to leave, we learned more about what they valued and what they'd learned, how they'd changed, and how "success" can look different for different people.

A contestant whose blood pressure meant he was forced to leave after more than two months said he could not have tried any harder. Despite the fact he didn't win, he said he was grateful for the experience. He'd also come to appreciate, more than ever, that family matters most.

Another said that while she'd been determined to stay to the end, her focus was never on beating other people. "I really wanted to show that there is a way of being at home in the wild, there is a way of connecting with an ancestral way of being that isn't about dominating nature," she said. "I want to thank the palawa for the tens of thousands of years they've lived here in right relationship and harmony with this country, leaving footprints for me to follow." I loved this reflection, and the fact my son had witnessed it as well.

Alone with our thoughts

After finishing the Australian season, my son and I promptly started, and have since finished, the first season of the US version. As with the Australian show, a recurring theme was how confronting it can be in our distracted age, to be alone with our thoughts.

One of the final four characters in that series said his time in the woods had forced him to "really look" at his life and himself. In that place, on his own, he couldn't "stuff" emotions away; he couldn't use food or another relationship or his phone or the internet to distract him. "I have to look at it," he said. In the process he was confronted by his insecurities and forced to reflect on his priorities; at one point he'd broken down and "wailed." I was pleased that my son could witness a strong, capable man speak openly and emotionally about his feelings.

This same character had made multiple shelters, culminating in a spacious yurt complete with shelves; a canoe that sailed; and a musical instrument. His handiwork was a delight to behold, but the psychological work he did, the self-reflection, seemed an even greater achievement.

The longest-lasting participant in that season, a middle-aged man who recited poetry, sang with operatic gusto, and very much missed German chocolate cake, knew the biggest challenge would be psychological, and that he would ultimately be competing against himself. Just as in one sense, the participants were competing against themselves, in one sense, they were alone. But in another, they did have company; they did have someone to talk to: us.

The cameras meant the contestants could talk without feeling crazy; in fact, they were expected to. Medical checks aside, there were no real-time, in-person conversations, but they knew their words would reach people in time. Eventually, the footage would be seen and their words would be heard.

Much of it wouldn't make the final cut, but all of it would be reviewed by someone, and some of it would be seen by many. I found myself wondering: if this were not the case, would they have lasted like they did? I wager not.

There was the odd complaint about the camera gear and the work of recording—for all I know there were many more that didn't make the final cut—but I suspect this "work" gave more than it took. The talking, the story-telling, the meaning-making, helped contestants to process, persevere, and learn.

And it gave viewers the chance to learn a little too—not only about physical survival in the natural world, but about human psychology. We were able to gain insight into people's attitudes, values, priorities, struggles and limits, and in doing so, to reflect on our own. We were able to look at our lifestyles with a new appreciation of how easily our basic needs are met, and how many "necessities" are really luxuries. Above all, we were reminded that humans were not made to be alone, but to love, and to hold our loved ones tight.

Everything all the time all at once: Who needs a multiverse when you have multiple kids?
The Guardian, 2023 (Published as: "My brain can't handle all of the school emails! Why I've enlisted kids to preserve my sanity.")

I sat our three (primary-aged) kids down the other day and told them . . .

Actually, that's not true. I didn't even *try* to sit them down. But I did catch their attention when they all happened to be in our kitchen/living area, at various stages of getting ready for school.

So no, the kids weren't all *sitting* quietly, looking up with large, attentive eyes—but at least I wasn't, as I'm prone to do when busy, yelling through the house.

Once I had their attention, I told them that I needed their help—not just "help," but *theirs*. I didn't go so quite far as to say I wasn't coping with the pace of life, but that was the gist. I warned them that my brain was currently behaving like a sieve, that my inbox and calendar were out of control, that even if the school sent me three important reminders about this or that, and even if I read them all, there would be no guarantee I would remember what I was supposed to, when I was supposed to. I can't remember if I added that their dad was also unable to cope with the tsunami, or if that was a given.

Long story short: I was absolving us from full responsibility for "all the things" (times three), and giving some to them.

I love my children's school, and the time its teachers take to keep parents in the loop. I'm not against reminders, or newsletters or updates or FYIs. I'd certainly prefer too much communication than too little. I'm just not keeping up with all of it right now. And once it occurred to me that maybe, right now, I can't, it made sense to take a breath, explain, and ask for help.

The problem is, we live in an age where it's just as easy for someone to contact fifty people as it is for them to contact one, where there's no limit on how many demands can be made on us, because all it takes is a click of a button to make them. At the same time, there are no more hours in a day. We can upgrade the hard drives on our computers, we can improve their memory, their capacity, their speed, but we can't upgrade our bodies or our brains. We can only be in one place at one time.

Sometimes information is nice to know, but it's not information I need to know, and I needn't feel guilty if I don't have time to process and action *all* of it. Sometimes, I *am* the person who needs to know something, but sometimes, I'm not. Sometimes, the (little) person it concerns can take responsibility themselves.

And often, that little person is better equipped to remember library day and cupcake day and free-dress day than I am, because they might actually care *and* they might actually succeed. Their brains are at a stage where they can absorb entire languages, I struggle to remember people's names. Also, they're at a stage in life where they only *really* have to manage themselves. They're not subject to requests and demands and expectations from what seems like all directions all the time. They have capacity that I do not.

I think of myself as being naturally quite diligent, and not very rebellious. Sometimes, the fact I could *not* do something I've been asked to do—or expect myself to do—doesn't even occur to me, even if the request or expectation is unreasonable. I'm also prone to feeling guilty, even over the smallest things.

But the more I think about it, the more important my sanity is, for me and for my family. Preserving it by lowering expectations (my own and other people's) of how much I can manage shouldn't induce guilt.

Perhaps you can relate. Perhaps you have more than three children or more than you can manage in the time you have each day. Perhaps you also need to admit defeat and ask for help.

I'm yet to determine how effective downward delegating will be, but I'm hopeful. After talking to the kids, I asked them if they understood, and they said they did. Time will tell. But what's the worst that can happen? School uniform on a free dress day? No money for a cupcake stall? Reading the same library book two weeks in a row?

They'll be just fine.

Do yourself and other parents a favor—lower the bar
The Guardian, June 2023

One of the most memorable birthday parties I've hosted was also one of the easiest and cheapest. Our eldest son was turning five and wanted to invite his whole class. I wasn't willing to host a party with twenty-plus five-year-olds, but I was willing to invite them for a play in our back garden after school.

I made a call: no games, no prizes, no party bags, no banquet. Just an invitation to swing by on their way home from school, hang out, and have some cake. I added a firm "no presents please," so it was easy for the guests as well.

The result was short, and it was sweet. The kids amused themselves, the parents watched while chatting, the birthday boy had a ball. Then—be still my beating heart—they all went home.

No one expected more, so no one was disappointed. The bar was low; stress levels were as well. It wasn't "the best party ever"—and it wasn't meant to be. It *was* good. And good was plenty good enough.

Of course, it could have been simpler still. A handful of friends, or even one. Some don't do a party every year—how radical! And how reasonable! We might think of this as breaking vital rules, but such rules are mostly self imposed; we have a choice.

It's one thing to throw a party because you want to, because it will bring joy to your child, your family, and your guests; it's quite another if you're driven by rules and expectations you secretly resent, if you're paying for trimmings you really can't afford, if the process makes you snappy and stressed out.

Perhaps if we spent more time doing things the way that works for us, our families and our budget, and less time trying to do things the way we think we're supposed to, we'd be more relaxed and more sociable.

Sometimes a bar we're aiming for makes sense, but sometimes it's a result of precedents we perpetuate unthinkingly, or assumptions about others' expectations that we've never sought to question or to test.

Whatever the case, it seems to me we can be a little *too* diligent when it comes to meeting expectations, and not diligent enough when it comes to questioning them.

Will fellow parents *really* judge us harshly if we do things differently? Will our children *really* care if their party doesn't have *all* the trimmings? If they do, it might disappoint them—and it might build character. It might be an opportunity to direct their gaze from what they want, to what they have.

If parties are all-or-nothing affairs, we might end up throwing them in the too-hard basket; if they're casual and fun, we might not dread them, we might even enjoy them—which will make guests more likely to as well.

I once received an invitation for a party at a park that asked kids to bring their own drink bottles. It was a great idea; it saved the hosts from buying drinks and made sense from an environmental perspective. I can imagine some parents would worry this would be too much to ask of a "guest," but why shouldn't we seek ways to simplify and share the load?

Sometimes parents tell their kids to "use their words." If we're *really* worried that bucking a tradition will cause awkwardness or confusion, if we want to do something differently but also want people to know what to expect, we can use *our* words.

We might be worried the word 'party' means we're obliged to provide lunch, a cake, games and lolly bags. These may well be expected, but expectations can be changed.

"Hey friends! Johnny's turning five! We've decided to go for simple this year. No 'party,' just a play at the park after lunch. No presents please. xx."

It feels ridiculous to say something so obvious, but also strangely necessary: communicating can change expectations. Our words can engender understanding, dispel awkwardness and confusion, change onerous traditions, and make life easier.

We teach our kids that they don't have to do things just because their friends do, that they don't have to be like everybody else, and that if they're struggling, they need only ask for help. We encourage them to "use their words." And then we do the opposite ourselves.

By choosing not to meet this or that expectation, I can make *my* life easier, I can be a more relaxed parent, and I can lower the bar for others. Some parents might judge me, but I'm willing to bet that most will rejoice.

Everything is easy after camping
The Guardian, December 2023 (Published as: "Camping is challenging, but worth it—any other trip will feel like the lap of luxury.")

Even if you're *sure* you'd *hate* camping, I recommend you try it at least once. Because after camping, you'll notice that aspects of every other holiday, from packing to unpacking, from showering to sleeping, will have elements of luxury.

I can't remember my first camping trip. I grew up with a mother committed to ensuring her children saw as much of their home state as possible, even if this involved excessive drive times to the middle of nowhere. I was also a Brownie, then a Girl Guide. I liked camping and had friends who liked it; later I married a guy who liked it, and we had kids who did too.

On one hand, who wouldn't? Stunning views in the day, starry skies at night; beautiful beaches, and/or bush; time to read, to wander, to walk, to swim, to think, to talk.

Then there are the double-edged swords. No reception feels freeing—unless someone gets hurt or the car breaks down; food somehow tastes better, but unless there's a shop within cheating distance, you have to BYO *everything*. If there are toilets, you have to contend with the smell, and if there aren't, you have to find a spot that's secluded enough to avoid getting seen, but not so secluded you end up getting lost.

There are aspects of camping I don't like at all. Packing is a pain. It doesn't just involve clothes, bedding and food. Tents, tarps, a camping stove, fuel, lighter, esky, pots, pans, bowls, knives, spoons, washing-up liquid, towels, tea towels, soap, chairs, wash-stand, chopping boards, suncream, mozzie repellant, hats, coats, jackets, beanies, scarves, swimmers, boots, torches, batteries for the torches, first-aid supplies . . .

Sometimes there are predatory insects: mosquitoes, flies, leeches, jellyfish. Possums are endearing unless they spend the night unzipping bags, stealing food, and fighting more viciously than cats. Native mice are cute, unless their scuttling, and the fear they will soon crawl over your face, interrupts your sleep. And snakes, spiders and ants sometimes bite.

There are moments of exciting exploration and blissful relaxation. But boy do you have to earn them. You have to pitch a tent before you can sleep, you have to set up a makeshift kitchen before you can cook, to pack supplies—even a *map*—before you can hike. You'd think that by the time you roll into bed you'd sleep well, but even if the wildlife behaves, lying in a bag of synthetic fabric that makes a noise every time you move, on an air mattress that feels less like the air than like the ground, in *very* close proximity to other family members, isn't necessarily restorative.

There is also the work of leaving: trying to stuff sleeping bags into sacks that seem half the appropriate size, cleaning the tent, drying the tent, packing up the tent. And then, when you get home, another round of unpacking and cleaning and putting away.

By the time you've let the (brown) bath water out of the tub and scrubbed the filthy rim it left behind, you might vow never to camp again. But the experience could yet pay off. Next time you go away to stay somewhere with walls and beds, electricity and shops, you won't *believe* how easy it is.

I was struck by this the last time my family had a weekend away—at a *house*. Rather than make an extensive list of necessities in advance, and check off items as we packed ahead of time, we just chucked some stuff in bags on the day. Rather than pack for the kids or at least supervise their packing, I just told them how many nights we were going and left them to sort themselves out. Rather than plan our meals, shop, and pre-prepare, I grabbed some food from the cupboard and some from the fridge; supplies could be replenished easily.

On the way, I said I knew this haphazard approach would mean we'd forgotten stuff, but reasoned it wouldn't matter so long as we all had undies. At that point I realized I had not in fact packed undies and added a slight detour to our route. A subsequent discovery was that our six-year-old had packed three pairs of PJs—one for every night—but no other clothes. Another child remembered thongs, but forgot shoes. If we'd been staying in the wilderness this would have been an issue, but we were staying in a *house*!

If you pack the wrong clothes for camping and get snowed in, you might risk hypothermia; if you haven't packed enough food, you might starve; if you run out of fuel, you can't cook; if all your torch batteries die, you can't light up the night. But if the nearest shops are a 20-minute drive, the stakes are gloriously low. And don't get me started on the luxuries: soft beds, electric lights, flushing loos, privacy, a fridge.

Even if you expect to hate camping, and while away regret choosing to go, it will pay off afterwards, when being in a normal house—even a rundown shack—feels like the lap of luxury.

I lost my kids in a crowd. Here's what I learned.
Scary Mommy, May 2021

It happened at the theatre. The kids and I had just seen a ninety-minute Peter Rabbit production and my ten-year-old said he was going to the bathroom. I told him there'd be a *huge* queue. We were heading to the library next, which was practically next door, so he could go there. In retrospect, I should have made sure that we were on the same page before I turned away. Instead, while I gathered my bag, their drinks, and my four-year-old's hand, he and his middle brother left the stalls and went downstairs. By the time we reached the crowded foyer, they were gone.

I didn't panic; I headed to the library, scanning the street, feeling slightly more cross than worried. We went upstairs to the men's toilets. My four-year-old peeped in to see if they were there, but no luck.

I headed to the holds section. We always have a stack of books to collect and it's usually the first place we go. The boys weren't there, so I left a note with our holds, telling them to *stay put!* I was checking the theater but I'd be back. As we left the library, I said a hurried prayer.

At this point I remembered to turn on my phone, which I'd put on flight mode for the show. As I approached the foyer it started ringing, and as I walked inside I saw them: my eldest holding the theater's old-school telephone, his eight-year-old brother holding back tears, three workers looking on.

I hope the staff saw the gratitude in my smile, because I didn't use words to thank them. Words followed, but they were all directed at the kids. Still hugging the eight-year-old, who was now letting himself cry, I explained that I'd been looking for them at the library. Then I listened.

My eldest said that after *I* told *him* to wait for the library loo, *he'd* told *me* that actually, he was still opting for the theatre. He knew *now* that I hadn't heard, he didn't know it then. They went together and upon emerging, realized I was gone and asked for help. I said I was glad they'd stuck together. I was glad they asked a staff member for help. I was glad the middle brother remembered my phone number.

And ultimately I was even glad it happened. The whole saga probably lasted less than ten minutes, I was never *really* worried, they were never *really* scared, and we'd learned a thing or two.

I tried to reinforce every important takeaway on the way home (*and* when we got home, *and* over dinner, *and* after dinner, *and* . . . you get the picture) I talked about the importance of staying together, of knowing my phone number, of obeying instructions; the problem of countering one statement with another; the problem of not making sure that a message was actually received; the benefit of asking then *listening*, versus telling then *doing*.

I also tested the kids on my phone number. I'd tried to teach them it before. I now knew the eight-year-old had it memorized, but it turned out that the ten-year-old did not. "I hate memorizing numbers," he said. "They're slippery and they fall out of my ears!" I pondered this. He needed motivation. The experience of getting lost would help, but dusty numbers might still "fall" from his ears. To retain my number, he needed to need it regularly. This gave me an idea. I would add a password to the kids' account on my computer—a number. A number they needed to know for more than just screen time.

The memory of this day and the things I tried to teach my kids might fade, but I'm willing to bet that if they have to type in my phone number to access my computer, *that* memory won't.

Only Three

January 2024

I catch myself feeling guilty that I haven't been to the supermarket, bought more of everything. The result: only three breakfast choices.

Sultana bran, homemade muesli, toast. "Only three choices?" asks a child.

Only three.

Guilt came needlessly from the "only." I caught myself, and I rebuked myself. Three is *abundant*, and if anything, guilt should come from that.

My family lives a sheltered life. I live a sheltered life.

That we would put an "only" before "three."

Lean into playfulness. It's the mature thing to do
Common Good, May, 2024

At first I said "no" when my eldest child asked me, at a family gathering, if he could play a joke. He wanted to make and offer round some cordial spiked with salt. Mine had attracted complaints because it was too weak. This would attract a taker because it would be strong.

I said a smiling "no" and then, noting he had asked at all, and that his proposed trick was pretty tame, I thought, what's the harm?

When the other kids were too suspicious to accept his kind offering, he turned to the adults. An uncle thanked him for the drink, took a sip, and frowned, confused. He took another sip. My son began to laugh then ran outside.

"Salt!" I said. "A joke!" I said. And then, from the child in me, there came two unexpected words: "Get him!" The mother in me didn't disagree, "Go on! Tip it on his head!" I said. "Don't kids need to learn about consequences? About cause—and effect."

His uncle needed no further convincing. Out he went and out the cordial went, flowing from the cup to my son's unsuspecting head, dripping down his unsuspecting face, leaving undissolved grains of salt scattered through his hair.

His response to the lesson was delight. Whoever said that learning—that teaching—can't be fun?

I realize this prank could have gone either way. Depending on the child and on the victim, it could have ended in anger, or tears, or both, but the risk was minimal. I knew the players. What they didn't know til later was that I was one as well. Two life lessons for the price of one.

*

Weeks later, a friend and her partner make an offer on a unit. When it's accepted, they're both thrilled and terrified. Though she's fast approaching forty, she tells me she's still not 100 percent sure she's an "actual adult."

Her: Am I allowed a mortgage? And a baby?

Me: Aren't all adults just kids in disguise?

We could have decided we had "imposter syndrome"—why else would two fully-grown women doubt their own maturity? Instead, we decided all adults are indeed children in disguise. This isn't to say we aren't also adults, more that the notion of an adult that we had as children as more "other" than "us" was ill-conceived.

We also agreed that sometimes adults are in denial about this; we pretend we're more grown-up, less childlike, than we are. We don a disguise, play a part—to impress, convince, persuade, both others and ourselves—to court "success." And we suppress our insecurities and quirks.

*

Writer Sheila Heti, after meeting an editor for the first time, wonders what we need to know about a person in order to like them.

Before she wrapped her leftover buttered toast inside a paper napkin, I didn't know whether I liked her or not," Heti writes of the woman she met in a cafe. *"Then, when she wrapped up her toast in the napkin, I suddenly loved her. Before she wrapped up her toast, she had been making an effort to show herself to be a sophisticated and an impressive young editor from a respected magazine. Then, when she did that, the performance dropped; not only was she underpaid, the gesture said, but she really liked toast. She liked toast even more than she liked being admired.*

This made me smile, and it made sense to me. The less a person performs, the less they try to filter their quirks and hide their vulnerabilities, the easier it is to get to know them.

*

There is a world of difference between performing a role out of obligation, insecurity, or necessity, and being playful. Play is more experimental, less self-conscious, more curious, less serious. Psychiatrist Stuart Brown, who founded the National Institute for Play in the US, did so because fifty years of clinical practice, research and scholarship left him convinced that humans—not children in particular, humans in general—are "built to play and built by play."

In a paper on leisure and play, Benjamin Kline Hunnicutt says Plato viewed play as the best way for adults to learn. Meanwhile philosopher John Wall has claimed the "fundamental obligation" of human beings is, "to play amidst differences of experience in order to create more broadly expansive human relations."

In their 2023 book Playfulness in Coaching, LEGO Serious Play facilitator Stephanie Wheeler and corporate coach Teresa Leyman say play is "rooted in authenticity," encompasses "a cognitive attitude towards exploration," supports shifts in perspective, and can help people access a state of learning, connecting and co-creating.

They suggest that, "an increasing acceptance in coaching and leadership that we need space for uncertainty, ambiguity, and the whole person" might lead more organisations to see the value of supplementing, "our rational and logical thought with playfulness."

I'm reminded of a quote from author Natalie Goldberg who, in *Writing Down the Bones,* talks about how one small prop can "tip your mind into another place."

"When I sit down to write, often I have a cigarette hanging out of my mouth. If I'm in a cafe that has a 'No Smoking' sign, then my cigarette is unlit. I don't actually smoke anyway, so it doesn't matter. The cigarette is a prop to help me dream into another world," she writes.

*

Being less guarded, less risk-averse, and taking ourselves less seriously might make us come across as less impressive to some and downright weird to others, but it can stimulate more creative and innovative thinking and problem-solving.

It can enrich our relationships, too. It allows people to "get" us more easily and relate to us more honestly. They might not find us as sophisticated as they would if we suppressed our quirks, but I'm willing to bet they'll find us more interesting.

For those of us who have suppressed quirks, hidden vulnerabilities, and playful urges for so long it's become second-nature, letting down our guard from time to time might be more difficult than leaving it up permanently. But becoming one kind of person—an editor, a homeowner, a parent—doesn't mean we have to stop being another.

As for age, we're never *really* just one number, we're never *really* all "grown up," so why pretend otherwise? My middle-aged mind still contains and has been shaped by the memories, experiences, and views of my younger selves. I still have in me an urge, from time to time, to play. And, as I continue to grow up, I intend to foster it. It's the mature thing to do.

The challenges of self-assessment
Eureka Street, May 2022

My kids brought their report cards home last month. I'd been thinking about the election campaign, and about society's obsession with productivity. I'd been wondering how "the unemployed" and "pensioners" might feel—like a burden? Like a problem to be solved?

I'd been thinking about my own productivity too, as an employee, as a freelancer, as a parent; about what left me feeling satisfied, worthy, competent, or guilty, unproductive, unfulfilled.

I'm convinced we should value people for who they are, not what they do, or don't or cannot do. And yet I often catch myself thinking about how much I have or haven't *done* on any given day, and forgetting to reflect on how I have behaved, on the kind of parent, wife, colleague, friend, daughter, neighbour, stranger, that I've been.

Such thoughts were on my mind when those reports landed on our kitchen bench. Ten "learner dispositions," three possible ratings. I wanted our children to "actively participate in learning" and "aspire to do their best," but more than that, I hoped that they were kind. I wanted them to be good students, but more than that, good friends.

I skipped past "uses time effectively" and "works well independently," to "softer" (and yet harder) skills: "responds respectfully," "listens to others," "works well in groups." Were they working towards expectations? Meeting expectations? Exceeding expectations? But also: was I?

If I cared more about the kind of people they were than how they were performing, what about myself? How would I evaluate *my* performance? And how would they evaluate me? I wondered, and then I dared to ask.

My ten- and eight-year-olds were all too happy, *all too happy*, to oblige. They didn't hesitate when it came to working well independently and using time effectively: "exceeds expectations." Apparently I'm also very good at working in groups (*'cos of all the time you spend with your friends!*).

But in other areas, including listening to others, I was just "meeting expectations." And when it came to responding respectfully, I was merely "moving towards" them.

When pressed, they pointed out that I wasn't always calm and respectful when things went wrong. I thought about my tone when we were running late; when I randomly declared a harmless mess intolerable; when my frustration about something they did nothing to provoke landed on them. They had a point.

I could be listening better too. I often felt frustrated when they seemed to ignore *me*, but how often did I tune *their* voices out?

Why is it so easy, I thought, to be a hypocrite? To say or think one thing, then blindly do another? To forget what really matters and fixate on what does not?

Why do politicians so rarely say they're sorry, they messed up, *before* they are found out and they are forced? Perhaps they too forget to think not only about *what* they have achieved, but how they have behaved, about the kind of person they have been and want to be.

I want to care more about my character than my productivity or performance, more about others than myself. I'm destined to fail. But I can keep "working towards expectations." And at the end of every day, I can ask myself how well I have loved instead of how much I have done.

I can also practice saying sorry, and dare to hope that my failures really are forgivable; not because I am deserving but because I know, full well, that I am not.

Love &

. . . learning

We will make mistakes in life and work, but we should expect and own them
The Guardian, December 2021

According to a friend of mine, when I talk about feeling embarrassed, ashamed or misunderstood, my hands become claws and I run them down my face with exaggerated angst. I hadn't realized, but as soon as she said it, I knew it was true.

While still performing that move, we identified another: reeling in rope, cast too far out, at frantic speed. Both feature often when I talk about my writing, about the risk of sharing words I might regret.

If I want to write about what I really think, this is a risk I must accept. Sometimes my thoughts will go against the grain, will prove unpopular, will make me feel unpopular. And sometimes I'll look back on an opinion I expressed and realize it has changed. I'll want to pull it back.

Those gestures came to mind when I heard a celebrated US writer had bought back the rights to his first two books—for about ten times what he was paid to write them—so he could revise and reissue them. In the process, he cut some essays completely. I wondered why.

My first thought was that what he said then didn't align with popular opinion now. But in a *New York Times* interview, Kiese Laymon sounded less concerned about how those essays might now be perceived than he was about how his own perceptions had changed since writing them.

Laymon said he's always revising his work, and himself. He sees revision as an ongoing commitment to honesty, a perpetual process of "assessment" tied to the very act of living. He said the reason he removed essays from his book was that he could no longer "stand by" them.

He also said that the times he's been most "ethical" and "tender," whether in a piece of art or a relationship, had been the times he's looked back with a willingness to see if a kind of "harm" was done.

Reflecting like this can come at a price. There's a risk we will see something we don't want to see, in our words or in ourselves, that calls for change. We can't go back and unsay what was said, but if we see we were mistaken, and it matters, we can be the first to speak.

The way Laymon speaks of revision reminds me of the way George Saunders speaks of redrafting short stories. In his latest work, *A Swim in a Pond in the Rain*, Saunders discusses the power of careful, sentence-by-sentence revision in a way that makes editing a draft sound more important than writing one.

A work of art "has to surprise its audience, which it can only do if it has legitimately surprised its creator," he says. And, through repeated redrafting, it just might.

Like Laymon, Saunders takes this further: the unintended effect of trying, "per one's taste, over and over," to make better sentences might even be characterised as "moral-ethical."

Saunders illustrates his point by comparing the sentence "Bob was an asshole" with one that instead describes Bob behaving like an asshole and explains why. The person who wrote the revised sentence "feels like a better guy, somehow" than the person who wrote "Bob was an asshole," he says.

"I find this happening all the time. I like the person I am in my stories better than I like the real me. That person is smarter, wittier, more patient, funnier—his view of the world is wiser."

I'm no famous writer. Mostly, I relay the opinions of others, not my own. But I also pen the odd freelance piece. Through redrafting and revision I refine my words and thoughts until I can "stand by" an argument.

Rejection is disheartening, but acceptance is frightening. To have a piece purchased and published means it is no longer mine. Will a line or a word be taken the wrong way? Have I missed, or misunderstood, a vital point? Will I one day claw my face and pull imaginary rope—in vain?

Indeed I might. But if we let courting approval and avoiding disdain dictate our words, nobody wins. If we daren't speak with honesty—be vulnerable, take risks—the public square will be a dismal place indeed.

Motives matter. Sometimes I'm tempted to revise for the wrong reasons—not out of a desire to write better or more truthfully, but out of a desire to please, to play it safe. This is not "honest assessment." This is cowardice.

A revision that denies the past is too.

Writer or not, this is relevant to you: technology makes authors of us all, and who has never wanted to retrieve, revise, an email, text or post?

If we are human, we will make mistakes. There should be no shame in making an admission, in changing a stance, if a fault-line's been exposed—a nuance understood, a truth revealed. But sometimes we behave as if there is.

One thing is certain: we will never have all the answers. It's a fact we very easily forget, a fact that means staying alert to different ways of thinking is something we must cultivate, not fear. We have so much to learn. We will always have so much to learn.

We should expect to make mistakes. We should be willing to be honest when we see we're in the wrong and, when others do the same, we should be willing to respond to them with grace.

What color is a gumleaf, and what shape?
Contrary Magazine, Spring 2023

Some scattered thoughts, gathered.

Unless words count, I am not the kind of person who collects. But lately, I have found myself noticing—taking, treasuring—colored shapes I used to walk upon.

Perhaps I have the snake to thank. Before I saw it sliding fast across the path, before I froze and watched it simply melt away, I hadn't thought to fix my wandering gaze on the ground. Nor had I noticed what I had been stepping on.

I live on an island called Tasmania. It sits beneath, and belongs to, a larger island called Australia. The eucalyptus tree, which grows and thrives in many countries now, is native here. It boasts nine hundred species, and dominates the land that we call "bush."

I arrive home holding my new treasures loosely in my hand. I look at each in turn, afresh. Their curves: some easy, elegant, some pained. Their surfaces: some dotted, others dashed or spotted, faded, chewed; some rough, some smooth. Each is divided with a line that can be traced from tip to tail, not one is straight, symmetrical; none could ever be identical. I photograph them all. They will not keep, but in this way I keep them.

I live a short walk from Hobart's city center, all downhill. And closer still, uphill, there's native bush. At night, wallabies descend four blocks, bouncing down the footpaths, crossing streetlit roads to feast on moonlit lawns. By night they take from my garden, by day I take from theirs.

I was walking in the scrubby bush that crawls upon the hills behind our house. My eyes were on the path. This island isn't home to harmless snakes; all are venomous. And as it happens, the ground here is never dull. Looking down has made me notice and delight in something new.

As I finish individual shots, they form a pile. I photograph them all at once, a glorious, unruly mess. I wonder at their beauty, their variety, their brokenness, their grace. And I marvel at the fact I hadn't marveled until now. How did it take so many years to really look, to really see? I'm mystified. What other wonders do I overlook each day?

I used to think the Aussie bush a little dreary, somewhat dull. The greens and blues of gum leaves may prove bright and full of life up close, but from a distance they seemed lustreless and dull. Meanwhile I'd swoon over the luminescent greens of European trees in spring. And I loved the way in autumn they would burst, slow-motion, into flames. But recently, belatedly, I've seen that gum leaves come in many colors too—they also change and change again, are beautiful—even and especially once they fall, while they're lying quietly dying on the ground.

I love their blemishes, emerging as they age, as they're weathered, as they're bruised, as they're trodden, as they're eaten by disease and animals, as they twist and writhe then stiffen, unable to unwind, as they break and as they crumble, returning to the dust. I love the way they form a carpet, catch the light, reflecting silver-white or gleaming gold. They fascinate me most not when they're fresh and young and thriving on a tree, but when they've lived a little while; when just a little while remains.

The hitchhiker

Fortunate Traveller, October 2022 (but penned two years earlier)

We'd spent the weekend in Westerway, Tasmania, a town whose population could fit on a large bus. He was waiting on the main street, one bulging pack strapped to his front, another to his back, seemingly unbothered by the load. He was tall and strong with generic good looks.

I took one look at him and I knew his story. I knew the second pack belonged to his girlfriend—a tanned beauty with long legs and perfect teeth. I knew they were in their thirties—smart, with high-paying jobs back home, but also adventurous. I knew he was hitching a ride because she'd gone on ahead, though I didn't know why. In fact, I knew nothing.

His name was Jackson, and although he was from Montana, he didn't call it, or any other place, home. The second pack didn't belong to a girl; it was his, and it contained extra bedding. Jackson was more a tent-in-the-wilderness, than a bunk-in-a-hostel type.

We told him we could take him as far as New Norfolk and he asked us where we were from. When we told him Hobart, he smiled. "You're too clean to be from New Norfolk," he said. I wasn't the only one making assumptions.

In the thirty-odd kilometres that followed, Jackson treated us to a collection of stories so bizarre I knew that if I didn't write them down, I'd doubt my recollection. So, after we dropped him off, I did.

Jackson, you said this was your tenth trip to the state. You'd recently made your way to Westerway from Mount Field, having spent four days trying to hitchhike from Lake Pedder, and were now hoping to get to a caravan park in Launceston for a hot shower. I wondered why you had just accepted a lift in the wrong direction, and whether you were aware there were other hot showers in Tasmania, but didn't quite know how to ask.

I did ask where else your travels had taken you. Your answers raised more questions I didn't know how to ask. You said with casual calm that you'd backpacked across Africa and hung out with pygmies in the Congo. You told us the only way your parents knew whether you were alive or dead was when you made bank withdrawals, or when they consulted a psychic, and that when you fell into a bog and cut your leg from ankle to knee on the South Coast Track, it was the psychic who told them first.

You also said one of the reasons you kept coming back to Tasmania, of all places, was that it had a secret. "I guess I can tell you," you said, before we even had time to ask, speaking as if we were old friends who'd known each other for years, as if the honour had been earned.

Jackson, you told us your "secret": that thylacines are not extinct; that you saw one on your sixth visit to Tasmania and that you were determined to find proof. You reeled off some names of *National Geographic* editors who had given you the equipment to do it. You said you sometimes slept with ropes tied from your legs to dead wallabies (so you'd wake if an animal came to feed on them, of course). You told us about Andrew Orchard, "the tiger guy up north."

Jackson, we didn't know what to make of you, or your claims. I did look up Andrew Orchard, and find he'd been profiled in the *New Yorker*, of all places, but this was the only fact I could verify. Were your stories true? Did you tell them for our entertainment, or for yours? Did you believe them? Did you expect us to?

Jackson, I thought I knew your story. I made it up for you without even realising it, before I even met you. I still don't know what to make of your tales. I admit that the cumulative effect left me joking they were payment for the ride—entertainment in exchange for transport. Jokes aside, I will say this: just because I'm prone to concocting fiction and finding it more plausible than fact, doesn't mean that you are. Either way, you gave us quite the ride.

*Note: Because I couldn't run this story by the hitchhiker, I didn't use his real name.

Leading by example

The Guardian, March, 2024 (Published as: "Maybe I should have suppressed my shriek as the screen flooded with porn, but I was teaching my kids a life lesson.")

I was clicking a link that should have taken me to a review of a children's book, when my computer screen flooded with porn. I couldn't close the window fast enough or—judging by the speed with which other family members flocked to find out what on earth was wrong—shriek loudly enough. It was like the time I was stung by a bee and a neighbour who lives a street away not only heard, but was so concerned she knocked on the door to check no one needed an ambulance.

This time there was no bee—or burn, no broken bones, or even blood. I told the kids that I was fine. All that had happened was a link that should have taken me to one page took me to another, one with pictures that I didn't want to see. I can't remember if I used the word "nudity," or the word "pornography," or said something about "people without clothes on doing things I didn't want to see," but however I phrased it, they understood.

If I'd thought twice in the moment, I might have suppressed that shriek, but reflecting on it later, my husband and I were glad I didn't. Sooner or later, this would happen to the kids, and I'd reacted in the way we'd want them to. Sure, you can set up filters, but filters don't work every time, and aren't on every device they'll ever use. We wanted *them* to be prepared to filter too. Knowing when to look away, when to—if not shriek—raise the alarm, is a "life skill."

When you think about it, adults—parents in particular—are setting an example of one type or another whenever children are watching them. Sometimes we do so consciously, but especially when we're reacting in the moment, we might forget they're looking on. In those moments, our examples might be as much a lesson in what *not* to do as what to do.

If we're not careful, our behaviour might suggest the appropriate reaction to feeling stressed is to drink, that the appropriate response to frustration is passive aggression, that the appropriate response to feeling sad is buying things we do not need.

If we're not careful, a child might judge us for paying more attention to our phone than to the cashier who is serving us or the family member sitting across from us, or they might think that's just "what you do," and when they're older, do the same.

A related challenge is adjusting how we treat our children as they age. We have an instinct to protect our kids that won't always serve us, or them, well. If we want them to learn how to be responsible adults, it's our responsibility to gradually give them more freedom as they become more capable of exercising it, mindful that one day they'll have to navigate without our help. I struggle with this, especially when risk is involved, but I remind myself that shielding our kids now might do them a disservice down the track.

Another protective tendency is to shield kids from emotional struggles we might be facing which they might learn from. Last year when I received a distressing letter, I fought the instinct to flee the room to hide my tears, and stayed to explain them instead. I'd told the kids there's no shame in expressing and processing emotion; this was my chance to show it.

I fought the impulse to be closed instead of open again when, on another occasion, our eldest overheard me talking to his dad about someone who was interested in me a long time ago, and started asking questions. I could have shut him down, but because I don't want him to be secretive when he enters the world of romantic relationships, I spoke openly instead.

Knowing when to be more or less open with our kids, or when to give them more or less freedom, knowing what's "age-appropriate," would be easy—or at least, easier—if all children matured at the same rate, if all were equally responsible, equally trustworthy, equally risk-averse, equally streetwise. But like each parent, each child is different.

I suppose it's a matter of noticing them noticing us, of being a little more conscious of and intentional about what we're saying and not saying, what we're suppressing and expressing, and why.

No matter how strong our resolve, we'll still model bad behavior. The good news is that every time we catch ourselves, we have an opportunity to admit it and apologise. If our kids leave home with the ability to do the same, then for all that we've got wrong, we'll have got something vital very right.

When we assume someone that someone's judging us, it may be that we are unfairly judging them
ABC, November 2023

The main thing I learned in science class, apart from the fact teenagers can't be trusted with bunsen burners, is that experiments should begin with a hypothesis and end with a conclusion.

You can't jump straight to the conclusion. And yet outside of science labs, when we're making judgments in the world—especially about fellow human beings—that's what we tend to do.

I'm not saying we can, or should, devise experiments to somehow test our assumptions about each other; I'm just wondering how we come to such confident conclusions about what people are like, and why, with so little information. We seem to forget that what we don't know about another person far surpasses what we do. If we stuck to hypothesising, perhaps we'd be more curious, less prone to misconceptions and to judgement, quicker to extend the benefit of the doubt.

If we truly disapprove of judgmental attitudes and behaviour, we'd do well to examine our own. I know I have a tendency to give others less credit than they deserve, and to make more allowances for myself. And sometimes it's the people I know the least—in the case of famous figures, not at all—that I judge the most readily and the most harshly. I don't have the full picture; I'm trusting headlines, I'm filling gaps with guesses. Their most winsome traits might never make the news; this doesn't mean they don't exist. All this is easy to forget.

Why is it so easy to presume to know more than we do? So difficult to adopt the posture towards others that we want them to adopt towards us, or to put ourselves in others' shoes?

One thing I've come to realize as I've tried to be more aware of how and why I judge others, is that I often feel judged—or rather, misjudged, myself.

Sometimes it's to do with something trivial; I'll assume a stranger's stare means they're judging my children's "spirited" behaviour. Other times, it's to do with a polarising issue where sympathising with one "side" means feeling judged by the other, and not taking a side means feeling judged by both.

I might have the opportunity to add nuance to a conversation—then assume everyone has made up their minds, so there's no point.

In that moment, I presume to know what others would think and what they would say. I deprive them of the chance to hear another point of view, and myself of hearing how they would actually respond.

I see the irony. Or should I say hypocrisy? It's not very open-minded to consider other people judgemental without good reason. Feeling judged isn't the same as being judged, and it's certainly not evidence of it.

Assumptions and judgments are a part of life. When they're informed they're often right, and help us operate effectively. I'm not suggesting we should make none at all, or second-guess each one. But when we are making ill-informed, ungenerous guesses about other people's thoughts and motives—and treating them as proven conclusions—we should be wary indeed.

Working to imagine, when we feel judged, that it might just be a feeling, that we might be wrong, could make us happier, kinder people. We might become less defensive, more open and more gracious. Even if a person has been judging us, they might start to see us differently.

You don't have to believe that "the measure you use will be measured unto you," or that in judging others you "bring judgement on yourself" to resolve to judge less, and hypothesise more.

Perhaps you agree, perhaps you don't; perhaps you're judging me right now for quoting a religious text, or perhaps to judge someone for that would never even cross your mind. I could jump to a conclusion about what you might be thinking, or I could make a conscious effort to resist. I could remind myself that unless you tell me what you really think, and unless I really listen, I can't presume to know.

UNlearning
(Expanded and published by *Common Good*, May 2025, as "Why I, a Christian, don't always share my faith.")

Some Saturdays ago, I was sitting at a party with a group of "can't-dance" friends, discussing our woeful incompetence. Instead of just hitting the dance floor and moving with the music, we would think about what our bodies were doing or not doing, what others might be seeing or thinking—making carefree, casual dance impossible.

We had learned how *not* to dance; if we wanted *to* dance—naturally, unselfconsciously, without set steps—we had some *un*learning to do.

Later, I was reflecting on some verses from a book and from a song about how there is "a time for everything." I noticed there a time to dance.

No doubt the wedding where a Jewish man turned water into wine—his first recorded miracle—was one such time.

Jesus: who also told his friends, when they shooed some kids away, to let the little children come to him. Jesus: who cared less about appearances, than the heart. As an adult, I have come to speak of him with too much caution, and too little passion.

I was once a little child. I've since learned to hear a catchy song, and barely move at all. It makes me wonder: what else would I do well to unlearn?

To wonder still

ABC, August 2023 (Published as: "Learning how to linger with the wonder of the world.")

If you had asked me, "What color is a gumleaf, and what shape?" this time last year, I might have answered, "Green, or bluish green; and kind of like an elongated heart." If you had asked, "What is the color of a *dying* eucalyptus leaf?," I might have answered: "Brown? Or gray?"

I've since noticed just how differently each one is shaped, colored, and textured. The toil of living decorates their skin; it grows more detailed, complex, blemished, and beautiful with time.

These days I find that the eucalyptus leaves beneath my feet arrest me more than those still green upon the tree. I often pause, when walking in the bush, to pick one up. I place its skin against my skin, compare its creases and its veins to mine. And I imagine, based on its blemishes, the story of its life.

Discovering these wonders, which I trod upon indifferently for years, stirred a feeling Annie Dillard describes well. She writes of watching a stunt pilot dancing through and all around the sky, and feeling unexpected awe.

She'd known about such people and such planes, but knowing's not the same as noticing. In the days that followed, she kept thinking of the spectacle; she couldn't stop. The reason had to do with beauty, a kind she hadn't seen until that day. Dillard writes:

> *I had thought I knew my way around beauty a little bit. I knew I had devoted a good part of my life to it, memorizing poetry and focusing my attention on complexity of rhythm in particular, on force, movement, repetition, and surprise, in both poetry and prose. Now I had stood among dandelions*

between two asphalt runways in Bellingham, Washington, and begun learning about beauty. Even the Boston Museum of Fine Arts was never more inspiring than this small northwestern airport on this time-killing Sunday afternoon in June. Nothing on earth is more gladdening than knowing we must roll up our sleeves and move back the boundaries of the humanly possible once more.

I too have seen a person in a plane defying death—a team of six, in fact. I heard a sound; my children heard it too, we sought its source. I hadn't yet read Dillard, didn't know what to expect, and I am glad.

The sky above the city was their stage and from below, tilted faces watched in wonder. I was astonished by their synchronicity, their speed, their grace.

What moved me most wasn't what I saw, but that which was invisible: pilots who had worked and trained, had taken risks for years to make those strange contraptions dance in unison.

I imagined pulses pounding, grins growing, spirits soaring, as they whizzed and flipped, drew close then peeled apart. And I pictured them all back down on the ground: breathless and excited and relieved—relieved and yet impatient, to fly back up and do it all again.

I think about the feeling Dillard writes about so well: the joy of having seen a thing you've never seen, or never *really* seen, before; and how the revelation can make your mind expand, recalibrate. It is a sudden prising open: not completely, just enough to let new light, new air rush in.

I felt something like it when, some years ago, twelve boys and one young man were trapped within a flooding cave. Some watching from afar saw that their knowledge, skills, and experience might prove invaluable. Full of fear and doubt, they boarded planes. Can you imagine how they felt when that first young boy was carried out? When one by one, the other children were returned alive to frantic parents? Imagine what those divers learned about the boundaries of what might be possible, about what humans can achieve working as one; about how beautiful a thing like breath can be.

It can take effort to stand still, to stop and imagine, when distractions court us so relentlessly. It can be work. Sometimes we must "roll up our sleeves"—it's true! But oh what work! And there will always be more work to do, for there are untold stores of beauty in this world.

I think about the kind that shocks, the kind that we expect, the kind that can dawn gradually with time—and it seems to me supply outstrips demand.

There's a tradition at my children's school. Each year the grade one class pretends they're traveling overseas. The teachers make them passports, give them tickets in advance, and the children then make magic with their minds. On "the big day," there's an arrivals and departures board, a plane made out of numbered chairs, an aisle. Attendants take their tickets and help the children find their seats. In the air, they're given menus, order food, receive a snack and lunch, dessert. They travel from their hometown to a far-off foreign land. It's just a game; it's play—and yet it is work. If they don't use their imagination, and channel their attention, they won't travel anywhere. They will remain in plastic seats, in Tasmania, at school. But imagination is their specialty. The class takes off—and lands in Tokyo.

I'm not one to reread books; I think too much of those I'm yet to read. But I'm convinced there can be as much value in reading the same book repeatedly as choosing something new, as much to learn by staying in one country as traveling the world, as much joy in loving one partner as many.

A stunt pilot's breathtaking, death-defying show, and the thrill it can provoke, is a delight; a moving rescue, greater still. But there are many types of beauty in this world.

The secret is to learn to look, to linger, and then long after you pass the wonder by, to wonder still.

Dillard, after watching a stunt pilot from a runway on the ground, thought about the spectacle, "that night, and the next day, and the next."

This seems to me a worthy use of time.

On rhythm and judgment

Common Good Magazine, April 2024 (Published as "Break the pattern of judging one another.")

Before explaining how to read rhythm on a page, my children's piano teacher gave the class a challenge. She asked the kids to walk around the room without consistent steps—no repetition and no pattern. If you've never tried this, try it now. You might find you have to hop and skip and jump to keep your feet from falling—unintentionally, automatically, irresistibly—into a steady beat.

It's a simple challenge. And it's absurdly difficult. It shows that when we're walking normally, we do so rhythmically and unthinkingly. Even if we walk unevenly, our steps still fall predictably: ba-dum, ba-dum, ba-dum. It's natural, effortless.

That same week, I'd been thinking about how inclined we are to judge, even with no grounds. We judge each other's motives, behaviors, words, and even tastes. We do this naturally and unthinkingly as well.

A criticism I've often heard leveled at Christians is that they are self-righteous and judgmental. It's both strange and sad that belief in a higher power is often more closely associated with pride than with humility.

It's especially strange when the Bible makes it clear that God is the only one equipped to judge with perfect knowledge and justice, the only one whose view isn't clouded by ignorance, mixed motives, planks, or specks. The Bible also warns that in judging others, we invite God's judgment on ourselves; the measure we use will be measured to us.

The call to resist judging others if we don't desire to be judged reminds me of the warning that if we don't forgive others their sins, it's hypocritical to expect God to forgive ours.

If we unfairly label another person "judgmental," we earn the label ourselves. It's a challenge to us all. Feeling judged is not the same as being judged—and yet the feeling often leads us to call "judgmental" even those we *think* are looking down on us. Perhaps they are. But it's possible they're not. A person might have a furrowed brow for any number of reasons, and we may be the ones making it about us.

There's a parable I used to struggle with, about a farmer hiring laborers. In the morning, he offers people a fixed sum to labor for the day. They agree the sum is fair and get to work.

The day goes on; he hires still more workers. Yet at the day's end, he pays everyone the same. This used to seem unfair to me. But if the work is an honor and a joy—if the workers aren't hired based on merit, and the payment is an undeserved gift—it's not at all unfair. Besides, what right have I to judge the farmer if he chooses to be generous? Or to judge those who, for reasons I can't know, arrive later in the day?

If the farmer wants to measure payment not based on our (scarce) virtues or (feeble) toil, who am I to question him? When I stop and think about it, I don't want the wages I deserve; I'd rather have the gift.

You don't have to be religious to resolve to judge less, and extend the benefit of the doubt more. You might not fear that the measure you use will be measured unto you, but you don't have to be a "person of the Book" to believe that "doing unto others as you'd have them do unto you" is a goal worth pursuing.

And if you do believe that, at the end of the day, God has canceled all your debt and given you life to the full—you have even more reason to be gracious. The Bible says that God's own son—who unlike us had every right to be exalted—humbled himself. How much must those who claim to follow him do the same?

When pondering judgment and how readily we judge, I am also reminded of the Fall: the tale of people who, when tempted to judge good and evil for themselves, succumb. Their maker knows it won't end well, but they don't heed his warning. They choose to eat the forbidden fruit instead.

Could this story shed some light on why judging comes so very easily to us? On why we find it nearly impossible to keep in mind our blind spots and our biases, our mixed motives, our pride? And could it give reason for our tendency to presume our view is right? Resisting these natural tendencies is difficult. It takes concerted effort, like walking without rhythm, like holding in your breath.

And yet how wonderful it is when we're expecting to be judged, and the person who's observing us remembers their own bias, fortune, flaws, or ignorance. How wonderful it is when that person, instead of doing what comes naturally—ba-dum, ba-dum, ba-dum—skips a beat.

Even more wonderful is not expecting judgment when we die; not because we don't deserve it but because our loving judge has made a way—has offered, also longs—to take our place.

On connotations, and contentment
The Spectator, December 2020 (Published as: "Can't get no satisfaction? Try, for a happier New Year.")

The older I get, the less inclined I am to make New Year's resolutions. Perhaps I've developed an unconscious superstition that turning a personal goal into a New Year's resolution means I'm *less* likely to achieve it. After all, we joke about breaking them even as we're making them.

The classic health goals, for example, are usually either too vague—to eat healthier and exercise more—or too prescriptive—to cut out carbs *and* exercise for two hours a day—to stick to. There's a disconnect between the life we are living—with time restraints that make menu planning and grocery shopping haphazard and rushed; with social occasions that practically *necessitate* the consumption of alcohol, cheese, and cake; with fussy children who will only tolerate so much green on their plates—and the life where we're able to go to the gym, work out, go home, and prepare a healthy meal *every day* as opposed to once every few *years*.

The solution seems simple: to make our resolutions less ambitious and more practical, to make them compatible with the lives we are actually living. So why don't we? Why don't we stop dreaming big, and commit to achievable goals instead? Could it be that we'd *rather* dream big? That wanting is the point?

In Lin-Manuel Miranda's musical *Hamilton*, the protagonist describes his bride's sister, whom he has feelings for, as "a woman who has never been satisfied." He tells her: "You're like me. I'm never satisfied"—as if it is a virtue.

It reminds me of when Nadia in Brit Bennett's *The Mothers* reflects on how marriage has left her old flame Luke "satisfied."

"During long lulls in the afternoon, she thought about him, how peaceful he seemed. This had always frightened her about marriage: how satisfied married people seemed, how unable they were to ask for more."

In fact, he's not content at all, but her perception of contentment is telling. The passage continues: "She couldn't imagine feeling satisfied. She was always searching for the right challenge, the next job, the next city. In law school, she'd become prickly and analytical, gaining a sharpness while Luke has rounded and filled. She felt hungry all the time—always wanting, needing more—but Luke had pushed away from the table already, patting his full stomach."

It strikes me as strange yet familiar: the notion that contentment might be something to be feared or even despised rather than desired, that dissatisfaction might be cast as a virtue. It reminds me of the assumption that people who choose steady commitment over "playing the field" are somehow missing out, when the opposite could well be the case. It makes me wonder whether words like "satisfied" and "content" have begun to carry connotations that almost contradict their very meaning.

Could this explain our tendency to make New Year's resolutions a step too ambitious? Maybe we joke about breaking them, even as we're making them, because we expect to: they're an expression of desire, not intent. Perhaps, deep in our subconscious, we've started to value wanting and to shun satisfaction.

I'm sure this wasn't always the case. I think of the apostle Paul writing to the Philippian church all those years ago. Paul, who never comes across as lazy or settled—whose dramatic conversion was the original "road-to-Damascus moment" and who, from that day forward, was a man on a mission—claims to have learned the secret of contentment in all circumstances. It's clear he isn't expecting the word to carry negative baggage: "I know what it is to be in need, and I know what it is to have plenty," he writes. "I have learned the secret of being content in any and every situation, whether well fed or hungry, whether living in plenty or in want. I can do all this through him who gives me strength."

Returning to the present, I wonder whether part of the reason contentment is sometimes treated with contempt is that companies depend on, and marketers exploit (and even spiritualize) dissatisfaction. We can end up so consumed with wanting—more money, more things, more experiences, more "likes"—that we start despising the kind of satisfaction Paul describes. We're continually upgrading, discarding, and replacing technology that's *not* designed to last. Apps encourage us to sleep with people, but not to stay with them. Ads encourage us to throw money at New Year's resolutions, but not to keep them.

I suspect these trends are influencing the lives we live and the stories we tell, the promises we make and break, more than we realize.

If I betray a loving spouse, I can cast myself as a restless romantic, or a selfish coward. What's it to be? Did I have *an affair* or did I *cheat*? Is dissatisfaction a virtue, or a vice? Should contentment be sought, or scorned?

I suppose it depends on how we listen, how we unpack every word and test every assumption. As for how we speak—to others and ourselves—the choice is ours. We can use words to hide the truth or tell it. We can make resolutions we expect to break, or intend to keep. We can scorn contentment—or we can esteem it.

Not all older people envy youth

The Good Trade, August 2023

I realized something recently about my younger self. She assumed her elders wished that they were young again—her age or younger still.

I continued to assume this well into my thirties, all the while not envying a younger age myself. This lack of envy should have challenged my assumption, but I wasn't really conscious I was making it at all, so it remained.

I think I first noticed the story I'd been telling about youth versus maturity when cradling our youngest child. An older relative made a sentimental comment about mothering a newborn, *such a precious time*, then declared she'd no desire to do it all again.

How could someone whose children were grown-up—had *flown the nest*—not long to hold them close again? Not long to live that stage again? Not pine after their youth? I didn't have the answers; even so I didn't doubt her. I could tell she was sincere.

Now my kids are all in school and while I loved their newborn stage, I'm just as happy now. I don't lament the fact its joys and challenges have passed, or the fact I've aged. And I don't long to live my twenties or my teens a second time. A younger self might not believe me, but it's true.

Yes, my body's aging; I'm not thrilled about the signs. But even if I could go back, I'm too attached to all that I've experienced and learned to want to throw those years away, to rewind, repeat, replace who I am now with who I was. Even now at forty, I'm still yet to envy youth. The desire to revert to any younger self, the desire that I'd thought would surely come, still hasn't reared its head.

Today I wonder this: how many younger people now see *me* and those my age, and assume that we would prefer to be theirs?

Would they believe me if I told them I don't envy them their youth? Would they believe me if I told them I now see it's possible to relish later ages, later stages, of this life just as much as early ones?

And would *I* believe somebody who is double my own years, if they claimed they didn't envy *me* this age? I think that now I could; now I know: not all older people envy youth.

*

These thoughts returned to mind when I overheard a grade six boy, traveling in my car, talking to a friend and marveling at his younger self's "stupidity." Something he'd believed to be quite true just days before had turned out to be false; a conviction he had held with confidence was one that suddenly had fallen to the ground.

As he spoke he realized that much of what he *now* thought that he knew, would later make him laugh or groan or both. Time would prove him wrong repeatedly. He concluded he would always, in each moment, hold some views that he'd deem "stupid" later on, that he was therefore "stupid" now—and not just him, each one of us, to some degree.

How then could we trust our present selves, our views, at all?

I smiled at such a pessimistic view. Could not the fact we sometimes find we've been mistaken—about a person, or a fact, about a piece of so-called "wisdom" that seemed true—show that as we grow in years, we tend to grow in understanding too?

*

Later, I raised the topic with a friend. She spoke of "cringing" at past selves as a "developmental milestone"—an important one at that.

Perhaps the "cringe factor" is among the reasons I don't want to be a younger self again. There are things I thought many years ago that make me cringe a little now. There are things I care about now that I didn't in my thirties, twenties, teens, and there are things I cared intensely about then that matter little to me now.

In my early teens I was painfully self-conscious; a fleeting comment from a bully—about my teeth, my weight, my hair, my skin, my singleness—would have made me feel quite sorry for myself. Now I'd pity them—for having nothing better to think about or do, for having nothing kind to say.

And I remember liking songs that were the opposite of "cool," but keeping quiet; wanting clothes with certain brand names to "fit in"; *not* wanting to go partying, but feeling like I should.

Now I don't care for brand names and I'm fine with loving daggy songs, and puzzles, early nights, and cups of tea. I still want to be liked, but I know true friends will like me as I am. As for being different, aren't we all? And wouldn't life be boring if we weren't? Quirks make life interesting.

In some respects, I'm still the "me" I was in moments past. Memories and experiences from my younger selves still feed the way I see and understand the world; they give me lessons I can draw on and greater empathy and make me judge less unequivocally—but now they're but a part of who I am. Life isn't about pining for the past, but growing, changing, learning, and becoming; moving on.

There are things that I think true today, that one day I will realize just weren't so. That's not cause to doubt each thing I think I know. It's cause to be more open, cautious, humble, curious—it's cause to welcome, not lament, my mounting years, to realize and rejoice that growing old can be a gift, that not all older people envy youth.

On guilt, and doubt

Third Space, 2021 (Published as "The niggling problem of perfectionism")

There's a Franz Kafka character known only as "the officer" whose guiding principle is that guilt should never be doubted—even when the sentence is death. It's a chilling prospect. Shouldn't we always demand proof beyond reasonable doubt?

What of other kinds of guilt, lesser kinds with lesser stakes, guilt we feel ourselves? We joke about "guilty pleasures," we pay to offset carbon (guilt) when booking flights, we might even feel guilty about how (in)frequently we wash our sheets. How can we tell when guilt is "healthy" and when it's "unhealthy," when it's irrational and when it's reasonable, when it should be acknowledged, and when it should be doubted?

I don't question the guilt that strikes when I'm unkind or unfair, when I let someone down, when I feel and say I'm sorry. And I'm not inclined to feel much guilt at all if I indulge in a decent quantity of chocolate or neglect a decent quantity of washing.

The guilt I find myself questioning is the kind I wouldn't judge in others but condemn in myself, and mostly relates to parenting. I feel guilty for letting our children have screen time for longer than I read to them aloud, and I feel guilty for not forcing them to endure weekly piano lessons (*they'll thank you when they're older*, or in our case, won't). I even feel a twinge when I let them have honey on their Weet-Bix.

Then I think: Hang on! Their screen time is limited and often educational; just because it gives me a break doesn't make it wrong! Tasty food isn't immoral! *I* put honey on Weet-Bix, why shouldn't they? And while we *could* carve out time and money for piano lessons, it would take time and money from something else worthwhile, and then I'd feel guilty about neglecting *that.* Isn't the mental load I carry heavy enough without adding a load of guilt for not doing all the right things, all the time? Still, the feeling lingers.

Socially prescribed perfectionism

I suspect part of the problem is the influence of social media and "socially prescribed perfectionism" on my thinking. According to psychologists Thomas Curran and Andrew Hill, who broadly define perfectionism as "an irrational desire for flawlessness, combined with harsh self-criticism," the phenomenon is on the rise and with it, a tendency to overvalue performance and undervalue the self.

While I'm stressing about my parenting, the next generation of perfectionists is obsessing about their performance at university, in the workplace, and on social media. When they don't meet their own often unrealistic expectations, or secure the approval they crave, they feel "a profound sense of guilt and shame," Curran says.

Again I think: Hang on! If someone fails to meet a personal goal *despite their best efforts,* wouldn't disappointment or frustration be a more appropriate response than guilt and shame? They could even congratulate themselves for having done their best. If an unmet desire causes *guilt,* surely that guilt should be scrutinized? Doubted? Dismissed?

And if the desire is to be hailed as the smartest, the prettiest, the most popular—even the kindest or wisest—perhaps that should be scrutinized as well.

Overthinking some failings, overlooking others

In addition to the (questionable) guilt we feel when we let ourselves down, and the (often justified) guilt we feel when we let others down, what if there are worse failings we don't even *think* about? Failings we should feel guilty about, but don't?

Are there people I judge with such habitual self-righteousness, such unconscious bias, that I don't even realize I'm doing it? Or priorities I justify in the name of self-care when really they're just selfish? Do I hide my greatest failings from the world—and from myself—then ruminate on trivia instead?

The notion that there are different types of guilt certainly isn't new. Jewish law presupposed numerous categories; its extensive sacrificial system included rituals to atone for unintentional failings, even failings we remain unaware of. Animals were slaughtered, blood was shed. The lesson was clear: human guilt is extensive and diverse, a messy problem that cannot be ignored. Perhaps some guilt is unfounded, but if it's justified it cannot be dismissed; one way or another, it must be dealt with.

If the officer's guiding principle is that guilt can't be doubted, the Bible's is that guilt can be forgiven. As a Christian, I believe the reason Old Testament sacrifices are no longer necessary isn't that the system was misguided or uncalled for. I know that I've "done what I ought not to have done" and "left undone what I ought to have done"; a good and just God can't just let that go. But I also believe he provided the ultimate sacrifice—his son. Given once, for all; his blood for ours. All that came before foreshadowed this.

It's a messy solution with a clean result. Perfect, even. Forgiveness isn't dependent on a person's ability to list every failing, or feel appropriately sorry for every sin, or even have the emotional intelligence to be aware of them all. It's dependent on them depending on a savior to take their guilt—all their guilt—away, and on trusting, not with blind faith, but belief beyond reasonable doubt.

Learning how to break the rules
ABC, November 2022 (Published as: "It's about time we learn how to break the rules.")

It's funny how certain courses of action simply don't occur to us, especially in the moment. Even in retrospect we don't see all we could have said or done. We stay inside the square, behave in the expected ways, conform to expectations, follow written and unwritten rules.

What's more, we do so even when we have good reason to do otherwise. Or at least, most of us do, most of the time.

I recently heard the journalist David Brooks interview historian Kate Bowler. Bowler, who was diagnosed with stage-four cancer at the age of thirty five, told a story about a time three junior doctors approached her hospital bed, chatting among themselves as if she wasn't there. Bowler tried to interject, to give a friendly greeting, to mention her sensitive skin. But before she could get a word in, they'd stripped a layer off.

Many of us rule-abiding citizens, many of us model patients, would have suffered in silence. But Bowler did something that wouldn't have even *occurred* to me, at least not in the moment. She told the men to number off in terms of their seniority and rebuked them in turn: "Number One, obviously you need to set a precedent; Number Three, you need to be paying attention to your patients instead of sucking up to Number One; and Number Two, I have no idea why you're here."

I'm sure those doctors had attended many lectures, but I doubt any were as memorable or formative as Bowler's cheeky speech.

Now, I'm not suggesting that patients shouldn't respect their doctors, or that breaking unwritten rules and conventions is necessarily good. I'm just saying that sometimes it doesn't hurt. And sometimes, following them might.

*

I was in labor with our third child and my water had broken. I'd been assessed at the hospital and sent home to "rest" until the contractions became more regular. The problem was, they seemed to alternate—one was strong, the next was weak—so I deemed the weak ones cramps and only counted every other one.

My husband and I were playing Scrabble (I was scoring pretty well) when the less painful ones became quite painful and the painful ones became extremely painful, and I began to suspect they were all contractions all along. Still, I figured I had time to win the game.

After that we had no time to lose. As we raced to the hospital, we discussed parking options. The day-night carpark was two blocks away, but if we got a metered park nearby it would run out in an hour, two at most. We needed more than that. My husband could have dropped me at the entrance, parked, and then returned, but I could not bear the thought of being left.

I opted for the carpark. Those two blocks were quite the walk. By the time we got to the maternity ward, I was barely able to speak. Thankfully the staff took one look at me and knew everything they needed to know.

They showed us to a birthing suite. A midwife had me kneel upon the bed. She said that I should use one hand to see if I could feel the baby's head. I could. Minutes later, he was born.

It wasn't until much later that I realized how absurd it was to park two blocks from the hospital when I was, quite literally, about to give birth. If not wanting to give birth in the street wasn't reason enough to bend or break a rule, would I ever have reason enough? (I say "I" not "us," because my husband was following a different rule: never argue with a woman in labor.)

We could have left the car in a metered park for longer than the prescribed time. We could have risked a fine. We could have parked illegally. These possibilities did not even cross my mind.

*

One of my earliest childhood memories is of my mother breaking a rule, and letting me break it too.

My father was terminally ill and she was spending a lot of time caring for him. One day she asked me if I wanted to skip school and spend the day with her. The very thought shocked me. I guess I must have come around, because I still remember how special I felt sitting in a leafy cafe courtyard, savoring a tall glass of apricot nectar and, sweeter still, my mom's attention. Who would have thought such a thing was even possible when "the rules" said otherwise—when my classmates were in school?

What I didn't think about that day was the reason for such rules. They were written for our good, to meet our needs. And what that little girl needed most that day was not reading, writing, and arithmetic; it was her mom.

I'm often astonished by how quickly we let rules become an end in themselves, when what they should be is a means. Religious institutions seem especially prone to this very human tendency. The teachers of the law in the Christian scriptures were intensely rule-abiding. But consider the long-awaited Messiah's response. He didn't praise them for their great obedience; he condemned them for their lack of love. They kept their hands clean, they played it safe; he touched lepers, befriended "sinners" and non-Jews.

Such audacity. Such disregard for social convention. And such tenderness. It was the spirit, not the letter, of the law that mattered most.

My favorite part of Bowler's story about the doctors is what happened next. "Number Two" returned the following day to remove a tube from her stomach. She playfully critiqued his entry and suggested he try again. Number Two could have shut her down. He could have insisted that Bowler take him, and his job, more seriously. Instead, he played along.

There was a curtain, I remember he was like, Knock-knock! He came in, I was like, why are your hands like this? and he was like, I have to keep them sterile, and I was like, I would actually really prefer if you would pretend you were doing a magic trick.

And if you could see his face . . . he shakes his head. I was like, Make it so.

He left, he came back, and then he was like, I'm here to perform a magic trick, I'll be taking something out of your stomach, and I said, Great!

He told Bowler she'd feel a deep pinch then a hard pull.

And then when I opened my eyes, there was my blood all over his white gown and it looked like he was holding like 22 feet of tube . . . and then he goes, Ta da!

And we are friends to this day.

The thing I find most remarkable about Bowler's story isn't her boldness, her playfulness, or the "22 feet of tube"; it's the way she helped a doctor to really see his patient. She didn't let an established power dynamic stop her from speaking her mind; she didn't let a generic bed and gown make her a generic patient; and she didn't let anger or frustration eclipse her sense of humor.

Bowler disregarded an age-old doctor-patient convention. In doing so, she reminded three young doctors that their patient was a person just like them. I can think of no better proof than this: one is now her friend.

I have nothing against well-intentioned rules. I appreciate most of them, most of the time. But rules should be a means to an end and not an end in themselves. Context matters, motives matter, the big picture matters.

The thing is, it's often easier to do "the right thing" than to have the right motives. It can also be easier to follow a rule than to consider its intention and all the possibilities in play. But it isn't always better. And sometimes, it makes no sense at all.

Love &

. . . kindness

A strange kind of kindness
ABC, December 2021

We met over a damsel in distress. The damsel had just given birth to twins and urgently needed a bar fridge to store breast milk in. I posted a request on our neighborhood Facebook page. Within minutes, a lady named Veronika had replied offering a "lovely" fridge we could keep for several months—and call "Louise" if we wanted to. She was even willing to delay an outing for potting mix and chook food so I could pick the fridge up that morning.

Pick it up I did. As we lugged the thing out of an art studio, up a driveway, and into my boot, we bonded over the fact we'd both struggled in the newborn phase (who hasn't?), couldn't imagine how we'd have coped with *twins* (who could?), and still remembered the small kindnesses—a meal here, a word there—that had touched and surprised us.

I'll never forget the day my kinder kid came out from school with a shoelace undone. I was heavily pregnant at the time and his feet seemed *very* far away. Another mom, seeing my dismay, knelt down and tied it up. I didn't recognize her face or know her name. I wanted to hug her.

In her essay "The Sacrament of Divorce," Ann Patchett talks about the kindness she experienced when her marriage fell apart—in particular, the kindness of strangers who had also been divorced. A man from her insurance company, her lawyer's receptionist, and a woman processing her credit card application all showed unexpected empathy. The latter, after asking "Are you married or single?" and realizing Patchett didn't know the answer, dropped the questions and called her "honey." "Honey," she said, "I know."

One thing that makes kindness from strangers so touching—even if it's fleeting, and small—is that we rarely expect it. We want to show love to the people we love, and it makes sense to be kind to people who are kind to us. It even makes sense to be kind to people who aren't, provided we know and care about them, or have something to gain. But to show *kindness* to a stranger—to not just be polite, but to be kind—is to go beyond expected norms.

The recipient rarely asks for or expects such treatment, but as we see in Patchett's essay, they may be in desperate need of it. And as I know from experience—as I hope you do too—they won't forget it. Even if it's just three words ("Honey, I know"), or two ("I know"), or even just one ("Honey"), kindness can give comfort, restore hope.

And the person who is struggling the most, who is expecting it the least—the person who feels most unworthy, unlovable, alone—will appreciate it most. This person might not look sad or come across as needy; the one who shows them kindness might not realize what it meant, or that it meant anything at all. But the recipient will seize it, treasure it, for days or years to come.

If the stranger who knelt beneath my bulging belly to tie my little boy's shoelace knew I'm still thinking about her, now *writing* about her, *years* later, I wonder what she'd say? She's probably forgotten the small sacrifice she made that day. But I have not.

As I write, Christmas is approaching. There's chaos in the shops and in the streets, but it's not all self-serving. Some presents are bought out of obligation, but others are earnest attempts to say, *I know you; I love you.* Then there are the gifts bought for trees that aren't our own, for strangers we will never meet. Gifts that say, *I don't know you, but I do care.*

All the while an ancient book tells an absurd tale of an immortal God humbling himself, stooping down to become one of us, so we could know his love. The only thing more outrageous than the idea of God's son becoming man is the manner of his death. An almighty creator would owe us nothing. To not just stoop and serve but suffer so, would seem to make no sense. But maybe true kindness, true love, doesn't have to make sense or seem appropriate. Maybe that's the point.

Several months after I borrowed the fridge, a friend who was helping me return it asked me how I knew Veronika. I didn't, I explained, though she was probably one of my favorite strangers.

I must have started thinking of her as a Favorite Stranger after that, because later when I happened upon her in an op-shop, I found myself saying, "Hello, Favorite Stranger!" It took her a second to place me, and then she shot me one of her wild grins. I introduced her to my three-year-old, who was running riot with a little friend, and we chatted. Later, I wondered if *I* was anyone's Favorite Stranger—or at least, their Favorite Weirdo. I also considered the risk Veronika might lose her status. If we crossed paths again, if we chatted any more, she might become a friend.

Too good to make the news?
The Guardian, December 2022 (Published as: "What if altruism is more common than we think?")

I heard some good news recently. My ninety-one-year-old grandfather called me to test his new hearing aid. For the first time in a long time, he could hear my voice. It thrilled us both.

He and my grandmother had been trying to replace his previous hearing aid for more than a month, but confusing instructions, impatient explanations, and faulty hardware meant they'd almost given up. Now they had me on speaker-phone, and were giving me an update in excited voices. This time their story didn't evoke sympathy, but joy.

I soon saw that it wasn't just the hearing aid that had them grinning down the line; it was the person behind it—their new audiologist, Anna.

Unlike the previous providers they'd dealt with, Anna gave them two miraculous gifts: time and attention. She didn't, like one audiologist, assume that because a hearing aid worked while on his *desk*, it would work while in my grandad's *ear*, or that if *he* could make it work at the clinic, my *grandad* could make it work at home.

Anna not only ensured the new hearing aid worked as it should, she offered to go to my grandparents' apartment to show them—*really* show them—how to use it.

At first she suggested dropping by before she started work, but she worried that if traffic made her late they'd be too rushed. In the end she decided on a Friday after work. She'd pick up her son, then come straight to theirs. They protested. My grandad asked why she'd do such a thing. Anna's reply: Why *not*?

Such kindness might sound implausible, but I've since started wondering: what if it's more common than we think?

It started with research that showed people often underestimate the willingness of strangers to engage with or even befriend them. Then I came across a study that suggested news coverage of current affairs tends to be more negative than positive, because humans tend to give negative stimuli more attention.

From an evolutionary perspective, this makes sense: because positive stimuli doesn't pose a threat to our survival, it doesn't warrant as much attention. But if negative news is more attention-grabbing news, it will receive more coverage, and if it receives more coverage, we might start to think of the world as a more negative place than it really is. This will affect us at an individual level and a collective one.

I wonder how often my own attention leads me to focus on negative stimuli and stories at the expense of positive ones. I wonder if I'm more attentive to the negative stories my friends and family tell than the positive ones, and whether I'm more inclined to *tell* negative stories too.

What about all the little stories we only tell ourselves? Are they more negative than they need to be? What if you *didn't* offend this person or disappoint that one? What if that friend *hasn't* been holding a grudge? What if your parents *are* proud of you?

Negative stories can attract our attention, and prepare us for disappointment. But if we don't also engage with positive ones, they might lead us to be more cynical, more defensive, and less hopeful than we need to be; they might close our minds to happier, and just as likely, possibilities.

We might not think of being wrong as something anyone would want to be, but being wrong—even just the possibility—can be a wondrous thing.

Maybe no one's even noticed the flaw that, in the mirror, is the only thing you see. Maybe you could have got that job, maybe you will. Maybe that new neighbor would like to be your friend. Maybe that date will call you back.

And maybe there's still hope for the planet. Maybe some leaders do care, maybe we can make a difference. Maybe even little things—realizing we might often be wrong; paying more attention to good news; making a point of sharing it—*will* help.

Whether Anna arrived before or after 7 p.m. depends on who you ask, but my grandparents both testify with certainty that she stayed for ninety minutes. *Ninety minutes*, they told me, their voices filled with wonder and delight. What's more, she wouldn't bill them for a single one.

Anna understood that for someone with virtually no hearing in one ear and severely impaired hearing in another, speaking quickly was akin to speaking in a foreign language—and when she told my grandfather so, he finally felt understood. She not only knew he needed patience, she was willing to offer it. She spoke to him slowly, giving his brain time to fill in the spaces caused by words he could not catch. She listened; she sympathized; she treated him with kindness and respect.

Anna's attitude was remarkable. She went beyond the call of duty and, upon leaving, refused to accept anything but words as thanks.

Why do such a thing for virtual strangers? In Anna's words, why not?

And when we witness, or hear of a kind act, why not make a phone call, tell a friend?

Why not remind ourselves that for all the bad that's in the world and in the news, behind the scenes in people's ordinary lives, lie untold stories of extraordinary good.

An unlikely hero, an unlikely children's book
Spoonie Press, August 2022

I happened upon a wonderful book this week: a first-person account of an old man's rehabilitation following a serious illness. I found it at the library and later in the day read it to my kids.

The book—written by Michael Rosen, and illustrated by Tony Ross—begins with a drawing of a greenish-blue face emerging from a white sheet and the words: "I was ill. I was so ill I couldn't get up."

Later, an author's note will reveal the year—2020—and the illness—COVID-19. Rosen was so sick that doctors had to put him to sleep for forty days; when he woke he had to learn to walk again.

The second page introduces three masked rehabilitation providers. They come to Rosen's bedside, tell him it's time to get up, and lift him from the sheets. He says, "Please let me go back to bed!"

They do; he smiles. But the next day they are back—and the next, and the next—to get him up again.

In time they help him learn to walk again. He progresses gradually and comically: he walks with a frame, between bars, with a walking stick and then, at last, without.

Eventually he's well enough to go home. Suddenly we see he isn't just a patient—he has a family, a life beyond the hospital, even normal clothes—and it's almost a surprise.

Once home, and with his family watching apprehensively, he climbs the stairs, goes to the loo, and makes a cup of tea—gingerly, but by himself. The story makes it clear this isn't normal; it is remarkable.

The author's note at the end, which fascinates the kids—"so it's all *true?*"—gives some background on the story before addressing the reader: "Maybe you've been ill. Or maybe you know someone who's been ill. When we're ill, we change, don't we?"

I think of the pale ghoulish face peering from a bed on the first page of the story, and the happy granddad pictured later on. They look like different people, but as the story shows, as I hope my children saw, they aren't.

I put the kids to bed and open my laptop, wanting to know more. I come across a 2021 interview where Rosen describes his rehabilitation experience as so "utterly infantilising" that turning it into a children's book made sense.

He also talks about how one of the things we're always saying to children is "try harder."

> *We put in front of them great sporting successes—we're all watching them now at the Olympics. But I think if I had to list my greatest physical achievements in life, one of them would be learning to walk again this last year. This book is a reminder that there are very, very ordinary achievements that are amazing as well.*

I read this quote aloud to my husband. He suffers from such severe chronic pain that playing with the kids or cooking them a meal is an extraordinary achievement. I read it to our eldest son, who understands this now, and I manage not to cry.

Later, I share it with a friend who suffered a stroke in his thirties and is still re-learning ordinary skills years later—and with his wife, who has since become a speech pathologist and now helps others who have suffered strokes. They are ordinary-amazing too.

It's refreshing to read a children's book like this. There are no talking animals, no superheroes, no alternative worlds. There's just a person stuck in bed who needs some help, and some people who say, "We're going to get you up."

They say, "See if you can . . ." day after day and, day after day, he does.

There's no dramatic action, just slow transformation. Yes, Rosen gives his walking stick a funny name and his illustrator adds eyes and a mouth, but the magic of the story—for this reader at least—resides elsewhere.

After dedicating the book to his family, Rosen says it's also for, "all the doctors, nurses, physiotherapists, occupational therapists and hospital workers who saved my life and have helped me get better." My heart is full.

I can't decide who the hero of this story is: the character who perseveres, who learns old skills anew, or those who show him how.

It's a silly question. Of course the answer is both.

On the benefit of the doubt

The Guardian, October 2023 (Published as: "I didn't mean to crash into a stranger's car. What shocked me was that he believed me.")

One of the biggest shocks I had this year wasn't the sound of my car scraping against another car, and the realization that in an absent moment, I'd gone straight into someone else's lane instead of turning left. It was what happened next.

I pulled over and started vomiting apologies onto the driver of the ute I'd just scraped. I was sorry, it was completely my fault, I had no idea what I'd been thinking, or rather, I clearly *hadn't* been thinking, at least not about the task at hand, and did I mention I was sorry?

I braced myself for an angry response, but instead of unleashing a stream of abuse in return, the ute driver asked me if I was OK about as many times as I'd said sorry.

Perhaps this shouldn't have surprised me; surely most people care more about other humans being OK than about their cars being OK, but not only was he genuinely concerned for my wellbeing, he had a genuine lack of concern for his ute.

Granted, the scraping had done more damage to my sedan's side mirror than his sturdy flat tray, but either way, he didn't seem bothered. He didn't even want to swap numbers. I told him I couldn't imagine a better person to run into, and that he'd made my day; we parted ways laughing.

Perhaps part of the reason I found his response so shocking is my previous experience in this area. I'm embarrassed to admit that this wasn't my first collision; I've had a few in my twenty-plus years of driving, and in every other case, the part that shook me most wasn't the collision (every single one was at a ridiculously low speed); it was the other driver's indignation.

None of the others seemed willing to accept, let alone assume, that I'd hit them accidentally, preferring to treat my poor driving as a conscious decision to vandalize their property, albeit with limited success. The most striking example was the couple who, after I accidentally reversed into their car, told me they didn't understand why I would do such a thing to *pensioners*. It was as if I had identified their car as one that likely belonged to pensioners, then targeted it accordingly.

They didn't seem to realize I was just a terrified student who lacked spatial awareness; they didn't seem to notice my apologetic manner. In their eyes, I was the perpetrator.

But I was genuinely sorry. So sorry, in fact, that later that week I baked them a peace offering—they'd given me their address when we exchanged details—a recipe I've thought of as being for "pensioner cookies" ever since.

More than a decade later, in another local carpark (Hobartians beware), I managed to reverse into another unsuspecting car at extremely low speed. Neither I nor my "victim" could detect any damage, but I gave her my details all the same. That afternoon I received a phone call from the police. The woman on the phone told me she was with the lady whose car I'd run into earlier that day. I assured her it was an accident, but also asked if she had seen the damage, or lack thereof. No, she hadn't got that far. She rang off to check the car and didn't call back.

The ute encounter made me realize the extent to which those past experiences had rendered an understanding, sympathetic "victim" of my driving almost unimaginable. I had come to assume that all strangers would treat my mishaps as deliberate assaults.

I know that in theory there are many kinds of drivers in this world, and that when it comes to probability, rolling two ones in a row doesn't make rolling a third any more likely. Even so, the benefit of the doubt the ute driver gave me was not a possibility I'd dared to entertain.

I've since wondered what past experiences my other two "victims" might have had, on the road or off it, to take an accidental bump so personally.

I've also since wondered how different the world might be if more people responded to minor mishaps like that ute driver did.

Instead of assuming the worst of a stranger, he assumed the best, if not in relation to my driving skills, at least in relation to my motives—or lack thereof. I'm reminded of Hanlon's Razor: never attribute to malice that which is adequately explained by stupidity.

It's not an original idea to give people the benefit of the doubt—there's a sense in which it's just another version of "doing-unto-others"—but timeless wisdom doesn't date.

Of course, giving this gift means taking risks. Sometimes, we might extend the benefit of the doubt only to be disappointed, to find a person undeserving. But sometimes, more often than perhaps we might expect, the benefit will be warranted. In extending it, a person who's been wronged can make another person's day. And who knows, the other person's gratitude might just make theirs.

My aunt mistook a famous fashion designer for a fellow customer. Offense wasn't taken, photos were.
Common Good, November 2024 (Published as *"My aunt met a famous fashion designer, and all she got was this great story."*)

The photos arrived via SMS. They featured my eighty-seven-year-old great-aunt standing beside a world-famous fashion designer, beaming. In one of them, the designer is smiling at my aunt instead of the camera. In another, my aunt's head rests on the designer's shoulder. Each has an arm around the other. They look comfortable, relaxed.

If you hadn't heard "the story" before seeing "the photos," you might think the women pictured were old friends. If you recognized the designer, you might assume my aunt, who wasn't wearing fancy clothes, but whose sunglasses made a statement of their own, was famous too. But they weren't old friends, and my aunt isn't famous— at least, not yet.

"It was Christmas Eve and I went in to buy a voucher in a designer shop. Now I've never been in a designer shop in my whole life, and when I asked the price of the dresses, I nearly fell over," my auntie says.

She has texted me to say she has a story for me. I have called her back to hear and record the story.

"I was only going to buy a hundred-dollar voucher and I said to the girls: Do you *do* a voucher for one hundred dollars?" says my aunt.

There was something about their response, or rather, their lack of a response, that made my aunt start feeling mischievous. Or, in her words, "being a smart arse."

"These young kids . . . I've been in sales my whole life and I thought, you *talk* to the customer, you don't ignore them," she tells me. When she asked if she could buy a voucher that, compared to the price of dresses, cost a very small sum, neither said, "Of course!" with a reassuring smile. All she got was a perfunctory "yes."

"I think they thought I was a silly old bugger," my aunt says.

Still seeking a reaction, she asked if they accepted cash, then pulled out a hundred-dollar note. "I made this one this morning, hot off the press," she told them. Still nothing.

One of the girls started wrapping the voucher in a piece of paper—"just ordinary paper, not Christmassy or anything"—my aunt says. "And I said, 'Don't you have an envelope to put it in?'" The girl wrapping the voucher shook her head, but she did attach a little gold tag with the designer's name on it.

"I said, 'Gee, that's better!'; I accepted that," she tells me. What she didn't accept was the fact she still hadn't got a laugh out of either sales assistant, not even a pretend one.

"So I picked up these absolutely fantastic sunglasses, great big round funny-looking ones, and I put them on and said, 'These are great, I'd *love* these.'"

As she took them off, a lady standing next to her—a fellow customer, perhaps—said, "I'd like to buy those for you." My aunt politely declined, but the stranger insisted. "She said, 'I'd like to give you a gift of kindness.'" My aunt turned to the woman and asked for her name.

"[It was] the name of the designer label—she was the owner of the shop. I looked at the price, they were three hundred eighty dollars, and I thought, 'Oh my God, fancy paying that for sunglasses!' But she insisted, so I accepted."

My auntie can't remember who suggested a picture, but she came away with "all these photos of her and I together" on her phone. "She's a tall lady who carried herself very well, and here's little old me, practically under her arm."

Later, after looking through the photos, my aunt tried those "great big round funny-looking" sunnies on again. "And believe it or not, these glasses looked darned good on me! I thought: Darn it, I'll wear them on Christmas Eve!" And she did.

She's worn the glasses many times since. They remind her of how a stranger treated her—not as "a silly old lady," but in a way that touched her heart.

If my aunt received a hundred dollars every time she told the story, she'd be able to afford one of the designer's dresses by now. She told it so many times on Christmas Day that she overheard someone mutter, "it's getting a bit much," and resolved not to tell it again.

She broke the resolution when, at a restaurant the following month, she complimented a diner on her blouse. When the diner told her where the blouse was from, my astonished aunt pulled up a seat.

"I said, 'I've got to tell you a story.' So I sat down on the chair and told her my story, and they thought it was wonderful."

This is where the story ended the first time I heard it, but there's another chapter underway. My aunt has since written to the designer to thank her. True to form, she didn't just sign a generic message in a generic card.

I imagine the designer sometimes tailor-makes a garment for a client or a friend. I don't imagine someone's ever tailor-made, for her, a poem.

Life truly is "full of surprises." You never know when a stranger will give you a gift, or turn out to be famous, or suggest a photo, or write you a poem. You never know when a pair of sunglasses you first declared absurd will, upon reflection, look darn good.

Caution is killing compassion
The Critic, March 2022

A friend of mine who works on a university campus spends the start of every year meeting students. This year she reported that to her disappointment, no one asked her where she's from.

She said this was a first. Did it mean that after fifteen years living in Australia, her accent had softened to the point no one noticed it? Or didn't people care where she was from?

Meanwhile, a friend with literary ambitions had a short story published. He shared it with some family and friends. One or two responded with their thoughts—his father said he liked it, and stopped there—but most did not say anything at all.

Why *not* get back to him? Did they not like it, or not read it? Did they not have time to say? He wondered, but of course he didn't ask.

In both cases, I had another theory: that people were afraid they might offend, or come across as ignorant somehow; that people felt unqualified to speak.

I'm sure that at least some of the students on campus noticed an accent they simply couldn't place, and would have liked to ask, "Where are you from?"—then stopped themselves.

Perhaps they feared it would be heard as, "I can tell *you* don't belong here;" the reply might be "What accent?" and a scowl (like when you ask a bulging woman when she's due—when she is not).

As for the story, I'm sure some of those who read it found it interesting and had thoughts they could have shared—or questions about meaning and intent—but didn't dare. What if they said something that showed they didn't really understand the themes, the plot? What if their feedback was unwelcome? Surely it was easier to take no risk, to say nothing at all.

The problem is, of course, that avoiding one set of risks can give rise to another. The fear of sounding ignorant can lead to ignorance, while fear of causing offense can cause offense.

In a passing comment on a social media post, I mentioned plans to write this piece. One lady said I should and told me why: a student from a school that's very ethnically diverse recently told her that asking where another student's from is "very racist," the "worst" insult.

I can only imagine the damage this causes, the opportunities it crushes—to express and embrace diversity, to build friendship and understanding and belonging—and the silence it creates.

It's a very good thing that we see the risk of hurting other people with our words; it's a very good thing that we care. But silence can do harm as well as good. Sometimes we must do the work of finding different ways to speak, so that we can learn.

In the conversation about accents, we discussed alternatives. One friend suggested asking about a person's "origin story" instead of where they're from. The question's open-ended, could apply to any color or race, and is less likely to imply "you don't belong." Another suggestion was to say, "What accent am I hearing?" with a smile. I loved the smile, loved the reminder that our expression and our tone could show the good intentions of our words.

The smile reminded me of a conversation at a family lunch about how some people champion the phrase "person with disability" (because a disability shouldn't define who you are), while others prefer "disabled person" (because "disabled" shouldn't be considered pejorative), and how some, about to speak but unsure which is "right," fearfully abort.

My sister-in-law, whose daughter has Down syndrome, said what matters most to her is not a person's words—Down's child? Child with Down syndrome? Disabled child?—it's their intent. If she can see a person cares and is showing love, why take offense?

Sometimes tone is hard to interpret, especially if a comment is typed or the context isn't clear. But there's another way that we can show we care.

As someone who interviews people for her work, who has lost count of how many people she's quizzed or questions she's asked,

I'm embarrassed to admit that I forget this all the time: if we do not know, then we can ask.

"I'm not quite sure what words to use, can you please help me out?"

"Which questions upset you? Do you mind if I ask why?"

"And which ones do you wish someone would ask?"

The challenge—in using this approach, in saying something over nothing—is that it makes us vulnerable. This is a benefit as well. It opens up a door a little more.

Then there are the times when people are *looking* to take offense, when they care nothing about context or intent.

Some people are even *paid* to take offense.

"Sensitivity readers" are people tasked with detecting cultural inaccuracies, bias, and stereotypes in manuscripts. The manuscripts are usually unpublished, but in the case of Kate Clanchy's memoir, *Some Kids I Taught, and What They Taught Me*, it was a published—an award-winning—book.

Clanchy's publisher engaged sensitivity readers following significant online criticism, with a view to updating future editions. Issues raised in a subsequent report included her use of the word "disfigure" in relation to a landscape, and her use of the word "handicap" to mean "impede."

There were also concerns she'd invoked the "straight white savior trope" when talking about a (gay) student she was close to. Further, her concern he would get AIDS (it was 1992) came across as "homophobic" and "reductive." The readers suggested ways she could update the manuscript. She thought about them all but in the end, dismissed the lot.

In their defense, the sensitivity readers were paid to take offense. I can only hope the rest of us would take a broader view, a much more generous approach.

Why? Because if we go *looking* for problematic speech, we'll probably find it even if it was never intended. We might critique a person's words without bothering to look up at their face. Who knows what we'll see there if we do?

What if it's someone who is using awkward words, but with a smile that says they mean no harm at all? Someone who seems a little hesitant to speak? Someone who, wanting to be kind, is trying to be brave.

Do unto others
May 2024

At the shops I pass a woman who is talking to a man; she calls me back. She has unbrushed hair and tired eyes and I wonder if she is going to ask me for money; she has interrupted the man to talk to me. She leans toward me and quietly, kindly, tells me that my fly is not done up. Grateful and surprised, I say thank you. I walk on marveling. She had nothing to gain from telling me. This was a case of "do unto others" and, stopping her friend mid-sentence, stopping me mid-step, that's what she did.

The end of grief
CPX, April 2023

An older friend of mine, whose son died more than thirty years ago, works at a hospital. She once asked a downcast doctor, who had lost his teenage boy two years before, "And how are you?" An honest answer was invited, he could tell; and so he didn't just say, "well."

"People say time heals," he said, in a way that showed he was yet to fathom this himself.

Three words spilled from her lips: "It never heals."

Instinctively and full of gratitude, the doctor hugged her tightly. She hadn't offered reassurance; she had spoken honestly, and for a moment, the sorrow that still filled them both—sorrow for their sons, themselves, sorrow for each other, for this world—was shared.

If our existence ends in death, the only way to overcome such profound loss is death. Blood might stop flowing from a wound and pain might ease with time, but for however long a grieving parent survives their precious child, the wound remains.

The only way that "time" can truly "heal" is for the griever to die too—*if* existence only, always, ends in death. I can't help but doubt that it does. I can't help but think that our souls live on somehow.

The Easter story makes an even bolder claim: that physical "perishable" bodies can be raised; that we weren't made for death, but life.

It has something to do with a creator entering creation—"putting on flesh"—to serve us, to weep with us, to suffer in our place, to show us love. It has something to do with sharing our sorrows, bearing our wrongs to make them right, and everything to do with grace.

It might all sound too strange to even entertain. But is it any stranger than the notion that a person's life and death are happenstance? That once they are forgotten, they're no more? That death is "natural," that it's the end? Instinctively, I think we sense it's not.

Undeserved gifts

2022 (Reworked and published in December 2024 by *Eureka Street* as *"The delight and discomfort of undeserved gifts."*)

On the challenge of receiving when we can't give back.

Two of the dearest neighbors my family's ever had have been elderly widowers. Byron shared a fence with us, and Mario lived opposite. Both were eager gardeners, both loved our kids, and both showered us with gifts.

Byron, a retired police officer, often popped up from behind his fence to chat. He'd comment on the weather and the news, and on the lotto jackpot that he never won but often spent, pledging us a very generous share. He'd pass us vegetables, slowly grown but quickly given. Also, there were ice-creams—whole boxes of choc-wedges—for the kids. He'd joke they'd fallen in his trolley at the shops, acting all surprised; the kids would play along with happy grins.

Meanwhile I'd pass him generous "single" portions of whatever I'd been baking, which he'd praise excessively. I still felt in his debt, but I knew he wasn't keeping an account.

Then there was Mario, who could build anything from an elaborate rat trap to a boat, and had the garage to prove it. When he saw us walking past his house, he'd intercept and usher us inside. When we reached the kitchen, he'd open a top cupboard, take down "chokkies" for each child, then take me to the garden for some greens. While Byron would accept small offerings in return, Mario consistently declined. But he wouldn't let *me* refuse him. Even when my youngest was too small for solid food, he would get a chocolate bar as well. Toblerone will always make me think of kindly Mario.

I understood this neighbor wanted just to give, not to receive—wanted nothing in return—but still I found it hard. We're so used to buying and selling, to owing and paying, to exchanging like for like. We're less accustomed to accepting kindness graciously, without expecting or constructing attached strings.

It's the time of year where gift-giving is on everybody's mind and, unfortunately, strings are often in play. I'm sure most of us know people who feel more—or less—loved depending on what we give them, and fear our offerings will disappoint. I'm sure many of us will be comparing what we give a loved one with what they give to us. Was the exchange even? Or did our gift fall short?

Last year my family had the humbling experience of receiving unexpected gifts from people we hadn't thought to buy for. I admit that although I thanked them warmly, I lacked true gratitude; I would have rather not received a thing.

We might seek to be humble, or at least to seem it, but no one wants to *be* humbled, let alone feel humiliated.

Meanwhile the Christmas story speaks of a God who willingly humbled himself by becoming human, who belongs upon a throne but came to serve, who deserves all glory and honor, but knelt in dust to wash his dear friends' feet.

There's a New Testament letter that describes Jesus as "the kindness and love of God." And reading through the stories of his life on earth—the "gospel narratives"—his kindness, his love, is not abstract; it's practical, tangible, real.

As if it weren't enough for God to show up in this place as one of us, Jesus went on to suffer death at human hands, shame and pain beyond imagining—part of a cosmic plan to save us from ourselves.

We struggle to understand our own helplessness, the fact that we need forgiving, the fact that we can contribute nothing, not one thing. It's we who should be humble, it's we who've fallen short, yet we who are, bizarrely, full of pride.

This pride, which causes us to question God, to presume that in his place we'd be more generous and kind, to presume that explanations we can't see or understand cannot exist, is profoundly misplaced.

The news that Jesus brings is that we can be redeemed, for he will pay the price. We needn't—can't—contribute anything.

Our pride makes this difficult to take. But if we see ourselves as we really are, weak and blind and heading towards death; if we realize how in need of help we are—we might dare accept the gift. Not with resistance or polite protests, not with resentment or attempts to earn the right, but with astonished and profound relief. With a show of empty hands, and tears of gratitude. With awe and with humility, with joy.

Love &

...literature

"Untalented": On defining creativity, and success
July 2023 (Published by *Mayday*, March 2025 as *"Author in progress."*)

Sometimes, others underestimate us; often, we underestimate ourselves.

When Megan Tudehope decided at age forty to write her first novel, she started reading and watching anything and everything that might teach her how, and noticed a common theme: people talking about how they'd wanted to be authors their whole lives, and had been writing since childhood; who'd drafted novels in their twenties, even teens.

Tudehope, who grew up convinced she couldn't draw or paint and therefore wasn't a creative person, never *thought* to write a novel in her twenties—but she did have an idea for one.

"I had read something in a newspaper and it had triggered an idea . . . it really stuck with me." It was a great idea, but *she'd* never use it; she wasn't *that* kind of writer. Tudehope was so sure of this that she didn't even keep her idea a secret; now she's a little apprehensive at the thought of how many people she might have told.

"For some reason I had this narrative about myself that I wasn't a creative person, that I was better at writing serious stuff." Perhaps it had something to do with winning a place at a writing camp as a kid, being "the youngest by far," and feeling so overwhelmed that she didn't write a word the whole time. She also had an idea that "serious" writing and "creative" writing were somehow mutually exclusive; she was good at the former, which ruled out the latter.

"I studied to be a journalist and then worked in politics and corporate communications and wrote about very serious things and, often, very boring things."

Tudehope was good at it, but she struggled with the fact that what she did for a living didn't always align with her values. And then she hit "mid-life," and realized that, "creative" or not, deep down she'd always wanted to write that novel—and if she didn't try now, she likely never would.

"I just had this realisation . . . I didn't want to get to the end of my life regretting not giving this a go. And I thought about all the other things I spent my time on that were less valuable."

Writing a novel was a daunting prospect, especially given all those stories about being "born" a writer and starting young. "I had to get over this feeling I'd missed the boat," she says. "I had this real sense of: if I was really going to be any good at this, surely I would have pursued it earlier in my life, therefore maybe I don't have any real natural talent."

Tudehope started to seek out stories of writers who came to their craft later in life—"because I felt like I needed to see people like me who'd pissed away their twenties and spent their thirties with their kids, and *now* were trying to do it"—stories that, even when she sought them out, were hard to find.

It occurs to me that this might be one of those stories, and that telling it before the subject has been declared "a writer," before she's been published, or nominated for an award, or achieved commercial success, is not the done thing. The profiles that proliferate are about ordinary people who have attained fame and fortune, thereby validating the labor that preceded it; whether or not this one will qualify remains to be seen. But does that make it any less legitimate? Isn't the tale of attempting something new and difficult for the first time, of taking a risk, of persevering in the face of uncertainty, worth telling too?

"At first it went pretty slowly, because my kids were really little," Tudehope says. "I thought, the only time I'm really going to get to do this is in the morning, [so] I'd get up at 5 a.m.—but I had a three-year-old son . . . Sometimes I would only get twenty minutes; I'd bash out two paragraphs in twenty minutes, and that was all I got." Occasionally she'd have until 6 a.m., but that was about as good as it got.

"Things went very, very slowly, but I just had this dogged determination: don't worry about the end product, just get up every day and do *something*; be disciplined in the process, and the outcome will take care of itself. And two-and-a-half years later, I'm still telling myself that when the alarm goes off at five."

When she started, Tudehope says, she had no idea what she was doing. "I got to 30,000 words and then realized I was not writing a novel at all, I was just writing a series of scenes that didn't connect to each other and had no character or story arcs, so I went back, after 30,000 words, and chucked probably 60 percent of it out and started again."

She got another rude shock when she finished her first draft. "I thought, 'excellent, it's just about editing this then I'm done'—but the editing process is much more complex than I understood." More than a year later, she's up to her sixth draft, which she's workshopping in a writing course.

"The premise is the same, the beginning is the same, the ending is the same, but the story in the middle is really evolving, and it's getting better and better and better as I learn." There are moments where she can see her skill and understanding have gone up a level, moments where she seems to have plateaued, and moments where she's struck by a pang of fear because there's so much, still, to learn.

It's scary and it's difficult, but she can see herself becoming a better writer. "It's a skill and craft I have to learn, through the discipline of getting up and doing it every day. It's less about how much time I get each day. It's the discipline of just getting up and doing it."

One benefit of having taken twenty-odd years to start working on her idea is that Tudehope has another twenty years of living under her belt. Writing characters that become more and more layered as they move through life, who are "good people" and "bad people" at the same time, is something she's not sure she could have done in her twenties.

And while she may not have spent those years writing fiction, she has spent them writing. Tudehope's professional life has taught her much that aids her personal pursuit—how to edit her work, how to sharpen her sentences, how to achieve clarity and economy. She's also written a lot of speeches. "That idea of pace and dialogue, and learning how to write how people speak . . . that's definitely helped."

If it weren't for all this, she can imagine having a much more complicated style, and considering that "good writing."

One major difference between corporate and creative writing has been the experience of having people read her work.

"There's a big difference between sending off a press release for someone to review, and pressing 'send' for the very first time ever to share your novel with someone else," she notes, describing the latter as "gut-wrenching."

As part of the workshopping process in the course, Tudehope has had to share her synopsis and her first five thousand words. "I didn't get great feedback on the synopsis . . . I was feeling a bit down . . . Should I start a new project? Was this something I should just file away as a learning process?

"Then I submitted my first 5,000 words and I got great feedback from the tutor. That really buoyed me to keep going. At the same time, I don't know if I can continue to go through this cycle being so affected by external feedback . . . I have to be able to keep going regardless of what the feedback is, and just have a real sense of confidence in my own work."

Despite this conviction, when she *does* catch herself feeling confident, Tudehope says part of her still wonders if she's like one of the contestants in the early seasons of *The Voice* or *Australia's Got Talent*, who never *really* had a chance, who were cast because they *thought* they were amazing, as a kind of cruel joke.

"There's part of me that's always wondering . . . Am I *really* good at this? *Can* I be good at this? Or am I just lacking the self-awareness to know that this isn't something that I should be doing? I don't have that lack of confidence at work."

Very occasionally Tudehope lets herself entertain the "ultimate dream" of quitting her job and spending all her time writing novels, but mostly, she's a realist.

"That is just so far away from where I am now I can't focus on that . . . At the moment, my focus is really on the discipline of just getting up and doing it, and being immersed in the process." If she doesn't enjoy *that*, she's kidding herself that she wants to do this for a living.

"[If], even when it's a bit torturous, I'm still enjoying it, then *maybe* one day I could have a life where I quit my job and do this every day," she says.

"It's funny, because before I started, I wished I'd done it earlier; now I've started, I don't actually think about that," she adds.

"I'm focusing so much on the process [that] the time-frames actually don't matter so much anymore. I'm not thinking about getting to this particular point by a particular age or time in my life anymore. It's just: the alarm goes off, I lay in bed for a minute, and then I tell myself, 'Get out of bed, Megan.'"

Whatever happens with the final manuscript, Tudehope says she won't regret the time spent writing it.

She recalls Ash Barty talking about how winning Wimbledon isn't her ultimate goal, because that's outside of her control. Instead, her focus is on what she *can* control: her mindset, her training regime, her day-to-day commitment.

Similarly, all the effort in the world might not result in Tudehope's book being published. "There's so much of that that involves luck: what's happening in the market at the moment, what's happening in trends in publishing," she says. Tudehope is well aware that she can't control those things. What she can do is create a novel that "makes sense from start to finish," that she's proud of, that she loves.

"I'll be proud of finishing this book whether it gets published or not, because it involves a level of discipline I didn't know I was capable of. Along with 'not creative,' 'un-disciplined' was another self-descriptor I've repeated over the years," she says. "Writing this book has taught me that I am both creative and disciplined."

I noted, earlier, that the writers we hear about tend to be those whose books are a "success." They are liked by lots of people, or they are liked by "the right people." Whether or not Tudehope's novel will be one of them, whether or not it's even published, remains to be seen.

But being published and selling a certain number of copies can be just as much a measure of luck as of talent. Perhaps, in narrowing our attention to stories of "success," in narrowing our definition of success, we're missing out. Creating a convincing world with convincing characters and a compelling story when you have a husband, two children, and a full-time job—not to mention discovering you *are* capable of discipline and creativity when you always thought you couldn't be—might be a story that's worth telling, in and of itself.

It all began, begins, with words
The Argyle Literary Magazine, May 2023

Every person who reads this, whether passionately religious or passionately anti-religious, will have beliefs about how our world came to be—about what is, and isn't, possible. To some extent, those beliefs will have been shaped by words. We use words to gain and share understanding, to make sentences; to make sense. We use different genres, too—from scientific theories, to historical narratives, to poems and allegories. Some are concerned with what and when, some with how, some with why, some with who. The following words focus on two texts which, while written by different authors, in different times and different genres, seem cut from the same cloth.

The Beginning

In the beginning—an ancient writer writes, evoking a poem written long before—*was the Word.* And so, with old words and with new, his story starts.

But first: long before this manuscript, that poem. That poem—the start of what becomes the book of Genesis—that speaks of how from nothing all things came, and came through words—that poem.

The poem declares there was no earth; there were no stars, there was no life. There *was* a speaker who then spoke, whose words evoked the heavens and the earth.

The poem describes a place that's not a place, that's formless, lifeless, dark. A God whose Spirit hovers, and whose commands create. A God who speaks.

In the beginning God created the heavens and the earth—with words.

Let there be, let there be, let there be.

The world is spoken into being. The creatures of the sea, the land, the sky. Surging oceans, dancing clouds, soil that teems with life and warmth, air that's filled with color, movement, noise.

Then comes a creature of another kind, the image-bearing kind, and a command to speak, to name.

In the beginning there were words; there was speaking and creating, there was naming and then . . . rest.

The world was authored, written, ordered; line by line, "day" by sweeping day—then done! A finished manuscript, a Work of Art, complete. And it was *good*.

Many words later—words thought, words spoken, words remembered, words forgotten; words sacred, words profane; words broken, words kept—the ancient poem's evoked once more.

In the beginning . . . another writes, in another time . . . *was the Word, and the Word was with God, and the Word was God.* It's the start of a biography that starts before the world.

And according to its writer—who some now call Saint John—*the Word* was, is, the Son of God and God himself. Human and divine, vulnerable, and invincible. Not either/or—both/and.

Through him all things were made; without him nothing was made that has been made.

In him was life, and that life was the light of all mankind.

In the beginning was *the Radiance of God's glory; the Exact Representation of God's Being.* In the beginning was the *Kindness and the Love of God.* These names, and many more, all came with time; all came after the Word entered the world—as one of us.

The Word became flesh and made his dwelling among us—an audacious, a bizarre, fantastic claim. He "put on flesh," received an ordinary name, lived in an ordinary town. He breathed. He ate. He walked. He slept. He learned to read.

And he loved. He hurt, he healed, he wept, he feared, he hoped; he spoke in parables, used metaphors. He wasn't handsome or attractive—*had no beauty, majesty*—but he could speak. And people came, in time crowds *flocked*, to hear his voice. The leaders of the day could not abide his popularity, his confidence, his claims, his wit.

In the end he was despised, rejected, mocked. And so, the story goes, the one whose word sustains all things, was killed. Also, the story goes, he rose. Said he would return—did not say when.

At the end of John's biography: the claim he did much more than can be written down or read. If it could, the world itself would not have space, could not contain, all of the books.

I picture them, spilling into space; drifting through the darkness; flaming when they float too near a star. So many books.

*

I wonder whether fiction writers, writers who create, who color, fill—who birth characters and lives—who craft beginnings, middles, ends—who use words to make us see and feel and think—often wonder at this impulse, where it came from, what it means.

In the beginning was the Word, and the Word was with God, and the Word was God.

Such a fantastic claim. And yet we live in a fantastic world, a world that speaks in every sense, that speaks to every sense, of wonder, order, and complexity. Its existence is implausible, absurd—and ours is too.

We can't begin, or can at best only *begin* to understand, this place—its origins, and ours. And we begin, time and time again, with words.

A Little Life: **On despair within, and hope beyond**
Eternity, June 2021

Regardless of whether you've read Hanya Yanagihara's 2015 novel *A Little Life*, chances are you've heard of it. It's been promoted as "an immensely powerful and heartbreaking novel of brotherly love and the limits of human endurance," and it's become notorious for testing many a reader's endurance.

Many, myself included, have described it as one of the most traumatic books they've ever read.

Over the course of seven-hundred-odd pages, *A Little Life* reminded me, again and again and again, that this world is wretched, depraved, and unjust. The book contains such appalling descriptions of abuse that I cannot recommend it. But it also contains such beautiful pictures of tenderness and love that I cannot regret reading it.

It's one of those novels that "forces demands on you that are so immense that you seek consolation from others," writes Brigid Delaney in *The Guardian.* "You urge your book club to read it (or you form a book club to that end); you post status updates, you tweet; you give it to other people to read, burdening them so that you're not left alone with this thing."

In a nutshell, the "thing" is the story of an abused orphan who goes to college, befriends three bright young men, and becomes a rich, successful lawyer. At its heart, it's the story of relentless pain, and love, and how impossible it is to ever escape your past or truly start afresh.

A dark past

The reader learns about Jude's past gradually—a wise decision on Yanagihara's part, as she inflicts more pain on him than some will be able to bear, and others, believe.

Abandoned at birth, Jude was raised in a monastery and abused by a series of pedophiles. Brother Luke promises to save him and claims to love him as a son, but after they run away together, he forces Jude to prostitute himself. He sustains Jude with the lie that when they can afford it, they'll live happily ever after in a cabin in the woods, but then shifts from casting himself as Jude's father to his lover.

Jude is eventually rescued by police, only to end up in state care where the abuse continues. He escapes but before long, another unconscionable predator takes him captive and almost kills him. He ends up alone and in the hospital with injuries he won't ever fully recover from, but goes on to attend college, make lifelong friends, and build a successful career.

The horrors of Jude's past, however, haunt him daily. His adult life is lonely and painful despite his vibrant circle of friends. He blames himself for others' crimes and believes he doesn't deserve to exist, let alone be happy; he lies to his friends instead of confiding in them, and seeks solace in self-harm. His first lover turns out to be yet another abuser, and his second dies in an accident.

It is plain to the reader that for all their faults, Jude's friends love him and would never blame him for his past, but it is far from plain to Jude. He cannot believe the abuse he suffered was not in some way his fault, that he is not worthless, that he is not "junk."

Many will find Jude's relationship with his best friend Willem, who becomes his lover, the most important in the book, but I was most struck by his relationship with one of his college professors, Harold.

A deep love

Harold and his wife Julia develop a lifelong friendship with Jude. They become like family to him and feel such strong, unconditional love for him that they want to formalize it. Even though Jude is an adult at the time, they propose adoption.

Yanagihara isn't writing as a Christian, but her depiction of a couple adopting an adult—not a baby but a scarred and troubled man—reminded me overwhelmingly of the Christian doctrine of adoption.

Jude is surprised and overjoyed by the proposed adoption; he's also reluctant to accept it. He tells Harold he's done things "that good people don't do," things he's ashamed of, that would make Harold ashamed. Harold says he can't imagine anything that would change the way he feels:

> *Jude, whatever it is, whatever you did, I promise you, whether you someday tell me or not, that it will never make me regret wanting or having you as a member of my family . . . I hereby absolve you of—of everything for which you seek absolution.*

Jude remains doubtful, as Yanagihara describes:

He felt he had failed once again: failed to confess properly, failed to determine in advance what he wanted to hear in response. Wouldn't it have been easier in a way if Harold had told him that he was right? That they should perhaps rethink the adoption? He would have been devastated, of course, but it would have been an old sensation, something he understood. In Harold's refusal to let go lay a future he couldn't imagine, one in which someone might really want him for good, and that was a reality that he had never experienced before, for which he had no preparation, no signposts.

The adoption goes ahead, and Harold and Julia love Jude with deep devotion.

Part of him, "will always be convinced that they will eventually tire of him, that they will one day regret their involvement with him," but the reader knows this can't be so. They love him and they always will.

An old problem

I spent much of this book lamenting Jude's refusal to entrust more of his secrets to his loved ones so they could challenge the lies he believes about himself and maybe even help him heal. Instead, behind closed doors, overwhelmed by shame and self-loathing, Jude cuts himself with razor blades.

Harold is appalled when he finds out, and asks Jude why he does it: "Sometimes it's because I feel so awful, or ashamed, and I need to make physical what I feel," Jude says. "And sometimes it's because I feel happy, and I have to remind myself that I shouldn't."

I couldn't relate to Jude's history of abuse or his addiction to self-harm, but I could relate to his astonishment when Harold and Julia proposed adoption. As a Christian, I not only believe that a perfect God adopts undeserving mortals; I believe he has adopted me.

It's not that I deserve it. I've done nothing to earn my Father's love and much to spurn it. Unlike Jude's misplaced feelings of shame and unworthiness before his adoptive parents, mine before God are appropriate. I've despised and rejected my Maker; I've loved myself and the things of this world more than him. I am unworthy. But I am also forgiven, beloved. It sounds too good to be true, but does that make it false?

A new life

Writing about *A Little Life* in *The New Yorker*, Jon Michaud says the book presents a godless world with no possibility of redemption and deliverance beyond tender moments, noting that Jude's tormentors aren't termed "evil," even by him.

In an interview published by *Foyles*, Yanagihara says she never considered giving Jude a happy ending: "I always knew that the book would be his slow awakening to the fact that he's just too damaged to recover, that he is, in a fundamental sense, irreparable," she says.

His past was destined to overwhelm him, to leave him with only one option, according to the book's author. "And I think it was the right one, the only one."

Jude is offered absolution from a man, but what he needs is absolution from God. *A Little Life* offers no such hope.

There is a book that does. It claims broken people can be redeemed, and that evil will be punished. There is hope for the Judes of this world, there is hope even for the Brother Lukes. Jesus came to seek and save the lost. If we fall on our knees before him, broken and contrite, he will lift us into his arms.

The idea of being bought, of belonging to anyone, might strike us as terrible if we think of God as a control freak or a bore, and ourselves as doing just fine on our own. But if we see ourselves as helpless and unworthy—if we see God as a loving father—it's a beautiful, astonishing relief.

Jesus said, "Come to me all who are weary and heavy laden, and I will give you rest." It sounds too good to be true, but that doesn't make it false. We deserve to be punished, but are offered grace; we deserve to be cast out, but can be adopted in.

Oh the pages you'll go!
Oh Reader, September 2023

What you read and where you go can sometimes be the same thing.

I was scrolling through my camera roll, looking for some summer snaps to send to my grandparents, when I noticed an unexpected theme. Interspersed among photographs of action, lit by sun, were just as many flat, uncolored images—ink on paper, black on white: photographs of text.

It didn't come as a surprise; I've had this habit for some time. I'll read a line or paragraph I don't want to forget—a passage that has moved me or intrigued me, a phrase that sounds especially beautiful or rings especially true—and make a copy I can keep. They're fragments I might want to ponder further, to reference in my writing, or to share with a book-loving friend.

I knew I'd been taking these photos. It hadn't slipped my mind, but it wasn't until I saw so many, interspersed with all my summer snaps—young kids cavorting, old friends posing—that I began to see them not as separate from "real life"—as somehow running parallel—but as part of it.

This meant that in recent months, while spending weekends at the mountains and the beach in my home state, I hadn't solely experienced those places. By reading, I'd been to Queensland and to New South Wales, to Massachusetts, Georgia, London, Gloucestershire. I'd spent time in big cities and small towns; I'd been to a university, a homestead, a convent; I'd even traveled through time, from the forties through to present day. The vehicles that took me all had names: *Either/Or* by Elif Batuman, *The Member of the Wedding* by Carson McCullers, *Leaping into Waterfalls* by Bernadette Brennan, *The Mint Lawn* by Gillian Mears, *Tell Me Again* by Amy Thunig, *The Bell* by Iris Murdoch.

That summer, a dear friend and her son had come to visit us; we'd spent a weekend in the mountains with four other families, and two weekends by the beach. I'd caught up with old school friends several times—but also, I'd met nuns and priests, students, teachers, abusive husbands, disillusioned wives. I don't like to play favorites, but of the (fictional) characters I spent time with, I found Harvard University student Selin Karadağ from *Either/Or*, who I'd already met some years ago (in Batuman's *The Idiot*), and twelve-year-old Frankie Addams (the passionate protagonist in *The Member of the Wedding*), most endearing—and most amusing.

Flicking through the many photographs I took when reading Batuman's *Either/Or* (I loved it so), I paused on one taken at 3:13 p.m. Selin, who's been reading *The Portrait of a Lady*, is reflecting on "how relevant and applicable" it is to her life. She talks about how she and Isabel are the same age, and how only "some" people think her beautiful, too. Isabel's values also make sense to Selin.

> *She valued reading, travel, and relationships with radically different people: the kinds of people who didn't necessarily get the point of each other. At some point, Ralph asked what Isabel saw in Henrietta, and Isabel said that she liked people to be different from each other, and that, if a person struck her in a certain way, she liked them. I, too, had friends who found each other annoying and incomprehensible, and some of them really could be annoying, but they all struck me in a certain way— and that was why I loved them.*

And I you, Selin.

I took *The Member of the Wedding* on a weekend away with my husband, our kids, my brother-in-law, and two of his children. I forgot to bring my pajamas, but did not forget my book. We were staying at a house surrounded by sandy soil and scrub. A wild beach lay five minutes' walk in one direction, a subdued lagoon five minutes in the other. I took photos of the kids paddling at the lagoon and catching waves at the beach, and photos of the pages of my book. A few pages here, a square of chocolate there, a board game, a trip to the beach, more chocolate—the stuff of dreams.

Among the pages I stopped to photograph is one I also stopped to read out loud: Frankie, after she's teased about a "crush," threatens to throw a knife. When the housekeeper, Berenice, tells her to lay it down, she responds with characteristic defiance.

The knife hit the middle of the stairway door and shivered there. She watched the knife until it did not shiver any longer.

'I am the best knife-thrower in this town,' she said.

Berenice, who stood behind her, did not speak.

'If they would have a contest I would win.' Frankie pulled the knife from the door and laid it on the kitchen table. Then she spat on her palm and rubbed her hands together.

Berenice said finally: 'Frances Addams, you going to do that once too often.'

'I never miss outside of a few inches.'

You know what your father said about knife-throwing in this house.

I loved the passing revelation that twelve-year-old Frankie, a child full of confusing emotions—strange ambitions, restless dissatisfaction, deep passion, unanswered questions—not only threw the knife on *this* occasion, but apparently threw knives frequently. While my husband and I regularly rebuke our kids for such crimes as eating with their mouths open and bickering, Berenice regularly rebuked Frankie for *throwing actual knives*; the kind that just don't hit a wall and fall, but pierce it.

I remember witnessing some spectacular sunrises that weekend. One morning, I left the children watching cartoons in their PJs, slipped out, and walked along the quiet lagoon where I watched muted colors absorb gleaming rays of gold and come alive.

Later in the day, I beheld Georgia's summer skies in my mind's eye. Skies that, "day after day," are "clear green-blue, but filled with light, the color of a shallow wave." *Light the color of a shallow wave*—I read that line again to hear it sing a second time, and then a third. Further on, when it's almost five o'clock in Frankie's world—when "the geranium glow" has faded from the sky, when she's missing a dear friend, when "the last pale colors" are "crushed and cold on the horizon"—the book ends.

The reason I was reading this novel that weekend—a novel far too dark and dated for the usual "summer reading" lists—is that I happened to have read, in Bernadette Brennan's biography of Gillian Mears, *Leaping into Waterfalls*, that Mears was most impressed by McCullers's novel. Later, it happened to be on the shelf at my local library, and I was curious.

Brennan's biography, written after Mears's death, portrays the author as strong-willed, sometimes impulsive, not always a safe person to be around. She didn't throw knives like a certain twelve-year-old, but she made many who were close to her suffer.

I was astonished, when reading Mears's novel *The Mint Lawn*, of the parallels between its abusive husband—the young protagonist's piano-teacher-turned-spouse—and Mears's real-life ex, who was initially her schoolteacher. The husband in the novel is increasingly despised by his young wife, who has come to look upon him and his body with disdain. Under his nightshirt she pictures his belly looking like "raw sausage," his glasses are "smeared with mold and grease."

Mears's uncle once wrote to her saying that "artistic license" isn't "freedom to skewer all those people to whose lives you have access," and that portraying identifiable relatives with "a curious amalgam of ingeniousness and viciousness" left no trust between them. Her aunt, who used to write to her, never did again. It can't be easy, walking the line between letting real life inspire fiction, and passing real life off as fiction.

In contrast, the line between real life and reading is distinct—or at least we make it seem that way. But looking through my camera roll, seeing images from the real world *and* the inner worlds I entered that summer, I realized this: the text that "interrupted" proper photographs, the pages that I planned to file elsewhere, made my record of that time more representative and more complete.

I think about how Frankie, who is a romantic, and Selin, who is a realist, both as a result miss something vital about the world—because both fact and fancy contain essential truth, if not about the world, at least about ourselves. We break so many contrasts neatly into either/ors when so often things are messier: overlapping, gray, both/and.

We pretend distinctions are straightforward when they're not. Real people, places, and experiences inform all works of fiction, while fictional people, places, and experiences inform readers' imaginations and perceptions—they can change real minds, provoke real tears.

Perhaps those photographs of words *did* belong with the photographs of people I had met and places I had been that summertime.

The time I spent in inner worlds conjured up by books, while not the same as time spent in the physical world, had influenced me, too. It, too, had taught and shaped and moved me, made impressions, left me changed.

After a summer break, there are people who ask you what you read, and there are people who ask you where you went. But there's a sense in which the books we read are also places we have been. And thanks to the marvel that is a library, travel can be free. A mind can be expanded, even changed. All it takes is words upon a page.

Talking to ourselves, thinking to God

Eternity, September 2021

I've often wondered what it would be like to read a mind: to access a person's unfiltered consciousness, to compare it to my own. I imagine the experience would be a bit like reading character-driven fiction, and a lot like reading Lucy Ellman's *Ducks, Newburyport*.

Ducks, Newburyport is a novel based on a stream of consciousness that runs without ceasing for more than a thousand pages. The stream contains no pauses, no paragraphs, and only one full-stop.

It's a daring experiment that Ellman's regular publisher rejected—an understandable decision, but one they doubtless regretted when it made the 2019 Booker shortlist and won the Goldsmiths Prize.

In one sense, the book's relentless form is familiar—it mirrors the frenetic, erratic nature of thought itself—but it's completely unlike the prose we're used to consuming, in fiction or anywhere else.

Technically the narrative is a single sentence, but the repeated phrase "the fact that" functions as a full-stop of sorts, and a more conventional story (about a mountain lion, of all things) interrupts from time to time to change the pace.

Ellman wrote the first draft over a seven-year period and says that once she started, it was difficult to stop; she even added thirty thousand words after submitting it for publication.

"I wanted to get in every single thing I knew about America, or thought I knew," she says. This explains why, though fiction, it also reads like she's collected every idea and opinion, every scrap of thought, she could. It also explains why the novel already feels like an important cultural artifact.

Broken and bewildered

I'm only three hundred pages in, but I was exhausted long before. I decided early on that it's a novel every fiction-lover should start, but not necessarily finish—though the more I read, the harder it is to stop.

It helps that I find the protagonist—a wife, mother, and former college teacher who now runs a baking business from her home—endearing. I can relate to her thoughts and often agree with her opinions. It would be a difficult read if she were narcissistic, arrogant, and proud, but she's empathetic, insecure, and funny, devoted to her husband and her kids.

I feel for her, too. She's suffered the loss of both her parents, a marriage break-up, and cancer; now she fears (among *many* other things), losing the teenage daughter who appears to despise her. As she bakes, she frets: about "the fact that it's probably aged me ten years, making this darn tartes tartin, and what for, for no reason, the fact that what use am I to my family or the community, the fact that I wanted to help *everybody* when I was younger, and all I do now is study smoke and steam coming out of apples . . ."—and so on.

Sometimes she's angry, sometimes she's resentful, but most of the time she seems "bewildered." There's a sense her life is happening *to* her and she's struggling to control it, let alone make sense of it.

She's also bewildered by the world at large—a place where "they still don't know who all the victims were from the latest Navy SEALs raid, but they do know they were mostly *little children*," where "nothing you do seems innocent anymore," where Donald Trump, of all people, could become the *President*.

How can she make sense of it all? She can't.

As she goes about her day—baking for the day's deliveries, going to the dentist, dropping her youngest child at playgroup—one thought leads to the next, to the next, to the next. They're banal one moment ("the fact that I wonder whatever happened to that book") and poignant the next ("the fact that you lose everything in life, everything"). I'm not waiting for anything in particular to happen, but the fact any *thought* could happen is compelling—perhaps the more ordinary a person and their day, the more room there is for interesting thought.

The Christian's "stream"

The sense of possibility intrigues me, but what fascinates me most about the novel is wondering how closely Ellman's depiction of a person's thoughts might resemble reality. I'm pretty sure every stream-of-consciousness is frenetic, eclectic, and chaotic to some degree at least, but there must be an astonishing diversity in the content and character, form and tone; in the phrases and themes that recur—or don't; all of which might vary wildly over the course of an hour, or a day, or a lifetime, depending on what a person is feeling or remembering or experiencing.

To what extent, I wonder, do our streams of consciousness bear the image of our Maker, and to what extent have they been shattered by the Fall? Has our rebellion not only corrupted the content of the "stream," but also disordered its form? And what difference does conversion make? What happens when God, the Holy Spirit, flows into the stream?

I've been a Christian for most of my life. I still find it difficult to pray and read God's word without my mind wandering, to remind myself of his truths without letting all my doubts creep in as well. I still forget important lessons and resolutions, and I still put myself before others. My thoughts are still disjointed and distracted. I'm still all too familiar with the law of sin at work within me.

And yet, the Bible says I'm being sanctified. When I think about it, my thoughts *are* less plagued by guilt and shame, fear and uncertainty, than they once were—are more hopeful and loving and free.

They're also more purposeful.

Thinking to God

As Christians, we don't just think to ourselves, we think to God. Now that we dwell with Christ, the center of our thoughts isn't always us; we know the source of all that's right and good and true. And we don't just pray for ourselves; we pray for others and our world.

Preachers sometimes call on us to imagine our inner thoughts exposed—the *shame*—to demonstrate how sinful we are. But surely there are moments when our inner thoughts laid bare would be selfless, otherworldly—beautiful? Moments when we truly rejoice in our Father's love—in what he's done, in who we are—when gratitude and awe take center stage?

As we fix our eyes on Jesus, as we worry less, and dwell more on what's lovely and excellent, God lightens our mental load; as we turn from this world towards him, our minds are transformed, renewed.

Our streams-of-consciousness are still broken things in a broken world, a mess of fragments, shards, and scraps—but some are being sanctified, a taste of what's to come.

Attention in a hostile world
Antithesis Journal, November 2022

There are people in this world who spend their days watching people, making people up, and trying to read minds. They are intent on knowing who these people are, and how they think, and why. This fascinates them utterly.

The Pulitzer Prize-winning novelist Elizabeth Strout often talks about this fascination, which she's had since she was young, in interviews. In a 2017 *New Yorker* article she recalls attending to a stranger so closely she almost felt "her *molecules* move into me—or my molecules move into her."

In Strout's latest novel, *Lucy by the Sea*, the protagonist says that's what made her a writer: a "deep desire to know what it feels like to be a different person." At the time, Lucy is watching a policeman who's parked in the car beside hers, unable to stop "feeling a fascination for this man, who seemed to be in his fifties, with a decent face and strong-looking arms."

Her attention is arrested, not because of anything he is doing, but because she wants to know who he is.

"In a way that is not uncommon for me as a writer, I sort of began to feel what it was like to be inside his skin. It sounds very strange, but it is almost as though I could feel my molecules go into him and his come into me," Lucy says.

One wonders just how many "molecules" this writer shares with Strout.

*

Many have argued that paying close attention to another person, or even a single task, is now a dying art. In *Stolen Focus: Why You Can't Pay Attention*, Johann Hari talks about how technology monopolizes our attention—to a damaging extent—because it's designed to.

Similarly, in *You're Not Listening: What You're Missing and Why it Matters*, Kate Murphy observes how hard it is to concentrate on the real world "when you're preoccupied with what could be happening in the virtual one."

One thing that can focus our attention is curiosity. But in *Curiosity and the Ethics of Attention*, Zachary Wojtowicz and George Loewenstein suggest that, like many drives, it weakens in response to high levels of prolonged stimulation. Satisfying it too quickly and frequently can reduce its potency. "This leads to the counter-intuitive result that the modern deluge of attention-grabbing content may in fact be creating a generation of less curious individuals."

If it is the case that we are becoming less curious, less attentive, less imaginative, and less empathetic than we ought to be—and if we want to regain what we've lost—then stories that arise from a fascination with what it means to be human, stories that expand the way we think, that show us how to slow down, how to look, how to imagine, how to see, might play a vital role.

Stories that give readers access to the experiences and perspectives of people who are not like them have been shown to help develop empathy, particularly when read rather than watched.

Neil Gaiman has famously claimed that reading for pleasure is "one of the most important things a person can do."

> *When you watch TV or see a film, you are looking at things happening to other people. Prose fiction is something you build up from twenty-six letters and a handful of punctuation marks, and you, and you alone, using your imagination, create a world and people it and look out through other eyes. You get to feel things, visit places and worlds you would never otherwise know. You learn that everyone else out there is a me, as well. You're being someone else, and when you return to your own world, you're going to be slightly changed.*

Strout's Lucy Barton novels are a case in point. They contain a cast of complex and compelling characters. Their narrator studies these characters, and herself, with curiosity. Observing how, and why, might help to teach a person in this world, to do the same.

*

Lucy By the Sea offers a window on creation and construction too, showing how a moment of curiosity can birth a story: a character who grows more complex and convincing with every detail its author determines, a character who Lucy later says she loves.

It begins when she's watching a stranger—the aforementioned policeman—oh *so* carefully. She wonders what it's like to be a cop, "especially now, these days," and what it's like to be *this* cop.

Almost as soon as he's back in the car, Lucy tells her ex-husband—and pandemic companion—William about the policeman, and that she intends to write about him. Already she knows that people call him Arms, that they call his brother Legs, that as a child he'd throw a football "like the wind."

By the time she sits down to write, she knows where his father worked and where his family lived, about his past and present struggles. She knows enough, and understands enough, to see him as a human, not a "type." But will her readers, too?

When Lucy finishes the story, she tells William she's written something that's "sympathetic toward a white cop who liked the old president and who does an act of violence and gets away with it"—and questions the wisdom of publishing it "right now."

She doesn't mention the death of George Floyd and the storming of Congress; she doesn't have to. William suggests the story might "help people understand each other," though Lucy has her doubts: "I knew that I could not trust myself—or other people."

There are many kinds of attention. Lucy's reluctance hints at the kind that's to be feared, the kind that instead of welcoming insight and possibility, takes offense and rules them out.

*

Lucy habitually notices strangers and imagines characters, but she pays particular attention to the people she is close to. She wants to better understand them and their reality. She also seeks to question, access, and better understand herself.

Lucy, though more prone to giving attention than seeking it, is not blind to the fact that at times, she craves it too.

At one point she reflects that it was a hunger for attention—the kind that makes us feel special—that drove her, following the discovery William had been cheating on her, to have a "disgusting" affair.

She attributes the mistake to being "showered" with attention. A kind that, while plentiful, was more likely prompted by self-interest than by love. Lucy is reminded of the experience when she realizes that her daughter, whom she observes behaving strangely, is on the brink of starting one.

Lucy can see that Chrissy is grieving successive miscarriages, and that her infidelity would be driven not by love, but loss. She demands her daughter's attention so that she can impart wisdom, and, to her great surprise, Chrissy gives it. Chrissy turns, she listens, and she keeps listening while Lucy speaks. This is no small miracle, especially because Lucy is her *mom*.

*

Elsewhere in the novel, Lucy says that she never imagined William would be unfaithful to her, because she never would have been unfaithful to him. In retrospect, she attributes this once-unquestioned assumption to the fact she was "thinking like [her]self."

The phrase "thinking like yourself" reminds Lucy of her deceased second husband; it was a saying between them.

If David wondered, let's say, why the conductor of the Philharmonic eviscerated the new violinist one night, I would say, "You're thinking like yourself, David." And he would laugh and agree. "Get inside his head, and you might understand," I'd say, and David would say that he didn't want to be inside that man's head.

"You're thinking like yourself," points to a tendency that can thwart our ability to understand another person or discern their true thoughts. It states an obvious fact: we think like ourselves. But we forget this, and assume that others think like us. It takes effort and imagination to think like anybody other than ourselves. Also, not everybody wants to be inside another person's head.

Paying focused attention is not a skill that's in any way unique to writers, though it is common to many. But while some attend to people with a genuine desire to understand them, others do so with a desire to use them.

In Nora Ephron's *Heartburn*, the narrator says of her ex-husband, a journalist, "I sometimes felt as if I were living with a cannibal; things barely finished happening before Mark was chewing away at them, trying to string them out, turn them upside down, blow them up into 850 words for tomorrow's newspaper."

Lucy attends to people, those she plans to write about and those she doesn't—with curiosity and courage, openness and generosity. Her main aim is not to use them; her quest for understanding calls to mind the "just and loving gaze" that Iris Murdoch has described—a distant cry from Ephron's "cannibal."

*

Lucy by the Sea ends on an unsettling note. Lucy and William are a couple again. William has told Lucy, and she has believed him, that the reason he went to her when he saw the pandemic coming was that he wanted to save her life, hers more than anyone's.

But her children wonder if their father has been completely honest. Perhaps he manipulated her: "to get you back with him so he doesn't ever have to be alone again," they say.

On the novel's final page, William and Lucy embrace on a New York sidewalk, and William tells Lucy he loves her. But the story doesn't end here.

"A tiny shiver of foreboding" passes through Lucy, "a shiver of foreboding for myself and also the entire world."

For everything this woman can imagine or discern, even confirm, there's so much more she can't, even with the person she knows best.

But what choice does she have, other than to keep on holding on?

So this is what she does. She holds William as though he's the last person left on Earth, as though, if they could only get close enough, he'd pass through her and her through him.

We can never truly know another person—understand them utterly, share "molecules"—but we can *try* to understand them all the same. And we can know enough to want to hold them close.

The more we do, in fiction and in life, the more habitable this hostile world will be.

Love &

...culture

March 2020: The strangest month of our lives
State Library Archives of Tasmania

In February, I spent a weekend in Sydney. I joked about the risk of Tassie closing its borders, of being refused re-entry. In March, the borders closed.

If you'd told me a month ago that I'd soon find myself taking a furtive last trip to the library, anticipating indefinite closure any day—or that while there, my son would ask for a tissue and I'd respond, almost hysterically, that blowing your nose isn't an option because you'll frighten people, *and* be unable to touch *anything* until you wash your hands—I would have doubted your sanity.

If you'd told me that taking a walk in the bush with another family would soon involve constant warnings—"Step back!" "Don't touch!" "Back off!"—as we sought to keep the children from touching; that meeting two adult friends for a coffee, or taking the kids to see their grandparents, or letting them jump the fence to play with the neighbors, would make me feel socially irresponsible and then, within days, breach strict protocols; if you had told me that going to the supermarket twice in one week would make me feel reckless, or that sending my kids to school would make me feel like a small-time criminal; if you had told me I would start teaching them at home, by choice—I would have laughed.

So many freedoms we took for granted have been taken away from us in such a short space of time, so many places have closed, so many events have been canceled, so many people have lost their jobs. There are now strict limits on how many people can attend a wedding or a funeral, how many people can exercise together, how many people can visit each other. From no overseas travel to no domestic travel to no unnecessary outings; from no hand shaking to no in-person socializing; from imagining invisible enemies lying in wait in every cough and sniff, to anticipating them in every touch, around every corner, on every surface, in every public place—the level and speed of change defies belief.

There has also been a corresponding rise in the use of technology. In the space of about a week, I attended my first "happy hour" with friends online, FaceTimed with various friends I've never even talked to on the phone, attended a church livestream and Zoom Bible study, joined a "prep friends" WhatsApp group, and participated in a Lego Masters challenge with eight other families online.

Last night, when organizing a group video-conferencing event, I joked that we should pretend we were meeting online because of a global pandemic that made gathering in person illegal—"too far fetched," someone quipped.

Can things get any stranger? And how will it end? One thing's for sure: newly acquired habits around hand washing and hand shaking, and newly acquired paranoia around surface contamination, will linger for weeks. The novelty—magic, delight—when we're finally allowed to breathe the same air as a friend, even rush to their embrace, will too.

Don't sweat that deadline; time "wasted" can be time well spent
The Guardian, August 2023 (Published as: "Don't sweat that deadline, time-wasting can be time well spent.")

A friend asked me recently how the freelance life is treating me. I thought about the days I work for my employer—when a story is assigned to me, when I write professionally, impersonally, efficiently—and the days I write for me; when I choose what I want to say and how, and who to send it to.

One is productive. It consistently results in published work and payment.

The other is hit and miss. Rejection and self-doubt abound. And it's tempting to procrastinate—take walks, do chores, text friends, read books . . . Even when I write a story that I'm happy with, I can't always give it the ideal "home." But sometimes—*just* often enough to make this crazy caper feel worthwhile—I can.

What is creative freelance writing like? Easy. Hard. Fun. Painful. Inefficient.

A story I've been drafting on my inefficient days, mentions how it's often cheaper to replace than to repair. It's made us quick to deem possessions worthless, to discard. To some, preserving what is damaged no longer makes much sense, but what is lost in sense is gained in meaning; in this culture and in these times, mending, treasuring, is a rare redemptive act.

Meanwhile, on "efficient" days when covering employment news, I've seen that inefficiency can, surprisingly, give more than it takes.

Employees, it seems, are often more productive when their managers show care, when they're willing to "waste" time: chatting, listening, giving their support. Some workplaces report that giving staff a whole day off each week while paying them the same leads to a *better* bottom line.

These "inefficiencies" might be ineffective on a given day or in a given moment, but can generate great value over time—better health, closer relationships, more discretionary effort.

Especially with creative work, some find that "wasted" time—in retrospect—fueled the work somehow, rarely in ways they could anticipate let alone plan. I find that pausing to take a walk or see a friend often doesn't, as I might expect, make for a less productive day. Where do ideas come from if not daily life? Solutions, too? They're just as likely to emerge when I am hanging out the washing or walking through the bush as when I'm staring at a screen.

The more creative the piece—the more it matters to me personally—the more procrastinating, rewording, and rewriting I seem to (have to?) do. Sometimes I spend half an hour on a paragraph I then delete, or ten minutes on one sentence. It is wildly inefficient.

But it's work I love. It's hard because I care. That is why it's inefficient; that is why it is frustrating when I feel I've wasted time; that is why making one sentence sing can make it all worthwhile.

Not all inefficiency is without gain. Sometimes it means a deadline or a target isn't met and time is wasted needlessly, but sometimes it plays a role that, looking back, proves indispensable; it improves or even "makes" the end result.

And sometimes, a tangent is more worthy of our time and attention than the goal was anyway. It depends on what we value most.

Yes, goals and targets, timing, output—they all matter too, but if we make them all-important we will pay a price. Our relationships will suffer, as will we; and depending on the nature of our work, it might as well.

Ruthless efficiency can cost us insight, innovation, inspiration, joy. An artist's work might lack beauty, meaning, soul; a patient treated as a problem to be solved might feel *more* ill.

In sacrificing time, giving attention—in squeezing a hand in solidarity, in finding out how a person *really* is, in soaking up beauty and truth—we might compromise efficiency.

But we might also gain it. Either way, how can time taken to bestow love or to feel wonder be anything but time that is well spent?

There are different types of inefficiency. We'd do well to do away with listless scrolling and to streamline bureaucratic paperwork, but we cannot do away with inefficiency itself, and we shouldn't try. Sometimes it is painful, pointless, and profitless, but sometimes it's the best and the only way.

On being a "Lone Ranger" in journalism's "Wild West"
Other Terrain, December 2024

In the famous phrase "murder your darlings," "you" are a writer and your "darlings" are the parts of a piece that, despite your love for them, must be scrapped. The work itself is the ultimate darling, which makes such scrapping possible. Once finished, the challenge is to find that work a home.

Before I started freelancing, I assumed my greatest challenge would either be the task of writing (and of murder), or of finding my writing a (paying) home. What I've since discovered is that, as hard as writing and rewriting is, and as hard as it is to find a piece a home, what happens next is often harder still.

It's one thing to grit your teeth and kill selected darlings; it's another to have a darling that you deemed essential murdered or mutilated by someone else.

Often the violence is justified; the editor deserves the writer's thanks. But sometimes, something valuable is lost. It might be rescued yet—if edits are proposed and not imposed, if the writer is invited to accept or to reject, if the editor respects their point of view—but, more often than most readers might assume, the writer only sees what has been changed when it's too late. Or, though shown the final copy when *in theory* there's still time to speak—decides to bite their tongue.

They bite their tongue because they fear that questioning a judgment call might cause offense, burn a bridge, or both. It might result in being labeled "difficult," and when an editor is spoilt for choice and pressed for time, why would they choose "difficult?"

*

I was a journalist—a staff-writer—for ten years before to-bite-or-not-to-bite-my-tongue became a regular dilemma. For years I was used to my editors detecting flaws and making improvements; I was used to feeling in their debt. Sometimes a change wasn't to my taste, but we didn't do bylines; my name was never attached to my stories, and because I wrote from interviews, court transcripts, studies, and reports, I was not attached to them. I wrote them, but I wasn't *in* them. They weren't personal; they were facts that I reported for a wage.

When, with my employer's blessing, I started freelancing in my own time, boundaries began to blur. I started writing stories about my life—stories based on my experiences and my relationships, on deeply-held opinions and beliefs; I started interviewing people I knew and cared about; I started taking risks. The greatest risk was one I never anticipated: the risk I took when I surrendered a finished piece I cared about to an editor I'd never met.

In what I've come to think of as the *Wild West* of freelancing, I discovered that some editors manage to *add* mistakes to a piece instead of removing them, and many don't run the final copy by the person who wrote it before publishing it.

I didn't expect editors to consult me when adding missing words or deleting repeated ones, when correcting grammatical errors, or applying their publication's style guide. I didn't expect to be consulted about minor changes to punctuation or structure or syntax. But I did expect to be consulted when an edit altered what I was trying to say, or how, in a personal essay or opinion piece. I expected a suggestion and an explanation of the rationale; I expected the opportunity to accept a tweak or propose one of my own. Many editors *do* collaborate like this, but I was naive to think all would.

*

The more personal the piece, and the harder a writer has worked to make each line "just so," the more it will pain them to stomach changes made against their will. I've suffered through edits that were insensitive to tone, rhythm, nuance, and voice, that disrupted the flow of a sentence or a paragraph or an argument, that put another's words into my mouth.

As for headlines—the only part some people read—I can understand why those who know what makes their readers tick and click better than I do would draft their own. I can understand why a stressed-out editor wouldn't make time to seek my approval before publication. But that doesn't stop *me*, the one whose name will be attached to it, wishing they would.

I've also found that many publications consider "exposure" ample payment for a writer's time. I once received an email informing me that a submission had not only been accepted, but had already been edited and published online. When I then inquired about payment, the editor informed me his publication didn't pay contributors. He offered to take the piece down, but by then it was too late to place elsewhere.

I suggested that in the future, the editor could tell contributors *prior* to publication that they wouldn't be paid for their time. The publication could also note this in its submission guidelines. (I've since checked; they haven't changed.)

Freelancers also run the risk that an editor won't respond to their pitch, or will reject it, only to use it themselves or assign it to somebody else. How can a writer who reads a story based on an idea they had, in a publication they pitched it to without success, tell if someone got there first, or if the article was based on their intellectual property? Much rests on editors being ethical. I like to think most are, but checks and balances are few.

Another point to note: an article that's suspiciously similar to one published elsewhere earlier might have been written first. Many editors say that due to the volume of pitches they receive, they can't respond to a writer unless they're interested. Those who send a prompt reply, even if it only says, "I'll pass," earn my heartfelt gratitude—I'd rather be rejected and move on than be left hanging, waiting, hoping, wasting time—while those who pass *and* take the time to explain why, fill me with hope for humankind.

It's worth noting that editors, especially if they're employees themselves, often lack agency too. They must conform to certain rules, meet certain deadlines, toe certain lines, and manage certain workloads to keep their job. Speaking of "certain rules," writers who submit to a publication with a writing style that makes them cringe can expect the edits to as well; we shouldn't blame an editor who's just doing their job.

Another issue is that while freelancers might generate the bulk of a publication's traffic, they're rarely told how well their stories do. I don't mind this very much; I don't want clicks to be my measure of success or of self-worth. But along with not knowing which pitches and submissions are actually read, and the reasons those that are ignored or declined didn't make the cut, it's another way in which we're often in the dark, blindfolded in the *Wild West*.

I don't want to make the writer-editor divide seem greater than it is. Many journalists are editors one minute and writers the next. I've worn the hat of editor myself—have seen first-hand how hard it is to please your writer *and* their readers *and* your boss. What I do want to do is give readers and budding writers a glimpse behind the scenes. I want you to know that just because a person's name is attached to a piece of writing, doesn't mean that every line is theirs, or that every line met their approval. This might work in the writer's favor—"their" best lines might be their editor's—but it can work against them too; the most dumbed-down or hyped-up sentences might not be theirs at all.

With all the risks and challenges, it's a wonder that lone rangers keep roaming the *Wild West*. In an article that asks whether freelance journalism is becoming unviable, staff-writer-turned-independent-journalist Ralph Jones says the writing isn't the tiring part. "What's tiring is that in order to do the writing you've got to do the pitching, the chasing, the dodging out-of-offices, the haggling, the compromising, the invoicing, the self-promotion, the work at weekends, the chasing, the chasing, the chasing." It is wildly inefficient.

Just as a writer can in theory ask an editor to respond to a pitch within a certain time, they can in theory impose conditions when an editor expresses interest in a piece. But the dynamic between freelance journalists and commissioning editors involves a significant power imbalance. Because most editors receive far more submissions than they can hope to use, freelance writers must pick their battles. In order to develop relationships and increase the chances of one acceptance leading to another, it pays to be agreeable. The newer the relationship, the more heightened the risk of appearing difficult, especially when interactions occur solely over email where rapport is hard to build. Even asking an editor respond to a time-sensitive pitch promptly so I can find another taker if they decline, or to "please run any edits by me," can feel like asking far too much.

Perhaps it's fitting that this article has been difficult to place. I was thrilled when a "dream" publication accepted a pitch for it last September. In October I sent through a finished draft. The editor said she liked the piece "tons" and had started to make a few edit notes; she'd get back to me soon. Weeks passed. When I followed up, which I did several times, I'd receive reassuring emails—"I'm just swamped," "please don't give up on me." Months passed. The following year, six weeks after an email that promised a reply "next week," I told the editor I was unwilling to be left hanging any longer. I wanted to write about the power imbalance, not succumb to it, and felt I had no choice but to cut my losses and try elsewhere. I was paid a quarter of the agreed amount—some publications wouldn't pay a cent—and I was back to square one. At least the piece was "evergreen."

Evergreen pieces—articles that aren't time-sensitive—are a much safer "investment" of time than harder-hitting stories that might pass their use-by date before you can find an editor to commission them. Another option is submitting finished pieces to literary journals instead of courting commissions from news outlets, because journals accept more esoteric, less newsy work, and tend to welcome simultaneous submissions. But these journals are often not-for-profit labors of love. They might be more likely to respond to a submission than an editor who's been contacted cold, but they usually take months to do so. Many don't pay writers a cent but do charge a reading fee; those that do pay writers can rarely offer much. And competition is fierce. The top journals are said to have acceptance rates under one percent. If I didn't steer clear of those that charge, I could find myself not only giving work away, but paying to.

I could up my freelance income by targeting publications I don't want to read, let alone write for, with content I have no desire to produce, but know will sell. But if I needed the money that badly, there would be much easier, less soul-destroying ways to earn it.

If I were the sole income-earner in my family, I'd almost certainly up my staff-writer hours, or take on copywriting work, rather than indulging in freelance writing. Many freelancers rely on other forms of employment to make a living; many give up entirely. According to author and journalist Katherine Lewis, this should matter to readers as well as the editors and publications that rely on them. Writing about the diversity independent journalists add to the media landscape, Lewis suggests the challenges they face—"being underpaid, exploited, ghosted by editors, and asked to do additional work beyond the scope of their assignments"—constitutes an "existential threat to a healthy and diverse journalism ecosystem."

Maybe some freelance writers could tell a different story. Presumably those at the top can call more shots than small-timers like me—but I'm pretty sure the majority have a lot less power than most readers would expect, especially if they are under financial pressure. The author of the next article you read might have more integrity than the piece implies, or less; more talent, or less. It depends on the compromises they made or refused to make, on the ultimatums they issued or didn't, and why. It depends on their skill, and on the editor's skill; it depends on much they can't control.

I sometimes think I'm not cut out to sustain a freelance writing career, especially when I'm writing something "from the heart." I care too much about what I want to say and how, about each word, each implication, every darling. At other times I think I *am* cut out for this *because* I care so much—about what I want to say and how, about each word, each implication, every darling.

This is why I'm so appreciative when I find editors who don't just tolerate collaboration, but invite it. They might ask me to compromise, but they also will compromise for me. Ink might be spilt and darlings murdered, but the process isn't painful, and sometimes it is fun.

I might call the place I freelance the *Wild West*, but when I'm working with an editor I trust, I stop being a lone ranger. I have a partner, and my partner has my back. The hats that we are wearing might be different, but the page that we are on, and the place we hope to go, is the same.

Is it any more "noble" to make art in secret, than for an audience?
ABC, November 2023

Last month I came across the story of an extremely "quiet" achiever: an Australian maths teacher who lived alone and, after retiring, started painting abstract art alone. Over a twenty-year period he produced more than seven thousand paintings—naming, dating, numbering each one.

After his death, his sister called them "rubbish" and told an estate auctioneer to get rid of them. But they didn't look like rubbish to him and, when he showed them to an experienced art valuer, she agreed.

The valuer, Elizabeth Arthur, said that when she first saw Robert Martiensen's paintings, she was speechless. She went on to study, catalog, and write about his collection. Earlier this year at the opening of *The Secret*, some gallery-goers, upon hearing the story, were moved to tears. When I first heard the story on the radio, before I saw a single painting, I felt moved myself.

It's often said that artists only become rich and famous after they die. The fact this man didn't seem interested in riches or renown is one reason the story is such an unusual one. It gives the impression of a kind of purity, of creating art for art's sake.

While *The Secret* was showing in Australia, a living artist—whose live paintings of subway riders and rags-to-riches story have attracted a massive social media following—had his first solo show in New York. Devon Rodriguez might have been a quiet achiever once, but he is famous now.

In a review of his show *Underground*, *Artnet* critic Ben Davis suggested the prominence of huge screens playing clips of the artist at work implied his social-media celebrity loomed "far larger than his accomplishments on canvas."

I think of Martiensen working in secret: no following, no feedback, no persona, no performance—no negative reviews. I wonder what he was trying to achieve and why, and how he measured success. I wonder if he ever suspected that anyone would take his work seriously when he died—and whether he'd have cared.

The idea of an artist creating without a crowd, of his work being untainted by popular opinion or his personality, drew me to the story. But despite (and because of) his death, Martiensen's persona is already inextricably tied to his work. Who can say which is more extraordinary: the story, or the paintings themselves? Davis's review of *Underground* raised the question of whether Rodriguez is an exceptional painter, or just an exceptionally popular one. But Martiensen's success may be no less connected to his persona than Rodriguez's. His persona might be even *more* influential because it's posthumous; the less a person can tell their story, the more we can construct our own.

If I was overly romantic about Martiensen, perhaps I was overly cynical about Rodriguez. My cynicism had less to do with the staged nature of some of his "spontaneous" videos than with an assumption that you can't have millions of social media fans without it going to your head. One artist struck me as a quiet achiever, the other as a star, and I'm a cheer-for-the-underdog type.

But was Martiensen's approach *really* more admirable than Rodriguez's? It's easy to assume the "influencer" would be far more motivated by the pursuit of fame, fortune, and acclaim than a desire to make art for more noble purposes. That's one possible scenario, but it's far from the only one. Besides, desires can be mixed. I can't know what each artist's motives are, let alone what proportion are self-serving, or self-less. What I can know is that Rodriguez isn't hiding his work away, and that Martiensen did.

When I heard Martiensen's story, I immediately assumed his secrecy was the result of humility. But who's to say Martiensen didn't keep his work to himself out of pride? Perhaps he was the only viewer he really cared or thought about. Or perhaps he cared deeply—even more than Rodriguez—about what others would think. Perhaps he was so afraid of critics saying that he should have stuck to maths, that he planned to one day burn his house of art so they wouldn't have the chance.

A writer-musician friend of mine once likened the difference between performing a song and writing a novel to baking a cake and eating it with a friend, and baking a cake and leaving it on a friend's doorstep. One is delightful because the friend's pleasure is witnessed; the other because it is anticipated. The baking delivers some satisfaction, but the sharing is what it's all about.

It is possible Martiensen planned to take his secret to the grave, to destroy all of that "cake," but I prefer to think he wanted it enjoyed—not just by him, by other people too.

There's something authentic—romantic—about the idea of an artist creating in solitude: art for art's sake, no audience, no ego, no interest in fortune, no desire for fame. But when we make something that delights us, that might delight others as well, there may be virtue—and vulnerability—in sharing it, whether the wall is in a kitchen, or an art gallery, or online; whether the audience is one person, or many. Not because of what the artist stands to gain, but because of what they hope to give.

Why should art matter to people? It matters to God.
TGCA, July 2023

Peirce and Christina Baehr, along with their growing family, run a hostel in Tasmania's Huon Valley. It attracts backpackers from all over the world and throughout the peak (fruit-picking) season, they host regular dinners with their guests. One would think that in the "off season," they'd enjoy a break, and to some extent, they do. But they also use that time to round up an army of volunteers and stage a multi-day art exhibition, complete with workshops, performances, and prizes.

All this might sound like a recipe for exhaustion. Sometimes, it is. But they're not doing any of it on their own. Sometimes it wearies them, but sometimes it doesn't feel like work at all. After all, they're living their dream.

The dream started to take shape more than a decade ago when, just after marrying, the pair prayerfully considered how their gifts might fit together. They decided that, God-willing, they'd build a family-run hostel that would offer distinctly Christian hospitality to travelers, and a residency program to artists—a place not unlike Francis and Edith Schaeffer's L'Abri.

Raising the necessary funds and starting to plan and build Pilgrim Hill took years. In the meantime, they started a family; they started showing hospitality to travelers in the Huon community by running free dinners in existing venues; and they started supporting Christian artists by running the Pilgrim Artists' Festival.

At first, Peirce and Christina thought of the annual festival—a public exhibition of Christian artworks and a selection of free workshops and performances—as a temporary substitute for the artist's residency they planned to build one day.

They're still yet to build an artist's residence on the hill, but even when they do, they expect the festival in the town to continue—it's become "its own thing."

When I ask the couple why art is so important to them, they answer that art is important to God. Christina notes that the means by which God communicates to us today—a collection of books that includes sweeping historical narratives, wisdom literature, poetry, prophecy, letters, and apocalyptic writing—is through a work of literary art.

"It doesn't just have propositional, logical arguments," she says of the Bible. "There's story, there's poetry . . . In times where people become more rationalist and utilitarian, they often struggle with that, like, why is Song of Songs in the Bible? Do we really need so many Psalms?!" Peirce adds that the instructions for art that would adorn the Temple and Solomon's palace contained intricate detail for works of great beauty, and that the Holy Spirit himself aided the craftsmen.

The fact beauty matters to God is clear from the Bible and from the world, Christina says.

"When you look around at the world, you'd have to really be quite blind not to understand how important beauty is to God. The world is full of completely useless things . . . There's so much lavish, extraneous beauty around us; it would be really hard to argue that beauty or art are not important to God."

Closer to home

The Baehrs also see "extraneous beauty" play an important role in their home life.

"For instance, we designed the large living space in our home to be a place where people would feel welcomed to come in and share meals with us and share the Bible with us," she says. Part of this involved hanging original art on their walls. They didn't first think, "What art can we hang on our walls that will make people understand what we value?" Christina says. "But by hanging beautiful art on the walls that does reflect our values, it has actually become a huge talking point, and also just a way that people can understand who we are."

Peirce notes that none of the works they've hung are "overtly religious." They're mostly portraiture by Christina's mother and artworks by their children, though there are two somewhat unusual oil paintings by a local artist.

"Peirce was insistent we get these two pieces by Emily Jones. I was like, this is a little surprising . . . Do I really want a picture of a trash can and an ATM on my wall?" Christina says. But she went along with it, placing the paintings above a portrait of her and one of their children, "and it's become a really wonderful thing to contemplate."

"It's a very Ecclesiastes pairing of pictures," she says. "It reminds me of times when Jesus [says], don't worry about tomorrow, the body is more than clothing, and life is more than what you possess; it reminds me that human beings are eternal, it reminds me not to worry."

"It spoke to me very deeply," Peirce says, of the futility of consumerism. "We buy, we trash, we buy and we trash; [but] the human life is not like that."

"It has also been a great talking point for the travelers," Christina says. "When we were discussing Ecclesiastes recently, I could just point to these paintings, and everyone completely got it; instantly."

A way to bless artists, and the community

Christina says a key goal of the Artists Festival—which exhibits a curated selection of entries from Christian artists of all ages—is to support established artists and inspire potential artists.

"We've seen a lot of ways in which artists have been encouraged: how they've been encouraged in their gifts [and] how they've been encouraged to meet with other Christians who are artists," Peirce says. "I think it was festival three that we started to step back and see: this has developed its own community. It's no longer just us, there's actually a community here of artists who are interacting with each other."

The opportunity to submit and exhibit work is unique, and has seen many Christians motivated to create works that wouldn't otherwise exist. Peirce and Christina are also aware of friendships and collaborations that have formed as a result of the festival, which has created "an atmosphere where things were able to germinate faster, or in ways that maybe wouldn't have happened before," Christina says.

This means a lot to the couple, who realize that time spent creating art isn't always rewarded, financially or otherwise.

It can also be undervalued by fellow believers who question whether it's a godly use of time that could be spent in other ways.

"The church doesn't always understand, and the art world doesn't always understand," Peirce says.

"I wish we could encourage them more," Christina says. "I wish more people would come and buy the art, because honestly, the most encouragement that you can give a Christian artist is actually to pay money for their work."

"Sometimes people are like, 'Oh, I'll pay you with exposure,' so we're trying to not be that, we're trying to be a bit more substantial than that by actually offering prizes, and hopefully encouraging people to buy their work, and also just with the validation of saying, we see you, we value you, and your craftsmanship is worth pursuing for God's glory."

Although Christina describes the volunteer-run festival as "very local, very grounded, very grassroots," it has attracted international support, entries, and visitors. It also features thirty (mostly cash) prizes, including a one-thousand-dollar people's choice award.

"We welcome submissions from anywhere," Peirce notes. "Technically it's a bit challenging to get the actual physical submissions, but we have had some from other countries come through, and the literary prizes are easy to apply for from any place on the planet."

While the festival is designed to showcase the work of Christian artists (entrants are asked to affirm the Nicene creed), it also seeks to bless the local community more broadly. As far as Peirce and Christina can tell, it's doing that too; they're fairly certain that most of the people who walk into the exhibition off the street aren't church-goers.

Some look at the art, some cast a people's choice vote, some attend a workshop.

"They're not necessarily going to get the entirety of the gospel, but they might get a piece of it," Christina says.

"They might come out and go, 'woah, Christians care about justice,' or oh, 'wow, these Christians are really good at noticing the beauty in the world,' or they might come in and go, 'oh, I thought Christians were very closed and insular, but they're really welcoming and they're offering this stuff for free.'"

She recalls a top graphic novelist from overseas who came across last year's festival by chance. "He just walked in and went into a self-publishing workshop that one of our Christian authors was running, and he was blown away . . . He was definitely not a Christian, but he came in and we were able to serve him, we were able to help him. He spent ages looking at all the art . . . he read the stories, he was voting on stuff, he was deeply engaging with all of the work."

A world infused with beauty

Not everything that's submitted to the festival makes the cut—teams of volunteer "curators" filter the entries each year, but Peirce says there are always works that amaze him.

Each entry is assessed based on three criteria: how well it fits the prompt, how skillfully it's made, and whether it's saying something true.

This year's theme is "beauty in the everyday."

"In the past, sometimes we've gone for really big, expansive, epic themes, like 'justice and mercy,' and some of our artists have thrived on that," Christina says. "But other artists, maybe their genres are like textiles or still life, they've kind of gone, how am I going to do 'justice and mercy?'"

"This year is great, you can essentially go big or small as you want, and beauty in the everyday is something that most people can identify with through any genre and any medium," she says.

"And it gives us a chance to recognise the fact God has given us this world, that is just so insanely infused with beauty."

Easter: A welcome holiday, a wild story
TGCA, March 2024

Easter is approaching, and while we don't all believe, or even know the "Easter Story," I think we're all on board with the holiday part. But as far as stories go, it *is* one worth hearing—full of action, tragedy, mystery, and unexpected twists.

It's about how a small-town Jewish guy who makes *the most* outrageous claim—that he is God—somehow grows so popular, and arouses so much jealousy among the religious leaders of his day, that they have him killed. But that's not all! Three days later his body disappears and he starts popping up all over the place—he's mistaken for a gardener, he's seen eating fish, he shows a skeptical friend the marks in his hands . . . Turns out the whole crucifixion thing was God's plan all along.

Not long after all this, there's a scene where the dead (?) guy's mates are rounded up and brought before an assembly of religious leaders. They've already been jailed once, but there was an issue with the locks—or divine intervention?—and they escaped. When the apostles are unapologetic about the trouble they're causing—they "obey God, not man"—the appalled leaders want to not just jail them *again* but put them to death.

But one of the leaders' number disagrees; this guy urges his peers to let the apostles go instead. He reckons that if their claims are a crock, they'll be forgotten soon enough. But if they're somehow from God—are somehow *true*—there'll be no stopping them; the religious leaders will only find themselves "fighting against God" (not a good look for religious leaders).

A couple of thousand years later, the claims the apostles made about Jesus—that he really did die and really did come back to life, that he really was divine—are still being made. Christianity might be declining in some places, but it's thriving in others. That outrageous guy whose body never was found is worshiped still—not just by a handful of kooks, but by people all over the world.

It's bizarre to claim that death is not the end and yet, isn't it bizarre to claim it is? Author and journalist Helen Garner, when recalling a visit to Melbourne's Springvale crematorium, wrote about this realization:

> *I didn't start shaking and crying till two days later. And on my way home, I had, for the first time in my life, a conviction—I mean not a thought but knowledge—that life can't possibly end at death. I had the punctuation wrong. I thought it was a full stop, but it's only a comma, or a dash—or better still, a colon: I don't believe in heaven or hell, or punishment or reward, or the survival of the ego; but what about energy, spirit, soul, imagination, love? The force for which we have no word? How preposterous, to think that it could die!*

There's this prophecy in the book of Isaiah, written long before Jesus was born, about how the coming Messiah would be despised and rejected. It's preparing the Jews for a king who won't come in glory, but humility; who will be crowned not with gold but thorns; who will die a slave's death. You could argue this prophecy reached its fulfillment when Jesus was crucified. But you could also argue it's fulfilled every day. You could even argue it's fulfilled every time someone mutters or shouts *"Jesus Christ!"*

Whether you curse his name or revere it, there's something to be said for those ancient predictions. And there's something to be said for the theory that if the claims about Jesus weren't from God, they'd have been lost to history long ago. Instead, whether in praise or in cursing, his name is spoken every day.

Easter is still unbelievable
Common Good, March 2024

I still remember my astonishment when an Australian PM, at a campaign trail event—the kind where hands are shaken, babies kissed—picked up a raw onion and took a bite from it.

If I saw the clip of that farm visit now, I might declare it a deep fake. Could someone really be so determined to please, so delighted by fresh produce, or so sleep-deprived—that they'd not only bite an onion but, still smiling, swallow too? Surely it was just an apple, digitally manipulated for a laugh.

Seeing isn't quite believing anymore—but not believing our own eyes is nothing new. Easter is approaching, and the story it commemorates is full of people who, though seeing, don't believe.

I have to say, I sympathize. If I watched a close friend die, then saw them standing by their grave, walking down a road, or appearing in a room, I wouldn't trust my eyes; I'd favor a logical explanation over a supernatural one. And that's what people did.

Even those who called Jesus of Nazareth "the Christ," even those he'd let in on a secret—that he'd be killed and in three days, return—expected nothing of the sort.

These were the people who knew and loved him best, who had good reason to think he wasn't just talking about a heavenly resurrection. They knew he'd performed miracles; they believed he was God's son.

To be fair, their friend could be obtuse. As his death approached he told them, "In a little while you will see me no more, and then after a little while you will see me." That could mean anything.

But their idiosyncratic leader—who often spoke about himself in the third person, who sometimes called himself "The Son of Man"—could also be direct: "The Son of Man is going to be betrayed into the hands of men. They will kill him, and after three days he will rise."

He could even be specific: "We are going up to Jerusalem, and everything that is written by the prophets about the Son of Man will be fulfilled. He will be delivered over to the Gentiles. They will mock him, insult him and spit on him; they will flog him and kill him. On the third day he will rise again."

Even so, the disciples probably thought their friend was speaking metaphorically, something he did *a lot*.

You might ask how a twenty-first century reader could presume to know that the disciples didn't catch Jesus's drift. Luke, a physician who made a "careful investigation" of these events before documenting them, says as much: "The disciples did not understand any of this."

In their defense, he adds, "Its meaning was hidden from them"—as if they weren't to blame. Whatever the cause, he's clear about the result: "they did not know what he was talking about."

The disciples did not expect their leader to die the way he did, and afterwards, they didn't expect him to return to his body the way he did.

Mary Magdalene, when she saw the empty tomb, didn't think, "He's risen!"—she assumed someone had taken her friend's body away.

As she's weeping by the tomb, Jesus appears, and she mistakes him for a gardener. Later, when he strikes up a conversation with two of his disciples walking down a road, neither of them recognizes him.

It's not until after they've walked and talked and asked him if he'd like to share a meal, until he breaks some bread, that they realize who he is.

To be fair, Mary's eyes were blinded by tears; when she hears Jesus say her name, she knows him instantly. And in both cases, there are hints of supernatural subterfuge. In John's account of the disciples on the road, "their eyes were kept from recognizing him." It wasn't until Jesus broke the bread that "their eyes were opened."

It's almost comical that after the disciples who are eating with Jesus recognize him, the moment they *finally* see, he disappears from view. But by that point they don't need their eyes; by then they *know*.

They ask each other, "Were not our hearts burning within us while he talked with us on the road and opened the Scriptures to us?," and then set off to spread the news.

Lucky for them, Jesus appears a few more times to verify their claim. According to the gospel accounts, some eat with him, some touch him, and many see him. Also extraordinary is that some who didn't see him—quite a number, actually—believed.

And some—quite a number, actually—have believed since. I count myself among them.

Much is unbelievable when you first hear talk of it. Imagine growing up learning that the earth is flat, only to be told that it is round, or thinking that walking on the moon never could be done, then hearing news of those first steps. It's not unreasonable to question strange and unexpected news.

But just because you didn't see something coming, or see it for yourself, doesn't mean it can't be true. The explanation might be utterly bizarre—it's *not* a hoax?—but so is, such is, life.

Between two flickering worlds
Ekstasis, March 2022

The stars were so bright that instead of looking where I was walking, I kept looking at them. Then I stopped walking—maybe even breathing—and stared.

I'm no expert on the constellations, but I was sure that if the sky usually contained a line of about a dozen stars, I would have seen it before. And then I noticed the line was moving.

I blinked. I exclaimed. I looked around for someone to tell, but it was before sunrise in the suburbs on a *very* icy morning; there were no fellow walkers in sight.

Later that morning I told my husband, who was as baffled as I was. The story was not one I planned to broadcast on social media; the fact I was out walking in the dark in Tasmania in late autumn *by choice* was strange enough without the UFOs. But I did text a friend who works at the Commonwealth Scientific and Industrial Research Organization: "If someone told you they saw a line of what looked like 10-15 stars but were presumably satellites traveling/drifting across the sky (in a roughly spaced line!!) while walking at 5:35 a.m. this morning, would you have an explanation? Asking for a friend."

Within minutes I had my answer: "Probably Starlink. Low orbital internet satellites. They're a nuisance for astronomy. It's the only satellite system I know of that's orbiting in close groups like that. They fit a whole bunch on each rocket . . . over time they should space out from each other, while staying in the same orbital plane."

Google filled in the gaps: what I saw was a "satellite internet constellation" constructed by the Elon Musk company SpaceX. It wasn't invaders from another planet or even spies from another country, but a billionaire's space toys. No need to wonder about all the other possibilities, including my own sanity; mystery solved.

*

It seems fitting that my own small mystery in the physical world was solved online through immaterial means. It's easy to think of the online world as one place and the real world as another, my mind as one thing and my body as another—to forget such things are intertwined.

The internet is part of the world, our minds are part of our bodies, and whether our thoughts are posted to the masses or spoken in private, their source is the same. And yet, I am between two worlds.

I don't expect death to transport me to another planet, but I do believe that one day this broken world—this fragile body and troubled mind—will be renewed. What I saw in that dawn sky wasn't aliens, but there's a sense in which I do believe in them—a sense in which I am one myself. The Scriptures I've been reading since childhood liken believers to strangers, foreigners, *aliens* in this world. What's more, the Bible explains that from the world's perspective, my beliefs are foolish; I am a fool.

*

I might be between two worlds, but I don't want to be two people, to hide my beliefs in some spaces and let them out in others. I don't want to be one person in *real life* and another *online*, one in my mind and another when I speak, one in this social circle, another in that.

Doubt wants me to carve myself in pieces, to show one side here, another there; to always play it safe. Faith says that my final judge will not be my friends, my family, or the crowd; I'm called to love, not please. Doubt says I should follow all those spinning satellites; there are no absolutes. But faith says there's a truth older than time. The ancient constellations might be harder to discern in today's sky, but they're still there.

Technology helps mortals transcend limits of embodied interaction, time, and space. Our bodies remain still while what we type takes flight. Yet, this boundlessness imposes limits too. It robs us of the richness of true togetherness, flattens interactions, dulls imaginations, and divides.

It's one thing to assume that a flat, faceless majority will be hostile if I speak about my faith; it's another to assume that people

I know, and who know me, aren't interested. I realize I've made assumptions about my friends' assumptions. We've spoken face to face, walked side by side, discerned each others' feelings without words. They've never asked me to keep anything from them. Why wouldn't they be intrigued, open to another view—another world?

*

In *The Freedom of Self-Forgetfulness*, Timothy Keller says that it's possible to be free from caring about what others think of us, or even what we think of ourselves. He examines how the great apostle Paul could earnestly profess to care very little about being judged by any "human" court; could call himself the "chief" of sinners, and yet declare, "I do not even judge myself."

Paul is well aware of both his failures and his accomplishments, but "he does not connect them to himself and his identity"—or to his self-worth. It's one thing for an intelligent and influential figure to keep their ego in check; it's another thing altogether for them to stop thinking about it.

"True gospel-humility means I stop connecting every experience, every conversation, with myself. In fact, I stop thinking about myself," Keller says. This means criticism no longer devastates, not because pride and arrogance make a person unwilling or unable to hear it, but because hearing it, even accepting it, doesn't jeopardize their self-esteem. Their worth is rooted firmly in God's love.

It is a sobering truth and a wonderful relief. Sobering that a holy, perfect God is my true judge; a relief because this judge is just and merciful, for he sacrificed his son to set me free.

*

I'm reminded of a night several summers past. I was so uncomfortably hot that instead of sleeping I lay texting, trying to entice a friend to join me at the beach. Eventually, she complied. I dressed and she picked me up. We parked beside the promenade and headed to the sea.

We expected the water to be warm, but we did not expect it to be glowing. The bioluminescence amidst the waves had us skipping, playing, shouting with delight. But it wasn't until I put my goggles on and sunk below that I realized where the real show was.

Under the water's surface, away from streetlights and passing cars, against quiet silky blackness, there were no vague shimmers, only intense sparkles. Each flick of my fingers released a dancing spray of glitter. I shot fireworks from my fingertips and toes; I swam and spun, then watched the sparkles radiate and fade. I was a painter, a magician, an astronaut, a captivated child.

Resurfacing, I gave my friend the goggles, thrilled that this was something I could share. Seconds passed. She resurfaced, gasping for air and bursting with excitement, marveling at the magic. We took turns after that, swimming underwater, painting, playing, popping up and swapping, exclaiming with amazement and delight.

Later, when we walked towards the shore, I saw some people in the shallows. I called to them and handed them my goggles, urging them to take a look below. I didn't know them, and I didn't care. I knew that what I offered was a sight they would remember all their lives. I didn't hesitate; I wasn't shy; I didn't wonder what they'd think of me.

I wanted them to see this other world. Starstruck, I forgot my very self.

Love &

. . . loving

Love & knitting
Peppermint Magazine, May 2023 (Published as: "Stitch by loving stitch")

The first present my grandmother gave my grandfather, which he received in the post for his seventeenth birthday, was two knitted vests and a knitted cardigan. "The first thing I thought was: how long does it take to make three? Three!" Grandad recalls. He's almost as astonished now as he was then.

My Nanna tells me she didn't *plan* to make so many. She just kept on knitting them. She didn't say: "I'm going to make three." She "just" started, then she "just" kept going. "In Guyra, what else do you do? You just keep knitting."

If Theo had doubted Helen's affection, the present would have given her away. But Grandad says he knew she was sweet on him from the day they met.

It was a Sunday in 1947 and he was passing through Guyra with his uncle. They stopped by a shop owned by some fellow immigrants and he wandered out the back. Upon seeing my fifteen-year-old grandad, my fourteen-year-old grandma fled the room. But then she reappeared. With her hair done and a favorite outfit on, she walked up to him and said two words: "I'm Helen." The rest is history.

The knits, Nanna's first attempts at anything so difficult, were a perfect fit, Grandad recalls. "A *perfect* fit." What's more, they arrived in a high-class, *real leather* suitcase. I know from Nanna that the wool was high-class too: *bluebell crepe.* What she can't recall is how she saved enough while working in her parents' shop to pay for it.

I ask my grandfather how often he wore the knits. "Do you know how cold it was in Katoomba?" he asks. Often, I conclude.

They'd been writing to one another for about two years by that stage, but there'd been no grand declarations of love. I like to think of those three knits, of all the thought and time and care woven through each one, as Helen's first.

After that, she knit another cardigan, and then another. *Full cardigans*, my grandad notes. This wasn't just some fling; this was serious.

Years later their eldest son, while a second-year doctor at Launceston Hospital, would meet a first-year girl who knitted too, a girl who within months would begin to knit for him.

*

I can't ask my father how he felt when he first received a sweater from my mom; he died when I was five. But I know from our old photographs and slides that he wore them all the time.

When I ask Mom whether she started knitting for Dad before or after they started dating, she laughs. She remembers liking my loud, gregarious, practical-joke-loving dad well enough, but is adamant that she didn't have feelings for him right away. "It takes a while to knit a sweater, so they might have developed over time," she laughs.

While the state of the young doctor's existing sweaters, which were wearing through at the elbows, might have provoked a powerful urge to knit replacements right away, Mom resisted. But one thing led to another, and within four months of meeting, they were dating.

There was no stopping her now. Without delay she surreptitiously measured one of his old sweaters and chose a pattern. She remembers knitting on a break one day and admitting to a registrar the sweater was for Dad. "Entrapment syndrome," he said. She insists that this wasn't the plan. But by the time it was finished, they were engaged.

"I would have started maybe in March and got it done in six weeks," she says. "I finished that one and pretty soon afterwards I started another one. His birthday wasn't till September; there was no reason," she says.

Later, after they were married and they were working as flying doctors in the Northern Territory, she remembers knitting to distract herself in small rickety planes. Later still, she recalls knitting, praying, knitting, at a hospital as surgeons cut into my father's brain, then stitched it closed again. My younger brother was there too, being knit together in her womb.

*

I ask my mom what my dad's reaction to that first sweater was. "I think he was pretty pleased—he must have been, because then I started knitting him another one. The other one was 'fair isle,' so it was tan and red and brown."

"Actually, he's wearing it in photos the year that he died," she notes. "They wear well."

I want to know what brought more joy: the knitting—the anticipation—or seeing the sweaters worn.

"I think when I was knitting the first sweater, I would have been thinking a lot about the pleasure he would have in getting it, and the surprise," Mom says. "It's always fun to be planning a surprise for someone." There was added pleasure knowing the gift would be useful and used.

"I've never been that interested in craft, where you just think: what do I do with it now?" she says. She'd much rather think: "what will they like, what color would suit, what would be practical?" The *best* part, however, wasn't the lead-up. It was seeing them worn.

"Not just for the look of it—for the comfort; knowing they're warm; because those sweaters are way warmer than what you'd actually buy."

I love this. I think about the comfort knitting brought my mom, the literal warmth it brought my dad, and the outlet it provided for Dad's mom, then for her, to channel love.

Wool is a material, needles are a tool, and neither is very special on its own. But in the hands of knitters, they're transformed. When you add time, skill, and affection, treasures that can warm another's body and their heart emerge; minute by minute, stitch by loving stitch, treasures that might last them their whole life.

Cost of living
CPX, September 2023

I know what's meant by "cost of living." I know it's about money, the economy, inflation, interest rates. But don't you think those words, so often chanted in the news, could be taken from or used to make a poem?

Cost of living. I think less about the rising price of rent, of petrol, milk, and bread, than of parents sick with worry, up all night, waiting for their teen to return home; a grown man, helping a father who no longer knows his name, to bed; a school girl who sees her friend "forgot" his lunch again, and pretends to not want hers. It reminds me of the always worthwhile, often costly task—of loving.

Cost of living. Like burden of care, like right to die, it's said so casually but it can make me want to weep. It reminds me of how bleak this life can be and often is.

It reminds me of a survey in which one in two respondents thought that disability should qualify an adult to ask for help to die. 43 percent deemed mental illness valid grounds; some thought homelessness or poverty were too.

It's one thing to cry, "My life is not worth living!" when you're facing profound hardship, when you're in relentless pain, but I wonder what it's like when others, rather than protest, agree.

We've all suffered in this place, some less, some more—and doubtless will. Thinking of "the cost" there sometimes is to carry on, stirs me to lament. But then my spirits rise with what comes next. The task: beautiful and noble, full of wonder, laced with hope—"of living."

Sex, love, and consent
CPX, April 2021

In Taffy Brodesser-Akner's 2019 novel *Fleishman is in Trouble*, there is a scene where the main character, Toby Fleishman, is having dinner with a woman he found on a hookup app, but has only ever met for casual sex.

> *As she studies the menu, Fleishman studies her:*
> *If you looked closely, she had about two centimetres of gray hair at her temples. She had said she was forty-five. She might actually be forty-eight. That's almost fifty . . . She reached across the table to take his hand. He squeezed hers back. He never realized her arms were so hairy. It was a dark, thick hair that grew somewhat wiry towards the wrist, like a man's. He tried to look back at her in the eye, but he suddenly couldn't bear her. What was he doing here? What had he thought he liked about her so much? She talked, a vapid prattle of superficial nonsense . . . She was newly shy, and newly confused, sensing an annoyance from him. He felt bad about it, but that's what sunlight does sometimes. It shows you what you couldn't quite see in the dark.*

On this occasion, consent won't be a problem because Dr. Fleishman pretends the hospital has called him into work. He has no real feelings for this woman. She's the object of his gaze, not his affection.

Throughout Brodesser-Akner's book we're confronted by a culture where we've become so casual about sex that we no longer consider looking at naked strangers or even sleeping with them, well, strange; where what is becoming strange is the notion of exercising self-control to abstain from sexual activity, or using boundaries such as a committed relationship to confine it.

Yet the novel also depicts Fleishman's shock when he finds his nine-year-old son has been exploring hard-core porn online, and his horror when he's told his eleven-year-old daughter has sent a photo of her nipple to a boy. The fraught connections between the mores we practice, and those we want for our children, play out before the reader's eyes.

In recent times, a succession of news stories about sexual harassment has many talking about the issue of consent.

There was the petition detailing thousands of alleged sexual assaults and a subsequent crisis meeting of NSW principals. There were nationwide protests calling for stronger measures to stop gendered violence and sexual harassment. There was the hasty, largely misguided suggestion that apps could be used to record consent.

It's one thing to teach children about consent, but if the culture around us suggests sexual encounters between people who don't really care about each other are OK, it's unsurprising that confusion about what's not OK is rising too.

Again, a novel offers further insight, in this case Delia Owens's *Where the Crawdads Sing*. It's not set in the present day, but we all know consent isn't a recent problem.

The main character is living a lonely, loveless life when, in a rare moment of human contact, a man she barely knows comes onto her. She's attracted to him too, but feeling used, she pulls away and runs.

"As long as she ranted, sobs couldn't surface. But nothing could stop the burning shame and sharp sadness. A simple hope of being with someone, of actually being wanted, of being touched, had drawn her in. But these hurried groping hands were only a *taking*, not a *sharing* or *giving*."

The italics are Owens's, but they serve me well. If we want to stop people from feeling used and being abused—taken, not given— we need laws and practices that flow from a deeply-held concern for the other, not the abrupt imposition of a shallow one.

We need to see a whole person, stop to consider them, and start to care about them. If we care with heart as well as mind, with body and with soul, if we feel respect for a person, treating them with respect stops being a counter-intuitive learned behavior. We stop doing it because we have to; we do it because we want to.

We're already asking our teens to insist on consent for themselves and obtain it from others. But are we asking them to care about the person they are sexually attracted to? To expect care from that person? To realize that treating another human being only as someone who may or may not give them what they want will likely lead to hurt, because that someone has feelings? Are we recognizing the fact that the most vulnerable people, the most insecure, might sometimes be the most likely to give consent?

If we really want to reduce the risk of people hurting and being hurt, we need to raise the bar. We don't just need to stop seeing people as objects, or start demanding "enthusiastic consent;" we need to stop separating sex from love.

Everything that isn't broken
Pilgrim Hill Literary Prize 2022 (adult nonfiction)

It wasn't until I was thirty-seven-years old, married with three children under ten, that I began to appreciate the fact that I had full custody of my children. Better still, I shared it with my husband who—and this suddenly seemed too perfect to be true—was also their father.

Custody. Such a cold, clinical word. I'd never really thought about keeping it because I'd never really thought about losing it.

I'd seen the different ways families could be torn apart and thrown together, but I hadn't fully realized it might happen to any couple any time, or rather, any couple over time.

I knew there were spouses who could no longer speak to each other, let alone live together; that some mothers and fathers had to fight for every minute they spent with their kids—but I hadn't seen it unfold up close.

Now, I knew multiple once-besotted now-estranged couples who were negotiating custody arrangements. Now, I had seen people I loved betray people they were meant to love. Now, I was hearing that terrible word again and again. And I couldn't look away; no close friend could.

I started to wonder how it might feel to be left for another, how it might feel if your children hated, even loved—even preferred—them; how you would bear it if your time with them was cut in half—*in half!*—when they're already growing up, up and away, so fast.

I started wondering these things, and wondering at the fact I hadn't wondered them before, and I realized the things you don't think about might be just as telling as the things you do.

They say you don't know what you've got till it's gone, and sometimes that's true, but sometimes you realize what you have while it's still there. And you see how undeserved it is, how precious and how fragile, how unlikely, how in need of tender care.

In a world where anything could happen any time, you realize every mercy is a gift.

My "invisible friend," our "normal" life: Learning to live with chronic pain
ABC, January 2023

My invisible friend has an office in the corner of our bedroom. On either side of his computer sit two pots filled with grass. He mows them with scissors. On the floor by his desk is a dark, glossy palm, and on our dresser is a fern with leaves that are translucent in the sun.

My husband's office doubles as a garden and a music studio. Between the plants there is a microphone, speakers, a mixing desk, keys. When he's not working for money, he's making songs for fun. On a good day, that is.

On a good day, he can move from the bed in the middle of the room to the chair in the corner. On a good day, he's still in constant pain, but can distract himself. On a good day, he's able to eat dinner at the table, not in bed. On a *really* good day, he's able to walk the length of our short street or hang out with our noisy, active boys.

My closest friend barely leaves the house. He doesn't drive or walk the kids to school. He doesn't come with us to dinners, parties, parks. He was isolating before isolating was a thing.

You wouldn't know if you could see him. You wouldn't know if you joined him on a call with colleagues from around the world, if you saw him solving problems with solutions no one else had thought to try. You might mistake the greenery for an interest in horticulture. You wouldn't know the garden grew from his frustration, at spending nearly all his time inside.

It's been months; no, it's been years. I've had time to make new friends. Some have been here on a day when he's been able to emerge and say hello; others haven't glimpsed him; some don't even realize he exists. The old friends know the truth, but it's hard to keep in touch with one who's stuck between four walls, to remember one who's always out of sight, to call and know quite what to ask or say.

A newer friend who's met him has a husband who works in the same field. He tried to find my friend online. But he isn't on Facebook, or Twitter, or LinkedIn. Her husband was unable to confirm that mine exists.

*

If we had known married life without poor health, his illness would have floored us. But we'd already had a taste of chronic pain. More than a taste.

It started just before we met. I'm told he was unstoppable: running, riding, dancing—always moving, never still. At first it was a headache, that was all. But it lasted days, then weeks, then months. We joked it was an allergy to me. But I was there to stay, and so was it.

The headache was relentless. He couldn't finish college, couldn't work. But he was young. Those things could wait till he got better, or so we thought. In time, his ability to push pain to one side led him back to study, then to work. He kept quiet about his pain; he didn't *look* to be in pain, so it was easy to pretend it wasn't so. Some friends assumed the "headaches" must have passed (few could comprehend it was just one that never stopped). Others just forgot he was in pain. Sometimes, I did too.

Two years after meeting, we married. I promised to love him in sickness and (we hoped) in health. A few years later, we moved to Sydney. We worked, lived the city life, and then moved home to have a child. We settled; we traveled. We had another child, and then one more. We started looking old. And through it all, his poor head ached.

Over the years he had scans, saw experts, tried everything from Botox to acupuncture to prescription drugs. Nothing worked, but looking back, *those were the days!* He was in pain, but could still walk and drive, leave the house, barbecue with friends, even travel overseas for work.

In a moment of hope—or madness or despair—he bought a little boat to fix and sail. But such projects took a toll; it gathered dust. Later, he found a Datsun to restore. It sat on our front lawn, obscured more and more by thriving grass.

A good day then was different from a good day now. On one of those days, he sailed the boat with our eldest son. He was back within the hour, but what mattered was he went. On another day, he tinkered with the Datsun; kids in the tray, "helping" with the tools; a dream fulfilled, in part.

*

Then he had routine surgery. His recovery was slow. His good days began to disappear; most days were worse days. Now he had a "new daily persistent headache" *and* post-surgical nerve pain. Now it hurt to stand, to sit, to sing, to walk downstairs to where his office was. But surely he'd recover; this new thing would pass. We maintained hope.

He saw his doctor. The pain persisted. He saw another doctor. The pain persisted. He had injections to numb his nerves. They didn't work. His brain seemed strangely determined to remember pain and keep on sending signals, even if a threat had passed, even if a wound had healed. They put him on one drug, then another, and another. He stopped driving, exercising, making his own lunch. We started to adjust. We didn't want to give up hope, but had to face the fact that this new pain and these new limitations might remain.

About a year after the surgery, he gave up on the Datsun. Then the sailboat. He started buying ergonomic pillows and pill boxes and track pants. He gave away his dress shoes and his jeans. He used the kind of table that you see in hospitals, to work from bed.

Before the pandemic, I went to one of his appointments. I wanted to make sure he wasn't downplaying his pain, and its effect on our lives. I worried that his stoic stance was leading those who treated him astray, that he bore too much too well. In front of a doctor and a nurse I'd never met, who I hoped might understand if I could give them the right words, I wept.

*

When we first married, we wondered when the headache would pass. Later, we found a way to live with it. We could still do "normal" things; they would just take a toll. Too much activity and the pain would escalate; he'd pay the price for days. Instead of going camping for a week, we'd try two nights; instead of going hiking, we'd choose an easy walk; instead of entertaining as a couple, I'd do more with my friends.

In time, we accepted that the way things were might be the way things stayed. We prayed. We trusted we'd been heard even if it didn't seem that way. Our deepest hope was not good health.

We didn't think bad luck would strike us twice. I didn't realize the oversight—the subconscious assumption we'd already had our turn—until it did. Now I know it might yet strike again. Getting better and not getting better are only two possibilities. Many more exist; we needn't entertain them all.

And who knows. Maybe we've had miracles as well. It seems incredible my husband can still manage full-time work, if not from our office, from our room. More remarkably, he's not depressed. But even if he were—even if he couldn't earn a wage, make music, trim his plants—he could still love and still be loved. There's meaning and dignity in that.

*

I wonder what you're thinking as you read this. Perhaps you've suffered so much that this doesn't sound like suffering at all; perhaps you're feeling empathy, marveling at your luck. By all means, feel for us, but you needn't pity us. Our sorrows don't compare to all our joys.

Yes, sometimes my dear friend—my husband, my lover—wonders if there's much more he can take. Sometimes, when I think about his suffering, I despair. And I dwell on what I miss: taking him places other than the hospital, spending time with other families *as* a family, being a couple in the world. I miss sharing the load of three active boys with their dad; I miss asking him for help, and just expecting it. I'm saddened by how much of our children's lives he's only seen in photographs, and by how much he hasn't seen at all.

If we believed this life were all there is, perhaps we'd panic or feel robbed, or become depressed. But we imagine and dare to hope that it is not, that even suffering might somehow be a gift.

*

I realize it's OK to lament loss—to long for better days, "normality"—but it helps to remember that I'm not *entitled* to any of the things I miss or want. Most of the time, I don't dwell on them. Most of the time, I dwell on the fact that we're surrounded by family and friends, by prayers and support, by loving care and offers of help. And when I'm weary of my "carer's" load, I remember that I'd rather be the one stuck with the *doing* than the one in constant pain.

I'm especially thankful that this other half of mine is still the person I married. If anything, he's a better person: stronger, humbler, more gracious, more wise. He doesn't ask, *Why me?* He asks, with otherworldly calm, *Why not?* He accepts that there are things we cannot know. He knows that he can wallow, or try to suffer well. He suffers well. He doesn't dwell on what he cannot do; he looks for what is possible, and acts.

My other half supports me in whatever ways he can. He tries not to complain, to ask me for too much; he doesn't try to keep me for himself; and he listens to me, loves me, very well. He works full-time despite his full-time pain so I can work less and have more time with the kids. He shares the mental load; he brainstorms ways to help me, writes them down; he's present for and patient with us all.

He's also a good patient. Even when the exercises from the physio hurt, when those from the psychologist take discipline and time, when benefits are slow to show—or don't—he perseveres.

He always has a goal. To find the "powers" for a board game with the kids. To walk around the block, to attempt some kind of family holiday—even if he's inside the whole time. And, effortlessly, almost every day, he makes me laugh. There's no car now, no little boat. But he's always got a project that he's quietly working on. A song. A new way to make new music from his bed. A program that solves problems others don't. A new idea.

Meanwhile, I run around busily and play around with words. When I say that I'm now writing about him and about us, he doesn't seem surprised. When I finish, I attach it to an email, write *I'm so scared to show you this*, click "Send." He doesn't open the attachment right away. Pain levels are high, energy is low, and part of him is surely scared like me, for reading it will be a little like reading my mind.

Days pass before he comes to me and says he's read my words. To my relief and his, those words ring true. The page that he and I are on—even after fifteen years—is the same one. We wonder: should we keep this story close? Or let it out into the world?

*

In the end we chose to let it out. I sent it to a magazine that knocked it back. I sent it out again and then again. Some editors replied, some never did. Some praised it *then* declined, some just said "pass." And time passed too. More than a year. In that time, he had some better days. Meditation seemed to help his mind to slightly dull the pain. He started walking round the block again. He moved his office back downstairs. I thanked God, and I thanked our praying friends. I thought with trembling: *Is this the beginning of the end? Will our lives be different now?*

The moment didn't last, but we made the most of it. As it began to slip away, he fought. He'd still start work in the office, even if he ended it in bed; he'd still set off on a walk, even if he turned right back around.

Since then he's had more bad days, but better days and weeks as well. We just spent two nights in a cabin by a beach. He only left it once, but still, he came! He even left it once! He ate fish and chips with us—outside! On grass! Our family was together in our car. We put on sunny songs, thought sunny thoughts, brainstormed "things that you could fit inside your nose."

I can't tell you how our story ends. I didn't plot it and I cannot flick ahead. But I trust the one who's writing it, an author whose intentions are mysterious but always good. An author whose face cannot be seen, whose love abounds, who fills bewildered hearts with hope.

Why fewer frills made our wedding day more fun
Hello May, March 2023 (Published as "Frills vs Thrills.")

My husband and I married young and on a budget. His late grandfather was known for saying people shouldn't make any major life decisions before they turned twenty; my husband was nineteen.

I bought a dress on sale for about one hundred dollars. It wasn't technically a wedding dress but it looked like one to me. We didn't want to choose which friends and family to invite so, despite our budget, we made it open-invite.

How could an open-invite wedding *and reception* be compatible with a tight budget? We held the wedding at a park and the reception in my family's backyard; we asked guests to please bring picnic rugs. Our wedding car was a friend-of-a-friend's combi. There was no three-course meal; instead we focused on afternoon tea: multiple flavors of ice cream, extravagant toppings, cups and cones, homemade wedding cake, tea—in bags!—and brace yourself . . . *instant* coffee.

There was no band; instead my husband sang a song he wrote for me, a gift better than any diamond ring.

My mother was concerned some guests would prefer savory to sweet, my father-in-law thought some would expect alcohol. We said they were welcome to arrange some sandwiches and wine; happily, they did.

Friends still tell me it was one of the best weddings they've attended, and I still believe them. It helped that we hadn't attended many weddings ourselves—while we broke some rules knowingly, we were blissfully oblivious to others. Either way, we trusted our friends and family to care about us more than the food or drinks or entertainment.

One of the benefits we enjoyed later was the leftovers: instead of returning from our honeymoon with debts to pay, we returned to a freezer full of ice cream and a cupboard full of (waffle) cones. Another, in the coming months and years, was being spared those awkward moments where you talk about your wedding to a friend, then realize they weren't invited.

A further benefit of having a low-key wedding day was that we could enjoy the lead-up more. We didn't spend all our time planning a wedding. We lay around listening to music and we hung out with friends; we looked forward to starting a life together without a distracting, perhaps overwhelming, to-do list.

The casual approach gave the ceremony prominence as well; the "frills" we added here and there did not outshine the moment where I said yes to him and he to me—the moment that the day was all about.

Dating advice from a clueless mom

2022

There are some articles I've only ever joked about writing, with no intention of putting pen to paper. An article about online dating is—was—one of them. I've only had two boyfriends in my forty years, and both were good friends first. I've never even used a dating app. I lack experience, let alone expertise. But here I am.

It started with a conversation with friends about looking for love in the age of the internet. It was a topic none of us knew very much about—all of us had stumbled upon love in more old-fashioned ways; we'd had "other halves" (and kids) for years.

Somewhere between wondering whether "trialing" multiple people at once could be considered OK, and at what point in a relationship you could be audacious enough to ask exactly where you stood, I made a ridiculous statement with great conviction. It was met with merciless laughter, deservedly so.

What I said was that, within the first date or two, I'd want to meet the person in their home.

In my defense, I was remembering (or misremembering?) a study where researchers compared information that could be gleaned about someone's personality by interviewing them, with information that could be gleaned by snooping around their house. The snooping was apparently much more telling.

I was speaking through laughter as I tried to justify myself: to explain how reluctant I'd be to trust anyone I'd met in a bubble; how quickly I'd want to test their claims, connect them to real people, real places, real life. Can't anyone claim anything, if it's just you and them and neutral ground?

But as these friends so rightly pointed out, if you don't trust someone, do you *really* want to be *that* alone with them?

I had alternative suggestions—surprise them at work, demand referees, insist on meeting their friends and family (and quiz them when you do)—but my credibility, shaky to begin with, was shot.

Another flaw in the get-inside-their-house-to-suss-them-out plan was that the person would likely be suspicious—and not without reason—of *you* (especially if they caught you snooping through their stuff).

Even if there were some kind of not-creepy, not-weird way to have a good snoop, there's no guarantee you'd learn anything useful, or that any conclusions you drew from your observations would be correct.

But I reckon the suggestions I made while backpedaling did have some merit.

Why not ask to meet their friends sooner rather than later? Why not give those friends a light interrogation? (I'm thinking, *how do you know X? Not, so . . . has X ever been arrested?*)

Yes, your date might feel scrutinized and think you weird, but surely it would speed up the equally weird *is-this-person-really-who-they-say-they-are?* stage—especially if you let them meet *your* friends too.

Granted, my first idea was a dangerous one, and my second suggestion an awkward one with plenty of potential for disaster—but so is keeping the people closest to us away from the people who might want to be.

I don't stand by my initial advice, but I do stand by this: Just as close friends can prevent us from thinking a terrible idea is a good one, they might also save us from a terrible relationship.

Sorrow in statistics
CPX, June 2021

I took part in a national survey about child abuse this week. To better understand the problem, its impact, and possible solutions, the researchers aim to interview ten thousand randomly-selected Australians.

The questions were very specific and intensely personal. I was asked whether a parent had ever told me they wished I'd never been born, whether a partner had ever blamed me for their violence, whether I'd ever been locked up or starved. I was asked about my height and my weight and my income and my health.

At the end, I was asked whether I'd found the interview upsetting. I'd answered "no" to all the awful questions, now I answered yes. The interviewer seemed surprised.

I was upset because the sheer detail and number of questions in the survey told a terrible story. A story of Australians who have suffered because people who are supposed to love them, who perhaps do love them in strange and messed-up ways, have deliberately hurt them.

I wondered how many participants had suffered, how many had spoken up, and how many, even with the assurance of anonymity, were still too ashamed or too afraid.

I also wondered how the researchers were faring. It's easy to celebrate the love and compassion humans are capable of, it's harder to scrutinize our failings. But to gain insight, to change for the better, we need to do both.

It's a tension I'm familiar with. My faith has taught me that while we can and should work to change ourselves, our efforts will always fall short in this fallen world. It's why my ultimate hope is not in humanity, but in a power beyond.

At first, she fled
Antipodes, Janurary 2026

Theo

The first time Theo saw Helen, she fled. But that's not where the story starts, Theo says.

It began about a year earlier, when he met her elder sister Rene.

She was visiting his parents' shop in Katoomba with his auntie Kalimeras. Rene and Theo started talking, and before long she was telling him about a sister back in Guyra who would suit him.

"She's good looking, she's blonde, she's got this nice personality, and she's not like me," Rene said.

Theo chuckles. "*She's not like me. I love that.*"

Twelve months later, in 1947, he had the opportunity to accompany his uncle on a trip.

"We were going to Grafton. And on the Sunday morning, I knew we were going to go through Guyra," Theo says.

He also knew they would stop by Rene's family shop on the way. Her mother and his parents were from the same small island and the same tiny village in Greece.

Theo remembers standing in front of a mirror in his hotel room, wondering if he'd meet this young girl Rene had "recommended."

"I was fifteen, and I combed my hair especially."

They arrived in Guyra at midday on a Sunday. They didn't realize it at the time, but they had a 12:30 p.m. deadline. Any later and the shop would have been closed for Sunday lunch, he says.

He's told the story a thousand times, but he still stops at this point every time, and marvels at his luck.

Helen

Helen remembers the day well.

Her mother always washed the sheets on Sundays, and Helen had just finished helping her hang them on the line. She was sitting in the kitchen with curlers in her hair, warming herself by the stove.

"The curlers were, I don't know if you'd remember . . . Well, years ago we used to get our apples sent from Batlow," she says. "They would pack the apples, and they would wrap them in tissue paper. We would keep it. Rene taught me how to do my hair."

She didn't bother every day, but sometimes liked to on weekends.

"So I'm sitting in the kitchen. We had a big stove . . . And on the side of the stove was a tank that was filled with water, so that was our hot water.

"It was a cold day—it was the middle of June—and I'm sitting in the kitchen, and I've got my feet up on the side of the urn there, and Theo opens the door.

"I take one look at him, and here I am—a head full—and I take one look at him and I just go whoosh! I'm out."

I ask her what she saw in that flash of time.

"I thought he looked pretty handsome," she says, smiling.

Did she have any idea what this stranger was doing in her kitchen?

"No, I didn't even know who he was. But I thought, for him to come to the kitchen, he must have to have the OK from Dad to make this distance. So I raced upstairs and I took my hair out, and I put on a nice brown skirt and a pink blouse, and I came downstairs. And your Grandad was out in the backyard, and I walked up to him and I said: I'm Helen."

Theo

"We got there just before the shop closed, which was the first stroke of luck," Theo says.

He walked inside and was introduced to "Mister Comino."

"I said, 'I know your daughter Rene,' and he said, 'Oh, well Rene's somewhere out the back if you'd like to go through the shop.'"

Theo left his uncle and the "old people" at the front and went through to the back.

"And I opened the door, and I saw this girl."

It was the middle of winter and it was freezing cold, he says. Her hair was tied up with apple papers and she was sitting with her feet up against a stove.

"And—I can't believe it—as soon as she saw me coming through the door, she looked around and just streaked past me," Theo says.

Before he knew quite what had happened, she'd run upstairs.

"Not a word. Just went straight past.

"Anyhow, I walked out the back and I was just standing out in the back garden behind the shop. And then after a while this girl came down—good looking, blonde, with a good personality—just walked up to me and said, 'I'm Helen.'

"What a memory."

Helen

I ask Helen if she suddenly felt as confident as those two words suggest.

She says she wasn't usually so assertive, but in that moment, she did have a strange kind of confidence. Perhaps it was the outfit, or the hair, or both. Whatever it was, the girl who'd run away moments before was gone.

"And then we started talking."

Later, Helen asked Theo if they would stay for a day or two. He said, "Oh, I'm going up to the coast," or maybe it was, "I'm going fishing," and she said, "Oh. You're going."

She was annoyed, she says. Already, she wanted him to stay.

Later, over lunch perhaps, someone else asked if they were staying; Helen blurted out, "No! He's going fishing!"

She asks if I've heard the story of how Theo went on the trip in the first place.

Theo, like Helen, lived above the shop his parents ran. He spent most of his time upstairs, downstairs, or at school, and not by choice. But his father's brother, who also worked in the shop, went to Queensland every winter. Theo, who'd always longed to get away, begged his uncle to let him tag along.

"He said he would wash the car, do anything," Helen says, and eventually, his uncle agreed.

"And Theo will tell you that the Sunday that I met him, they came at half past twelve," she notes.

His uncle could have easily said no and gone alone; they could have easily arrived five minutes later.

"But that's a different story. My destiny was for us to have the shop open and for Theo—your Grandad—to walk in."

Present day

It's a mild winter's evening when I interview my grandad. The place is Bondi Junction, the year is 2016, and instead of living above a shop, he and my nanna live in a high-rise apartment block surrounded by shops.

This Theo is in his eighties, though he's not unlike the Theo of his twenties. His hair's not as black as it once was, but he still has plenty to comb, and when he has Helen on his arm, they make a stylish couple.

Only last year a friend of mine compared a photo of Theo to Harrison Ford. Instead of being flattered when I told him, he feigned outrage: "Harrison Ford! Harrison Ford? Couldn't it be Gregory Peck or Carey Grant?!"

Technically, my grandad is an old man now. But if you talk to him you'll realize he's also a child, a teenager, and a young adult—he's thirty-three, and middle-aged, and more—because surely you're never just one age; you're every age you've ever been at once.

My grandparents, my mother, and I are sitting in their kitchen, the peak hour rush below us and towers of light all around. We've just finished a feast of roast lamb and vegetables, and now that the kids are in bed, we're sitting down to rizogalo with ice-cream and fruit and cups of tea.

I planned to start the interview later in the evening, but when Theo launches into a story, I tell him I'm pressing record.

"Isn't she alert, this kid?" he says, and continues.

In the minutes that follow he goes from talking about sudoku puzzles and how Helen "shattered" his ego, to why she resembles an Olympic champion and is "a ruthless killer." I'm glad I pressed record.

"So, two weeks ago we start," he says of the sudoku puzzle. "We start at half past six, and we work on it for half an hour, till Helen gets ready to go to the hospital.

"We're struggling. I come home in the afternoon, we both sit, and try and help each other.

"I tried the pencil. I rubbed it out with the guess I was making—for instance, a two can only go here or here—so I chose one position to put the two, then kept going. So, I rubbed it out ten times; Helen had a lot of trouble as well.

"Come nightfall, we're still attacking this puzzle. After about half an hour, Helen gets it out and triumphantly says, 'I've got it!'"

Helen interrupts with the punchline: "And I didn't use the pencil!"

"See, if you get it out without using the pencil, it makes you much smarter," Theo says to me; then to Helen: "You shattered my ego when you got it."

But this is not the demeanor of a man with a shattered ego; this is the demeanor of a competitor who's delighted by his competition, and a husband who's proud of his wife. Her achievements are his, and his are hers.

I ask whether Helen's become more competitive with age. He says she's been like that since they met.

"She's got the makings of an Olympic champion," he says, warming to his theme. "When you read the stories of Federer, when he was seventeen, he would cry—every time he lost, he'd start crying. And he needed professional help to stop him getting so upset when he lost."

Of course, my grandmother doesn't start bawling if somebody beats her in a competition, but she does have "that Olympic-type thinking," Theo says. "See, outside appearances, she's this lovely softie, but if you get her in a competition—if you get her in a competition . . ." I'm laughing; we all are. I ask if he can remember the moment he first discovered the trait.

"It was well before the wedding," he says. "I kept trying to beat her at tennis, and I tried every trick in the book to make her feel sorry for me—"

Helen: "No, I think when he found out was when we had a game of Monopoly."

Theo abandons the tennis story in favor of the Monopoly tale.

"I'm sixteen; Helen's fifteen. This ruthless killer! We're sitting here playing Monopoly, right, and I'm in trouble—I've mortgaged Mayfair.

"And I said, to who I thought loved me and was my girlfriend,
I said, 'Can you lend me two hundred pounds, just for one round?'"
He turns to his girlfriend. "You remember that one?"
"Yeah, I remember that one," she says, smiling.

Father, Stranger, Friend
December 2022

Some time after writing the following essay, I read The Bright Hour by Nina Riggs. Riggs, a mother who was diagnosed with terminal cancer at the age of thirty-eight, talks about how a friend-of-a-friend emailed her out of the blue one day about losing his mother when he was nine. "In the message, he lists all the things he remembers about his mom and all the ways she remains in his life: her favorite flower, the books she read him, her sense of humor," she writes. And then: "She is far from a hole in my life. She is an enormous presence that can never be replaced." My father died when I was five. What follows is a letter that I penned to him when I was thirty-nine. It's about love, loss, memory, friendship, hope; and "an enormous presence in my life that can never be replaced."

About six years ago, I asked your mom and dad if I could write about their lives. I'd often conduct interviews for work, and write articles based on strangers' words; but I was failing to uncover and preserve the stories that I wanted for myself.

Your parents were in Sydney, I was not; with your father hard of hearing, conversations had to happen face-to-face. And so the next time I was visiting, we set aside some time; I pressed record. I flew home with my luggage and their words—sound waves trapped, preserved. And then, although this had not been the plan, I started mining your wife's memories as well.

At the time, I was nearly thirty-four, your dying age. My eldest child was five, the age I was when last I was with you. Very soon I realized that my "project" wasn't just about my grandparents, or my mom; it was about me finding you, the dad I barely knew.

But no, that "barely" couldn't quite be true. When I thought about *my* five-year-old and *me*, I knew it to be wrong. Memory is a funny thing, preserving trivia while leaking gold. But the leaks cannot change history. Whatever memories I lack—however many I have lost—cannot change how well I knew you, loved you, then.

*

You were an active kid, I'm told; always on adventures. As you grew you ventured further, through the cities and through bush, interstate, and overseas, usually with friends. You had so many friends.

"As soon as he'd come back he'd make this one phone call," your father said to me.

"Max, or Andrew, or The Wombat . . . And for the next twenty-four hours, the phone didn't stop ringing. We never bothered answering. When he was in the house we never answered the phone. Not once."

Your wife—my mom—who you met when you were interns at Launceston Hospital, said you were always sending and receiving letters too. I think about the letters I once wrote to your parents and your auntie Jude, over many years; of brimming boxes they refuse to throw away. Did this tendency of mine originate with you?

You had so many close friends, my mother said. At first she almost doubted all were real. And when you weren't going on about old mates and past adventures, you were inviting new mates to join future ones. You were always *organizing* people; my friends would surely sympathize with yours.

Another thing about you, I've been told, was that you'd maintain these many friendships over many, many years. Is it coincidence that I do this as well? Just this month I went away with friends I met back in year one, and just today I spoke to friends made interstate twelve years ago. I have not, will not, let them go.

But you, you took things further, I am told. When your year ten English teacher moved to Canberra, she said if any student found themselves in town then they should visit her.

"Well," Mom says to me, "who would do that?"

You, apparently. Because one day she opened her front door and found your face, beaming into hers. You'd convinced a friend to join you and you'd cycled there from Sydney, just like that.

When I transcribed that part I laughed. I started reading it aloud, to my husband—who you haven't met but would, I've no doubt love—and ended up a sobbing mess.

Your character was building; my love, and a lament, were building too.

*

Your parents and your wife, my Nanna, Grandad, Mom, have always shared their memories generously; they made sure we kids, who cannot know you now, know who you were. They resolved to be intentional, to pass on every detail that they could. I used to take their tales for granted, the effort they put in; I listened as if nothing was at stake, as if their memories and mine would always be available. Now I saw that their stories were subject to decay, destined to break. If I didn't catch them and put them somewhere safe, there might be nothing left to grasp.

Another tale that made me laugh was about a car you bought without consulting anyone, much to your mom and dad's dismay. Grandad claims one patch had rusted through, that passengers could see a flashing patch of road beneath their feet. And legend has it that a friend once pointed out a dashboard light, blinking urgent red. You just put a band-aid over it.

Is this true? I like to think it is.

In frames, in albums, on the wall, I'd grown up with you. I'd seen you upon mountain tops, on bushwalks, on your bike, seen your wide and ready grin—the brightest thing in any room. I'd seen you and me together, too: me strapped in a seat behind you on your bike, or in your arms, gazing at your smiling, bearded face. I'd even seen a snippet of a grainy video, though the camera only briefly touched on you. Now your parents' words, your wife's, were bringing flat and feeble images to life.

I wasn't polishing *my* memories; I had so very few. I was mining theirs and making something new.

*

Mom says that near the end, when your appetite was waning but you could still feed yourself, you stopped bothering with dinner but still would embrace dessert. You chose the sweet over the savory; I do this too.

And like your parents, and like me, you loved to walk.

"What Jim thought was a really easy walk, other people would find quite hard because he was so fit," Mom said. "He'd always say, 'It's not far now, it's not far,' and it would still be miles and miles."

In your defense she said you were "a great encourager"—and that if anyone was struggling, you'd just strap their pack on your front and walk with two—but the way you defined "easy" was unique. I too have been known to display optimism that borders on delusion, to be asked to please slow down.

Hearing stories about you in adulthood now that I'm an adult too, made me think of you not so much as a father, but as a potential friend; someone my husband and I would be drawn to, someone our kids would love, someone who'd fit right in with our circle of friends.

It also made me proud. Proud of the man you were, proud you were *my* dad; proud of my grandparents, my mom. They were brave when they lost you and brave when I started asking about you; they were brave enough to read what I wrote, and brave enough to let me share it.

Dad, you'd be so proud of them as well. Mom was devoted to us kids. Your parents were devoted to us too. They flew us up to see them every year, and they flew down to see us many times. Also they spoiled us, not too little, not too much. Our childhood was so full of love, your absence wasn't often felt. We were so young, and you left this world so gradually. When you were gone we didn't weep and wail; we were still so very loved. And we no longer had to share our Mom with you. We were just kids; we didn't understand yet what we'd lost.

I'm nearly forty now, older than you ever got to be. Your mother says you weren't the kind of person she could picture growing old. She says that on their final trip to see you, driving through the dark, she saw a falling star and knew: this was the end. She wanted to be wrong but she was right.

Meanwhile my mother says you didn't really call this world your home; you would say that you were "only passing through." Death meant going to your Maker and you were not afraid; he loved you like a son. At your funeral we wore colors, bold and bright.

I know you loved us. I know you didn't want to leave us all behind. I can't imagine leaving three young kids, a spouse—

But based on what I know about you now—your passion for adventure, your deep faith—I wonder if you weren't at least a little bit excited too. One caper was concluding but another one was about to begin.

And because I share that faith, I believe we'll meet again. Perhaps we'll plan a great adventure and call a bunch of friends, make them promise to come too. And when we've finished making plans, with matching grins, we'll skip dinner and go straight to dessert.

Acknowledgments

Earnest thanks to every friend, family member, and editor who has taken the time to read my work and encourage me, and to our children, who never cease to delight and inspire me. To all who have helped me to improve a piece, or publish it, or both, thank you; I can't do this alone. Thank you especially to Huw, Mum, Mikey Lynch, Fiona Lockett, Dan and Miranda Shepheard and Natasha Moore for your feedback over the years, and Aaron Johnstone, Scott Stephens, Svetlana Stankovic, Sarah Haywood, and Jess Lewis for all you've read and edited. And thank you Jo, for the "day job" that made the freelance experiment possible, and for being the kind of boss I (still!) don't want to leave.

This collection was written one piece at a time and over years. I had no idea a book is what they would become. Further thanks go to Riley Bounds and the team at Solum, for making that happen.

Finally, thank you to anyone who has read this book—and anyone who is reading still! So many words! Such an investment, of such limited, such precious time! I don't dare dream that you enjoyed every last piece; but I hope you enjoyed most; and that there was one, at least, you loved.

Citations

Love & Friendship

On truth-telling and friend-making in fiction—and in life

Murphy, Kate. *You're Not Listening: What You're Missing and Why It Matters*. Vintage Digital, 23 January, 2020, 42.

Batuman, Elif, *Either/Or*, Jonathan Cape, 2022, 19.

My friend, the therapist

Brooks, David, *The Second Mountain: The Quest for a Moral Life* Allen Lane, 2019, xx.

Ryan Howes. "Who Doesn't Need Therapy?," *Psychology Today*, 1 July 2014, accessed 17 May, 2025, https://www.psychology today.com/au/blog/in-therapy/201407/who-doesnt-need-therapy.

Ephesians 4:15.

We can help older Australians by asking them for help

"A phone call each day to check you're OK," Red Cross, accessed 7 May, 2025, https://www.redcross.org.au/services/telecross/

Shankar, Maya, "A Slight Change of Plans: The Science of Connection," *Pushkin*, 31 August, 2022, accessed 17 May 2025, https://www.pushkin.fm/podcasts/a-slight-change-of-plans/the-science-of-connection

"About Us," Friendship Bench, accessed 17 May, 2025, https://www.friendshipbenchzimbabwe.org/about-us

Holland-Batt, Sarah, "Magical thinking and the aged-care crisis," *The Griffith Review*, 5 May, 2020, accessed 17 May, 2025, https://www.griffithreview.com/articles/magical-thinking-and-the-aged-care-crisis/

MacIntyre, Alasdair, *Dependent Rational Animals—Why Human Beings Need the Virtues*, Duckworth, 1999.

Exodus 20:12.

Proverbs 16:31.

Love & Technology

Say it in your own words: Email templates can save us time, but at what cost?
"How to say no," *Starter Story*, accessed 17 May 2025, https://www.starterstory.com/how-to-say-no

Crouch, Andy, and Toh, Justine. "Community and connection in a world of devices," *ABC Soul Search*, 14 August, 2022, accessed 18 May, 2024, https://www.abc.net.au/listen/programs/soul-search/community-and-connection-in-a-world-of-devices/14009734

Actual or artificial? As the difference becomes harder to discern, will we eventually give up trying?
Metz, Cade, "The Godfather of A.I. Leaves Google and Warns of Danger Ahead," *The New York Times*, 4 May 2023, accessed 18 May 2024, https://www.nytimes.com/2023/05/01/technology/ai-google-chatbot-engineer-quits-hinton.html

"Pause Giant AI Experiments: An Open Letter," *Future of Life*, 22 March 2023, accessed 17 May 2025, https://futureoflife.org/open-letter/pause-giant-ai-experiments/

"Statement on AI Risk," Center for AI Safety, 2024, accessed 2 June 2025, https://safe.ai/work/statement-on-ai-risk

Vincent, Michael, "Tech world warns risk of extinction from AI should be a global priority like pandemics and nuclear war," *ABC News*, 31 May 2003, accessed 17 May, 2025, https://www.abc.net.au/news/2023-05-31/techworld-warns-risk-of-extinction-from-ai-should-be-priority/102413250

Devlin, Hannah. "Model embryo with heartbeat replicates cells in early pregnancy," *The Guardian*, 19 June, 2023, accessed 18 May, 2024, https://www.theguardian.com/science/2023/jun/18/model-embryo-with-heartbeat-replicates-cells-in-early-pregnancy

Genesis 1–3.

Genesis 11.

Martinez, Rebecca, "preTenders. Outsiders," Rebecca Martinez, 2017, accessed 17 May, 2025, https://www.rebeccamartinez.com/pretenders-outsiders

Tobin, Grace; Donaldson, Amy; and Longbottom, Jessica. "My AI wife: Digital love affairs, deepfakes and deadbots—inside the generative AI experiment we're living in," *ABC*, 8 May 2023, accessed 17 May 2025, https://www.abc.net.au/news/2023-05-08/generative-artificial-intelligence-ai-deepfakes-four-corners/102288216

Rosenbergh, Josh, "Christopher Reeve Probably Would Have Hated His The Flash Cameo," *Esquire*, 16 June 2023, accessed 17 May 2025, https://www.esquire.com/entertainment/movies/a44225779/the-flash-christopher-reeve-super man-cameo-explained/

Fasanao, Joseph, "For a Student Who Used AI to Write a Paper," [also published on Twitter as: "'For Someone Who Used AI to Write a Poem"], Joseph Fasano, 16 February 2023, accessed 17 May 2025, https://josephfasano.substack.com/p/poetry-mini-lecture-for-a-student

Trust over tech: Confronting tertiary cheating

Christodoulou, Mario, "The billion dollar industry helping students cheat," *ABC Listen: Background Briefing*, 29 July, 2022, accessed 17 May, 2025, https://www.abc.net.au/listen/programs/backgroundbriefing/the-billion-dollar-industry-helping-students-cheat/13993086

"Academic cheating crackdown: 'Ruthless' websites banned in bid to disrupt criminal operations," *SBS News*, 5 August 2022, accessed 17 May 2025, https://www.sbs.com.au/news/article/academic-cheating-crackdown-ruthless-web sites-banned-in-bid-to-disrupt-criminal-operations/88a roqr6r

Sparrow, Jeff. "'Full-on robot writing': the artificial intelligence challenge facing universities," *The Guardian*, 19 November, 2022, accessed 17 May, 2025, https://amp.theguardian.com/australia-news/2022/nov/19/full-on-robot-writing-the-artificial-intelligence-challenge-facing-universities

Aquinas, Thomas. "The Summa Thelologica," *Documenta Catholica Omnia*, Accessed 17 May 2025, http://www. documentacatholicaomnia.eu/03d/1225-1274,_Thomas_ Aquinas,_Summa_Theologiae_%5B1%5D,_EN.pdf

"1 in 6 university students has admitted to cheating in online exams this year," *WONKHE*, 2 August 2022, accessed 17 May, 2025, https://wonkhe.com/blogs-sus/1-in-6-university-students-has-admitted-to-cheating-in-online-exams-this-year/

Sheep and mirrors: On being social

Internet Activity, Australia," Australian Bureau of Statistics, 2 October, 2018, accessed 17 May, 2023, https://www.abs.gov. au/statistics/industry/technology-and-innovation/ internet-activity-australia/latest-release

Bogle, Ariel, 'Fake news spreads faster online than the truth, finds biggest-ever study,' *ABC News*, 9 March, 2018, accessed 19 May, 2024, https://www.abc.net.au/news/science/2018-03 -09/who-spreads-false-news-on-twitter-bots-and-us-study/9519402

"The must-know stats from the 2018 Yellow Social Media Report,' *Sensis*, June 2018, accessed 17 May, 2025, https://www. sensis.com.au/about/our-reports/sensis-social-media-report

"Addicted," *Merriam-Webster*, accessed 17 May, 2025, https:// www.merriam-webster.com/dictionary/addicted

Cameron, Andrew J. B. *Joined-Up Life*. United Kingdom: Inter Varsity Press UK, 2011, 56–57.

Cameron, *Joined-Up*, 57.

Cameron, *Joined-Up*, 94.

"2016 Census data reveals 'no religion' is rising fast," Australian Bureau of Statistics, 3 June 2025, accessed 3 June 2025, https://www.abs.gov.au/AUSSTATS/abs@.nsf/media releasesbyReleaseDate/7E65A144540551D7CA258148000

E2B85

"Social media and narcissism," *McCrindle*, accessed 17 May, 2025, https://mccrindle.com.au/article/social-media-and-narcissism/

"Social media and narcissism," *McCrindle*.

Bright, Jim, "Diverse Curiosity," Australian Catholic University, http://www.acu.edu.au, n.d., archived at the Wayback Machine, https://web.archive.org/web/20181004232551/http://www.acu.edu.au/about_acu/our_university/publications/insight/2013/autumn/the_importance_of_curiosity

The Gottman Institute. "The Gottman Method," accessed 17 May, 2025, https://www.gottman.com/about/the-gottman-method/

Tangible, relational, unplugged: On raising 'tech-healthy' humans

"Richard Johnson Lecture: Disconnected," Centre for Public Christianity, September 2022, accessed 17 May 2025, https://publicchristianity.org/podcast/disconnected-why-technology-keeps-disappointing-us-2/

Sih, Daniel. Raising *Tech-Healthy Humans: How to reset your children's tech-habits and give them a great start to life.* Spacemakers, 2022, 36.

Sih, *Tech-Healthy*, 37.

Sih, *Tech-Healthy*, 36.

Sih, *Tech-Healthy*, 11.

Sih, *Tech-Healthy*, 11.

Sih, *Tech-Healthy*, 13.

Sih, *Tech-Healthy*, 14.

Sih, *Tech-Healthy*, 20.

Sih, *Tech-Healthy*, 15.

Sih, *Tech-Healthy*, 71.

Sih, *Tech-Healthy*, 48.

Sih, *Tech-Healthy*, 51.

Sih, *Tech-Healthy*, 39.

Sih, *Tech-Healthy*, 89.

An 'unchanged' habitat? Questioning de-extinction

"Thylacine," Colossal Laboratories & Biosciences, 2022, accessed 17 May, 2025, https://colossal.com/thylacine

Schultz, Isaac, "A 'De-Extinction' Company Says It'll Bring Back the Tasmanian Tiger," *Gizmodo*, 18 August 2022, accessed 17 May 2025, https://gizmodo.com/de-extinction-thylacine-tasmanian-tiger-colossal-1849426310

"Meet the Aussie scientist striving to bring back the Tasmanian tiger," *The Sydney Morning Herald*, 26 November, 2022, accessed 18 May, 2024, https://www.smh.com.au/national/meet-the-aussie-scientist-striving-to-bring-back-the-tasmanian-tiger-20221124-p5coxf.html

"Thylacine," Colossal.

"De-extinction," Colossal Laboratories & Biosciences, 2022, acccessed 17 May, 2025, https://colossal.com de-extinction/

"Woolly Mammoth," Colossal Laboratories & Biosciences, 2022, accessed 17 May, 2023, https://colossal.com/mammoth

Keaton Leander, Sandy, "Bringing back extinct species: If we can, should we?" *ASU News*, January 02, 2019, accessed 17 May, 2025, https://news.asu.edu/20190102-global-engagement-bringing-back-extinct-species-if-we-can-should-we

Shapiro, Beth and McDonald, Bob, "Why humans should embrace our role as meddlers of nature—so that we can do it better," CBC Radio, *Quirks and Quarks*, 17 December 2021, accessed 17 May 2025, https://www.cbc.ca/radio/quirks/july-30-best-of-quirks-quarks-holiday-book-show-1.6288812/why-humans-should-embrace-our-role-as-meddlers-of-nature-so-that-we-can-do-it-better-1.6288828

Appetite versus appreciation

Delgado, Pablo; Vargas, Cristina; Ackerman, Rakefet; and Ladislao Salmerón, "Don't throw away your printed books: A meta-analysis on the effects of reading media on reading comprehension," *Science Direct*, November 2018, accessed 18 May 2025, https://www.sciencedirect.com/science/article/

pii/S1747938X18300101

Deuteronomy 6:7–9.

Heerema, Esther, "What Is the Method of Loci?" *Very Well Health*, 21 April 2021, accessed 18 May 2025, https://www.verywell health.com/will-the-method-of-loci-mnemonic-improve-your-memory-98411

"Dementia facts and figures," Dementia, accessed 18 May 2025, https://www.dementia.org.au/about-dementia/dementia-facts-and-figures

Marschall, Sabine, "Memory objects: Material objects and memories of home in the context of intra-African mobility," *Journal of Material Culture*. February 2019, accessed 18 May, 2025,https://www.researchgate.net/publiction/331294043_'Memory_objects'_Material_objects_and_memories_of_home_in_the_context_of_intra-African_mobility

Love & Ecology

Should the human race lament extinction—or pursue it?

Powers, Richard, *Bewilderment*, Hutchinson Heinemann, 2021, 63.

Rutledge, David and Benatar, David, "The predicament of existence," *ABC Listen: The Philosopher's Zone*, 10 April 2022, accessed 17 May 2025, https://www.abc.net.au/listen/programs/philosopherszone/the-predicament-of-existence/13826088

DiCamillo, Kate, "Why Children's Books Should Be a Little Sad,'" *Time Magazine*, 12 January 2018, https://time.com/5099463/kate-dicamillo-kids-books-sad/

Job 38:2; 38:4–5.

Job 40:3–5.

Berry, Wendell. *What Are People For?*, Washington, DC: Counterpoint, 2010.

Winton, Tim, *Eyrie*, Penguin eBooks, 12 October 2013, part 3, chapter 9.

Fashion expert calls for radical reinvention
Tonti, Lucianne. *Sundressed,* Black Inc Books, 2022, 116.
Tonti, *Sundressed,* 121.
Tonti, *Sundressed,* 118.
Tonti, *Sundressed,* 123.
Tonti, *Sundressed,* 136.
Tonti, *Sundressed,* 30.
Tonti, *Sundressed,* 30.
Tonti, *Sundressed,* 9.
Tonti, *Sundressed,* 9.
Tonti, *Sundressed,* 28.

The story nature tells
Morris, Shane and Haines, David, "God's Other Book," Upstream, 1 February 2022, accessed 19 May 2024, https://upstreamcc.libsyn.com/gods-other-book-dr-david-haines
Psalm 19:1.
Rooney, Sally, *Beautiful World Where Are You,* Faber, 2021, 232-3.
Rooney, *Beautiful,* 233
Romans 1:20.
Winton, Tim and Smart, Simon, "Hope is Violent," *Life & Faith podcast,* 29 March 2018, by Centre for Public Christianity, accessed 17 May 2025, https://www.publicchristianity.org/hope-is-violent/

Ordinary wonders
Psalm 19:1–4.

Love & Parenting

Life's work
MacKellar, Maggie, *When it Rains,* Random House Australia (EPUB), 2010, chapter 16.

Why watching *Alone* with my son was time well spent
Fairall, Amy, "Our First Reactions to the 41 Approved Gear Items

for Alone Australia Contestants." We are Explorers, 2 March 2023, accessed 19 May 2024, https://weareexplorers. co/alone-australia-approved-gear-items/

Lean into playfulness, its the natural thing to do
Heti, Sheila, *Motherhood*, Harvill Secker, 2018, 15.
"About Stuart Brown," National Institute for Play, accessed 6 June 2025, https://nifplay.org/about-us/about-dr-stuart-brown/
Kline Hunnicutt, Benjamin, "Leisure and play in Plato's teaching and philosophy of learning," *Leisure Sciences*, 1990, 12(2), 211–27, accessed 6 June 2025, https://doi. org/10.1080/01490409009513101
Wall, John, "All the World's a Stage: Childhood and the play of being," in *The Philosophy of Play*, Routledge, 2013, 41.
Leyman, Teresa and Wheeler, Stephanie, *Playfulness in Coaching: Exploring Our Untapped Potential Through Playfulness*, Taylor & Francis, 2024, 82.
Leyman, Teresa and Wheeler, Stephanie, *Playfulness*, 36.
Goldberg, Natalie, *Writing Down the Bones: 30th Anniversary Edition*, Shambala Publications, 2016, 151.

Love & Learning

We will make mistakes, in life and work, but we should expect, and own them
McMillan, Tressie, Laymon, Kiese, "Two acclaimed writers on revising your life," *The New York Times: The Ezra Klein Show*, 9 November 2021, accessed 17 May, 2025, https://www.ny times.com/2021/11/09/opinion/ezra-klein-podcast-kiese-laymon.html?showTranscript=1
Saunders, George, *A swim in a pond in the rain: in which four Russians give a masterclass on writing, reading, and life.* Bloomsbury Publishing, 2021, 112.
Saunders, *A Swim*, 112–13.

When we assume someone that someone's judging us, it may be that we are unfairly judging them
Matthew 7:2.

To Wonder Still
Dillard, Annie, *The Writing Life*. HarperPerennial, 1990, 98.
Dillard, 98.

On rhythm and judgement
Matthew 20:1–16.
John 10:10.
Genesis 3.

On connotations, and contentment
Miranda, L, Lacamoire, and A, Chernow, R, *Hamilton: An American Musical*, 2016.
Bennett, Brit, *The Mothers: A Novel*. New York: Riverhead Books, 2016, 197–98.
Philippians 4:12–13.

On guilt, and doubt
Curran, Thomas and Hill, Andrew, "How perfectionism became a hidden epidemic among young people," *The Conversation*, 4 January 2018, accessed 17 May 2025.

Learning how to break the rules
Bowler, Kate, "Never, Ever Enough with David Brooks," Kate Bowler, accessed 17 May 2025, https://katebowler.com/podcasts/david-brooks-kate-bowler-never-ever-enough/

Love & Kindness

A strange kind of kindness
Patchett, Ann, This is the Story of a Happy Marriage, Bloomsbury, 2014, 64.

Too good to make the news?

Brooks, David, "Why Your Social Life Is Not What It Should Be,'"*The New York Times*, 25 August 2022, accessed 17 May 2025, https://www.nytimes.com/2022/08/25/opinion/social-life-talk-strangers.html

Sorok, Stuart; Fournier, Patrick; and Nir, Lilach, "Cross-national evidence of a negativity bias in psychophysiological reactions to news," PNAS, 3 September 2019, accessed 17 May 2025, https://www.pnas.org/doi/10.1073/pnas.1908369116

An unlikely hero, an unlikely children's book

Rosen, Michael and Ross, Tony. *Michael Rosen's Sticky McStick stick: the friend who helped me walk again.* London: Walker Books, 2021.

Ferguson, Donna, "Thanks for your help, Sticky': Michael Rosen on learning to walk again after Covid," *The Guardian*, 7 August, 2018, accessed 19 May 2024, https://www.theguardian.com/books/2021/aug/07/michael-rosen-sticky-mcstickstick-book-about-covid-recovery-covid

Undeserved gifts

Ephesians 2:8–9.

Love & Literature

It all began, begins, with words

John 1:1.
Genesis 1.
John1:1–4.
Hebrews 1:3.
Titus 3:4.
John 1:14.
Isaiah 53:2.

A Little Life: On despair within, and hope beyond

Delaney, Brigid, "*A Little Life*: why everyone should read this modern-day classic," *The Guardian*, 20 January 2020, accessed 12 August 2025, https://www.theguardian.com/books/2016/jan/20/a-little-life-why-everyone-should-read-this-modern-day-classic

Yanagihara, Hanya. *A Little Life*. Anchor Books, 2016, 198.

Yanagihara. *A Little Life*. 198.

Yanagihara. *A Little Life*. 209.

Yanagihara. *A Little Life*. 360.

Oh the pages you'll go!

Batuman, Elif, *Either/Or*, Jonathan Cape, 2022, 347.

McCullers, Carson, *The Member of the Wedding*, Dales Large Print, 2007, 60–61.

McCullers, *The Member*, 266.

McCullers, *The Member*, 269.

Mears, Gillian, *The Mint Lawn*, Allen & Unwin, 2011, 380.

Bernadette, *Leaping into Waterfalls: The Enigmatic Gillian Mears*, Allen & Unwin, 2021, 74

Talking to ourselves, thinking to God

Ellman, Lucy. *Ducks, Newburyport*, Galley Beggar Press, 2019, 208.

Ellman, *Ducks*, 191.

Ellman, *Ducks*, 197.

Attention in a hostile world

Brennan, Levy, Ariel, "Elizabeth Strout's Long Homecoming: The author of Olive Kitteridge left Maine, but it didn't leave her," *The New Yorker*, 24 April 2017, accessed 18 May 2025, https://www.newyorker.com/magazine/2017/05/01/elizabeth-strouts-long-homecoming

Strout, Elizabeth, *Lucy by the Sea*, Random House, 2022, 203.

Murphy, Kate, *You're Not Listening*, Vintage Digital, 23 Jan 2020, chapter 14.

Wojtowicz, Zachary and Loewenstein, George, "Curiosity and the economics of attention," *Science Direct*, Volume 35, 2020, accessed 18 May 2025, https://www.sciencedirect.com/science/article/pii/S2352154620301376

Gaiman, Neil, "Neil Gaiman: Why our future depends on libraries, reading and daydreaming," *The Guardian.* 16 October 2013, accessed 18 May 2025, https://www.theguardian.com/books/2013/oct/15/neil-gaiman-future-libraries-reading-daydreaming

Strout, *Lucy*, 204.

Strout, *Lucy*, 250.

Strout, *Lucy*, 274–5.

Ephron, Nora. *Heartburn*, Virago Press, 2018, 89–90.

Strout, *Lucy*, 281.

Strout, *Lucy*, 288.

Love & Culture

On being a 'Lone Ranger' in journalism's 'Wild West'

Jones, Ralph, "Is freelance journalism becoming unviable?" *Press Gazette*, 17 August 2023, accessed 18 May 2025, https://pressgazette.co.uk/comment-analysis/is-freelance-journalsm-becoming-unviable/

Reynolds Lewis, Katherine. "Diverse Freelancers Play a Crucial Role in Journalism," *Nieman Reports*, 11 March 2024, accessed 18 May 2025, https://niemanreports.org/articles/freelance-journalism-diversity/

Is it any more 'noble' to make art in secret, than for an audience?

Vreeland, Dellaram, "'This is not rubbish': retired Australian teacher painted thousands of works in secret," *The Guardian*, 27 October 2023, accessed 18 May 2025, https://www.theguardian.com/australia-news/2023/oct/27/this-is-not-rubbish-retired-australian-teacher-painted-thousands-of-works-in-secret

Arthur, Elizabeth, *The Secret: Robert Martiensen*, Australian Scholarly Publishing, 2020.

Davis, Ben, "TikTok Star Devon Rodriguez Is Now the Most

Famous Artist in the World. But What About His Work?"
Artnet, 6 October 2023, accessed 18 May 2025, https://news.
artnet.com/art-world-archives/devon-rodriguez-painter-tik
tok-underground-2373157

Easter: A welcome holiday, a wild story
John 20:11–15.
Luke 24:40–43.
John 20:24–29.
Acts 5:34–40.
Garner, Helen, "Death," published in *True Stories: Selected Non-Fiction*. Text Publishing, EPUB 2011.
Isaiah 53:3.

Easter is still unbelievable
John 16:16.
Mark 9:31.
Luke 18:31–33.
Luke 18:34.
Luke 18:34.
John 20:1–2.
Luke 24:16.
Luke 24:31.
Luke 24:32.

Between two flickering worlds
1 Peter 2:11 (translated "exiles" in the NIV, "aliens" in the ISV, NAB, NRSV).
1 Corinthians 1:18; 1:23.
1 Corinthians 4:3.
Keller, Timothy, *The Freedom of Self-Forgetfulness: The Path to True Christian Joy*. Booklet, 2012, 32.

Love & Loving

Cost of living
Canseco, Mario, "Most Canadians Back Status Quo on Medical Assistance in Dying," Research Co, 5 May 2023, accessed 7 June 2025, https://researchco.ca/2023/05/05/maid-canada-2023/

Sex, love, and consent
Brodesser-Akner, Taffy, *Fleishman is in Trouble*, Headline Publishing Group, 2019, 355.
"Women's marches are demanding change at Parliament House and across the country—here's what they want," *ABC News*, 15 March, 2021, accessed 19 May 2024, https://www.abc.net.au/news/2021-03-15/womens-marches-canberra-parliament-house-brittany-higgins/13248096
McGowan, Michael, "NSW police commissioner admits his sex consent app proposal 'could be a terrible idea,'" *The Guardian*, 18 March 2021, accessed 18 May 2025, https://www.theguardian.com/australia-news/2021/mar/18/critics-ridicule-nsw-police-commissioners-idea-for-sexual-consent-app
Owens, Delia, *Where the Crawdads Sing*, Putnam, 2018, 162.

Father, stranger, friend
Riggs, Nina. *The Bright Hour*. Text Publishing Company, 2017, 217–18.

Chapter Bibliography

All articles and essays to which the author didn't hold rights are used with permission.

...FRIENDSHIP

"This (plum) life," *The Weekend Australian*, 21–22 March 2020

"Instead of presents, I asked for . . . salads," *Cicerone Journal*, https://ciceronejournal.au/issue-6/instead-of-presents-i-asked-for-salads/, March 2023, accessed 26 August 2025

"R U OK? is the paper, listening is the gift," The Centre for Public Christianity, 8 September 2021, https://www.publicchristianity.org/ruok/

"Burden of care," The Centre for Public Christianity, 8 September 2021, https://publicchristianity.org/thinking/burden-of-care/

"Take me away (so I can go home), *Atomic Mommy*, 18 June 2023, accessed via Wayback Machine, 26 August 2025, https://web.archive.org/web/20230930123556/https://atomicmommy.net/2022/07/26/take-me-away-so-i-can-go-home/

"Why asking friends for help has helped my friendships grow," Australian Broadcasting Corporation, 13 August 2022, https://www.abc.net.au/news/2022-08-13/asking-for-help-from-friends-is-hard-as-an-adult/101318706

"'And even if it is, I love weird': On truth-telling and friend-making in fiction—and in life," Australian Broadcasting Corporation, 26 December 2023, https://www.abc.net.au/religion/truth-telling-and-friend-making-in-fiction-and-in-life/103257202

"Want to do something for a struggling mom friend? Try just-good-enough food," *Scary Mommy*, 13 April 2022, https://www.scarymommy.com/lifestyle/good-enough-food-gift

"My friend, the therapist," *Ekstasis*, 6 September, 2021, https://www.ekstasismagazine.com/kingdom-meets-culture/2021/9/2/my-friend-the-therapist

"The best thing about holidaying with other families can also be the worst," *The Guardian*, 10 November 2023, https://www.theguardian.com/commentisfree/2023/nov/10/the-best-thing-about-holidaying-with-other-families-can-also-be-the-worst

"We can help older Australians by asking them for help," The Ethics Centre, 26 August 2022, https://ethics.org.au/we-can-help-older-australians-by-asking-them-for-help/

"On saying 'sorry' most readily, when we least need to," The Ethics Centre, 23 November 2023, https://ethics.org.au/on-saying-sorry-most-readily-when-we-least-need-to/

"Not sure what to buy 'the person who has everything' for Christmas? Don't buy them anything," *The Guardian*, 18 December 2023, https://www.theguardian.com/commentisfree/2023/dec/18/not-sure-what-to-buy-the-person-who-has-everything-for-christmas-dont-buy-them-anything

· · · TECHNOLOGY

"Say it in your own words: Email templates can save us time and make us sound good, but at what cost?" Australian Broadcasting Corporation, 29 September 2022, https://www.abc.net.au/religion/email-templates-save-us-time-but-what-cost/14068998

"Actual or artificial? As the difference becomes harder to discern, will we eventually give up trying?" Australian Broadcasting Corporation, 25 July 2023, https://www.abc.net.au/religion/will-we-give-up-discerning-real-from-artificial/102643656

"Are machines becoming more like us? Or are we becoming more like them?" *The Opinion Pages*, 6 February 2023, https://theopinion-pages.com/2023/02/are-machines-becoming-more-like-us-or-are-we-becoming-more-like-them/

"AI keeps giving me melodramatic story ideas," *Arts Hub*, 5 March 2023, https://www.artshub.com.au/news/opinions-analysis/ai-keeps-giving-me-melodramatic-story-ideas-2617072/

"Trust over tech: Confronting tertiary cheating," *Eureka Street*, 1 December 2022, https://www.eurekastreet.com.au/trust-over-tech-confronting-tertiary-cheating

"Sheep and mirrors: On being social," *Quilette*, 8 November 2019, https://quillette.com/2019/11/08/sheep-and-mirrors-on-being-social/

"Tangible, relational, unplugged: On raising 'tech-healthy' humans," Australian Broadcasting Corporation, 13 September 2023, https://www.abc.net.au/religion/emma-wilkins-how-to-raise-tech-healthy-humans/102853346

"An 'unchanged' habitat? Questioning de-extinction," *The Smart Set*, 9 June 2023 https://www.thesmartset.com/questioning-de-extinction/

"Appetite versus appreciation," *The Smart Set*, 9 September 2023, https://www.thesmartset.com/appetite-versus-appreciation/

...ECOLOGY

"A teaspoon of soil," *Thimble Literary Magazine*, March 2024, https://www.thimblelitmag.com/2024/01/21/a-teaspoon-of-soil/

"Should the human race lament extinction—or pursue it?," Australian Broadcasting Corporation, 8 June 2022, https://www.

abc.net.au/religion/should-the-human-race-lament-extinction-or-pursue-it/13920498

"Glorious inefficiency," The Centre for Public Christianity, 11 August 2023, https://www.publicchristianity.org/glorious-inefficiency/

"'The house turned into an op shop!' How to host a pre-Christmas stuff swap," *The Guardian*, 22 November 2022, https://www.theguardian.com/lifeandstyle/2022/nov/22/the-house-turned-into-an-op-shop-how-to-host-a-pre-christmas-stuff-swap

"On Sundressed: Fashion, farming and sustainability," *Arena*, 18 May 2023, https://arena.org.au/sundressed/ (Fashion expert calls for radical reinvention)

"P & the hare," *Olit*, March 2024, https://www.olitmag.com/emma-wilkins-issue-6

"Ecologist uses jewelery to start conservation conversations," *Forty South*, 11 July 2022, https://www.fortysouth.com.au/ecologist-uses-jewellery-to-start-conservation-conversations

"The story nature tells," *Third Space*, 25 March 2022, https://thirdspace.org.au/blog/story-nature-tells

"This (Blossoming) Life," *The Weekend Australian*, 12 August 2023

"Ordinary wonders," *The Age*, 12 September 2023, accessed 25 August 2025, https://www.theage.com.au/national/victoria/the-ordinary-wonders-that-give-me-belief-like-the-dawn-of-each-day-20230825-p5dzhj.html

...PARENTING

"Rest(less)" *Five Minute Lit,* March 2024, https://www.five minutelit.com/five-minutes/rest-less-1

"Learning to walk (alone) again. This time without my kids," *Motherwell,* 17 March 2022, https://motherwellmag. com/2022/03/17/walking-alone-without-kids/

"Life's work," The Centre for Public Christianity, 23 March 2021, https://publicchristianity.org/thinking/lifes-work/

"City Boy and the thistles of doom," *The Sunlight Press,* 27 February 2022, https://www.thesunlightpress.com/2022/02/27/city-boy-and-the-thistles-of-doom/

"How I'm privately preserving my kids' childhood memories in the age of social media," *The Good Trade,* 18 July 2022, https://www. thegoodtrade.com/features/babys-memory-book-ideas/

"Why watching *Alone* with my son proved to be time well spent," Australian Broadcasting Corporation, 3 July 2023, 26 August 2025, https://www.abc.net.au/religion/why-watching-alone-with-my-son-was-time-well-spent/102555064

"My brain can't handle all of the school emails! Why I've enlisted my kids to help preserve my sanity," *The Guardian,* 29 March 2023, https://www.theguardian.com/commentisfree/2023/mar/29/my-brain-cant-handle-all-of-the-school-emails-why-ive-enlisted-my-kids-to-help-preserve-my-sanity

"Do yourself and other parents a favor—lower the bar," *The Guardian,* 5 June 2023, https://www.theguardian.com/commentis-free/2023/jun/05/do-yourself-and-other-parents-a-favour-lower-the-bar

"Camping is challenging but worth it—any other trip will feel like the lap of luxury," *The Guardian*, 27 December 2023, https://www.theguardian.com/commentisfree/2023/dec/27/camping-australia-tips-advice-campsites

"I lost my kids in a crowd. Here's what I learned," *Scary Mommy*, 9 May 2022, https://www.scarymommy.com/parenting/i-lost-two-of-my-kids-today-now-theyre-found-im-glad

"Lean into playfulness. It's the mature thing to do," *Common Good Magazine*, 13 May 2024, https://commongoodmag.com/lean-into-playfulness-its-the-mature-thing-to-do/

"The challenges of self-assessment," *Eureka Street*, 17 May 2022, https://www.eurekastreet.com.au/article/the-challenges-of-self-assessment

...LEARNING

"We will make mistakes, in life and work, but we should expect, and own them," *The Guardian*, 13 December 2021, https://www.theguardian.com/commentisfree/2021/dec/13/we-will-make-mistakes-in-life-and-work-but-we-should-be-wary-of-trying-to-revise-the-past

"What color is a gumleaf, and what shape?" *Contrary Magazine*, April 2023, https://contrarymagazine.com/2023/what-colour-is-a-gum-leaf-and-what-shape/

"The hitchhiker," *Fortunate Traveller*, 14 October 2022, https://www.fortunatetraveller.com/the-hitchhiker-by-emma-wilkins/

"Maybe I should have suppressed my shriek as the screen flooded with porn, but I was teaching my kids a life lesson," *The Guardian*, 18

March 2024, https://www.theguardian.com/commentisfree/2024/mar/18/maybe-i-should-have-suppressed-my-shriek-as-the-screen-flooded-with-porn-but-i-was-teaching-my-kids-a-life-lesson

"When we assume someone that someone's judging us, it may be that we're unfairly judging them," Australian Broadcasting Corporation, 30 October 2023, https://www.abc.net.au/religion/emma-wilkins-feeling-judged-is-not-the-same-as-being-judged/103038882 (Feeling judged isn't the same as being judged)

"Why I, a Christian, don't always share my faith," *Common Good Magazine*, 3 March 2025, https://commongoodmag.com/why-i-a-christian-dont-always-share-my-faith/

"For the untold stores of beauty: Learning how to linger with the wonder of the world," Australian Broadcasting Corporation, 23 August 2023, https://www.abc.net.au/religion/emma-wilkins-learning-how-to-linger-with-the-wonder-of-the-world/102767250

"Break the pattern of judging one another," *Common Good Magazine*, 4 March 2024, https://commongoodmag.com/break-the-pattern-of-judging-one-another/

"Can't get no satisfaction? Try, for a happier New Year," *The Spectator*, 30 December 2020, https://www.spectator.com.au/2020/12/cant-get-no-satisfaction-try-for-a-happier-new-year/

"Not all older people envy youth," *The Good Trade*, 4 August 2023, https://www.thegoodtrade.com/features/do-older-envy-youth/

"The niggling problem of perfectionism," *Third Space*, 21 December 2021, https://thirdspace.org.au/city/blog/niggling-problem-perfectionism

"Learning how to break the rules," Australian Broadcasting Corporation, 16 November 2022, https://www.abc.net.au/religion/emma-wilkins-learning-how-to-break-the-rules/14103282

...KINDNESS

"A strange kind of kindness," Australian Broadcasting Corporation, 7 December 2021, https://www.abc.net.au/religion/a-strange-kind-of-kindness-emma-wilkins/13666676

"What if altruism is more common than we think?" *The Guardian*, 24 December 2022, https://www.theguardian.com/commentisfree/2022/dec/24/i-witnessed-an-extraordinary-act-of-kindness-what-if-altruism-is-more-common-than-we-think

"An unlikely hero, an unlikely children's book," *Spoonie Press*, 23 August 2022, accessed via The Wayback Machine, 26 August 2025, https://web.archive.org/web/20220826170420/https://www.spooniepress.com/magazine/an-unlikely-hero-an-unlikely-childrens-book

"I didn't mean to crash into a stranger's car. What shocked me was that he believed me," *The Guardian*, 13 October 2023, https://www.theguardian.com/commentisfree/2023/oct/13/i-didnt-mean-to-crash-into-a-strangers-car-what-shocked-me-was-that-he-believed-me

"My Aunt Met a Famous Fashion Designer, and All She Got Was This Great Story," *Common Good Magazine*, 25 November 2024, https://commongoodmag.com/the-photo-and-the-story/

"Caution is killing compassion," *The Critic*, 30 March 2022, https://thecritic.co.uk/kindness-is-killing-compassion/

"The end of grief," Centre for Public Christianity, 7 April 2023, https://www.publicchristianity.org/the-end-of-grief/

"The delight and discomfort of undeserved gifts," *Eureka Street*, 18 December 2024, https://www.eurekastreet.com.au/article/the-delight-and-discomfort-of-undeserved-gifts

…LITERATURE

"Author in Progress," *Mayday Magazine*, 3 March 2025, https://maydaymagazine.com/author-in-progress-by-emma-wilkins/

"It all began, begins, with words," *The Argyle Literary Magazine*, 20 May 2024, https://www.theargylelitmag.com/nonfiction-1/it-all-began-begins-with-words

"*A Little Life*: On despair within, and hope beyond," *Eternity Magazine*, 30 June 2021, https://www.eternitynews.com.au/opinion/a-little-life-on-despair-within-and-hope-beyond/

"Oh the pages you'll go!" *Oh Reader*, September 2023, Issue 14, https://www.ohreader.com/oh-reader-store/oh-reader-issue-014

"Talking to ourselves; thinking to God," *Eternity Magazine*, 8 September 2021 https://www.eternitynews.com.au/reflect/talking-to-ourselves-thinking-to-god/

"Attention in a hostile world," *Antithesis Journal*, 29 November 2022, https://www.antithesisjournal.com.au/blog/2022/11/29/attention-in-a-hostile-world

…CULTURE

"Don't sweat that deadline, time 'wasted' can be time well spent," *The Guardian*, 13 August 2023, https://www.theguardian.com/commentisfree/2023/aug/13/dont-sweat-that-deadline-time-wasting-can-be-time-well-spent

"On being a 'Lone Ranger' in journalism's 'Wild West,'" *Other Terrain Journal*, 1 December https://emmahwilkins.com/on-being-a-lone-ranger-in-journalisms-wild-west/

"Is it any more 'noble' to make art in secret, than for an audience?" Australian Broadcasting Corporation, 27 November 2023, https://www.abc.net.au/religion/robert-martiensen-devon-rodriguez-art-in-secret-and-for-audience/103154414

"Why should art matter to people? It matters to God," The Gospel Coalition Australia, 30 June 2025, https://au.thegospel coalition.org/article/why-should-art-matter-to-people-it-matters-to-god

"Easter: A welcome holiday, a wild story," The Gospel Coalition Australia, 29 March 2024, https://au.thegospelcoalition.org/article/easter-a-welcome-holiday-a-wild-story/

"Easter is still unbelievable," *Common Good Magazine*, 27 March 2024, https://commongoodmag.com/easter-is-still-unbelievable/

"Between two flickering worlds," *Ekstasis Magazine*, 24 March 2022, https://www.ekstasismagazine.com/kingdom-meets-culture/2022/3/17/between-two-worlds

...LOVING

"Stitch by Loving Stitch," *Peppermint Magazine*, May 2023, Issue 58, https://peppermintmag.com/product/issue-58-digital/

"Cost of living," The Centre for Public Christianity, 29 August 2023, https://www.publicchristianity.org/cost-of-living/

"Sex, love, and consent," The Centre for Public Christianity, 20 April 2021, https://www.publicchristianity.org/sex-love-and-consent/

"Everything that isn't broken" Pilgrim Artists Festival, July 2021, https://www.pilgrimartists.com/2022-pilgrim-artists-festival/2022-lit-finalists/#non-fiction

"My 'invisible friend,' our 'normal' life: Learning to live with chronic pain," Australian Broadcasting Corporation, 19 January 2023, https://www.abc.net.au/religion/emma-wilkins-my-husband-and-i-learning-to-live-with-chronic-pain/101868742

"Frills vs Thrills," *Hello May*, March 2023, Issue 49, Why fewer frills made my wedding day more fun.

"Sorrow in statistics," The Centre for Public Christianity, 18 June 2021, https://www.publicchristianity.org/sorrow-in-statistics/

"At first, she fled," *Antipodes*, January 2026, https://digitalcommons.wayne.edu/antipodes/vol37/iss1/23/

www.ingramcontent.com/pod-product-compliance
Lightning Source LLC
Chambersburg PA
CBHW061415160726
47995CB00003B/617